THE CASE AGAINST THE MODERN WORLD

A CRASH COURSE IN TRADITIONALIST THOUGHT

By Daniel Schwindt

THE CASE AGAINST THE MODERN WORLD:
A CRASH COURSE IN TRADITIONALIST THOUGHT

Copyright © 2016 Daniel Schwindt

To request permission to make copies of any part of this work, please contact:

Daniel Schwindt
daniel.schwindt@gmail.com

*"THE MODERN WORLD SHALL NOT BE PUNISHED:
IT IS THE PUNISHMENT."*

~NICOLAS GOMEZ-DAVILA

Note to the reader:

This information was compiled mostly for my own use, as a sort of intellectual storehouse. It contains many ideas and arguments, which seem to me to be useful, valid, and powerful—all of them drawn from men who know what they are talking about. The present volume is the first of what I hope will become many. It is as systematic as a work of this type can be—which is to say, not very. At any rate, this information has served me well, and I place it at the disposal of the public in the hope that it might also serve others.

DS

Contents

Section 1: LIBERALISM

"But many there are who follow in the footsteps of Lucifer, and adopt as their own his rebellious cry, 'I will not serve'; and consequently substitute for true liberty what is sheer and most foolish license. Such, for instance, are the men belonging to that widely spread and powerful organization, who, usurping the name of liberty, style themselves Liberals."

~ *Pope Leo XIII, "Libertas"*

INTRODUCTORY

The first problem that confronts us regarding the question of Liberalism is its definition. Depending on where we are and whom we talk to, we will find that people attach different meanings to the term. Unfortunately, these meaning are often not entirely coherent, and they rarely take into consideration the historical development of the Liberal tradition, which is to say that the term "Liberal" is too often applied in an entirely conventional way. When used conventionally, it simply means whatever the speaker or group wants it to say, regardless of how confused or inappropriate this may be with respect to the original meaning.

To explain what I mean, let us quote from the Encyclopedia Britannica's entry on "Liberalism":

> "In the United States, Liberalism is associated with the welfare-state policies of the New Deal program of the Democratic administration of Pres. Franklin D. Roosevelt, whereas in

Europe it is more commonly associated with a commitment to limited government and *laissez-faire* economic policies."[1]

What we see here is that the Atlantic Ocean has somehow divided the philosophy of Liberalism into two philosophies seemingly opposing each other. Obviously this will not do for any precise discussion of our situation or the Liberal ideas that have formed it; and so, before we continue, we need to ask which of these understandings is correct, if either. To do this we need to go back to the origins of the Liberal creed.

Liberalism as a philosophical tradition begins at the Enlightenment, and more specifically with a philosopher named John Locke (1632-1704), who is considered the father of this school. The central principles were, originally: individualism, democratic elections, free markets, insistence on free speech and various other civil rights, popular sovereignty, separation between church and state, and a high emphasis on equality and liberty.

In American politics, these values are divided out between both parties, whether conservative or avowedly "Liberal." Both insist on individualism, free speech, liberty, popular sovereignty, and democracy. Each of them speaks endlessly of the "rights" which they believe to be owed to them.

In the end, in fact, we find that they differ only in certain minor respects: the Right emphasizes primarily an *economic* sort of individualism, and so market autonomy becomes their pet project, usually under the aegis of Capitalism; the Left, on the other hand, emphasizes a more domestic sort of moral individualism, and so gay marriage and secularism become their predominating values. *Both parties are, at heart, thoroughgoing Liberals, but they differ on the area*

---

[1] *Encyclopedia Britannica*, "Liberalism," Girvetz, Harry K.
https://www.britannica.com/topic/liberalism. Accessed March 02, 2016.

of application and the extent to which they are willing to remain consistent.

The Right is willing to sacrifice all values to their belief in the market, and in this they are profoundly Liberal, for Capitalism is economic Liberalism. Yet they contradict themselves by their efforts to promote religion in the public sphere and by denying the sexual autonomy of certain individuals.

The Left, on the other hand, is willing to sacrifice all values to their belief in personal autonomy, and so here they are truly Liberal; but, much like the Right, they also contradict themselves when they fight against inequality and environmental destruction, because a coherent Liberalism has no room for such a liberty-limiting concern for the common good.

In sum, when we speak of Liberalism in this study, we must step outside of the arbitrary usage that predominates in American speech, because the way it is used in that context is internally incoherent. From a historical standpoint, to use the term in this way is to render is completely meaningless. When we refer to Liberalism, then, we must be understood as referring to the continuous and wide-ranging tradition of the Enlightenment, a tradition which has gone to form the political and social consensus of the modern world, for there is no developed nation that is not a child of this original Liberalism. It informs and dictates the positions and goals of both the American Right and the American Left. If the former seems by its rhetoric to despise it, we must simply remember Davila's observation: "Today's conservatives are nothing more than Liberals who have been ill-treated by democracy."[2]

_____

[2] Nicolás Gómez Dávila, *Scholia to an Implicit Text*, aphorism 1208. [Please note that there are two editions used throughout this book. In this instance I have cited the 2001, Spanish edition, which contains numbered aphorisms. I will also cite from a 2013 English-Spanish "bilingual" edition which has the same title but different content and does not have numbered aphorisms. For the latter edition, page numbers will be referenced.]

Daniel Schwindt

Oswald Spengler also explained for us the existence of a so-called conservative party, saying that "there arises the defensive figure of the Conservative party, copied from the Liberal, dominated completely by the latter's forms, bourgeois-ized without being bourgeois, and obliged to fight with rules and methods that Liberalism has laid down. It has the choice of handling these means better than its adversary or of perishing."[3]

The Right calls itself conservative, but its conservatism is only a matter of temperament and not of philosophy. Its adherents are simply Liberals who prefer inertia.

THE DISCOVERY OF THE SELF

Argument:

> *"The student of the Greek Fathers or of Hellenistic philosophy is likely to be made painfully aware of the difference between their starting-point and ours. Our difficulty in understanding them is largely due to the fact that they had no equivalent to our concept of 'person,' while their vocabulary was rich in words which express community of being... Whereas Aristotle began from the polis, the city which to him was the natural unit of society, the 'classical' Western political philosophers (among whom one must count Hobbes, Locke, and Rousseau) assumed that the individual person and his rights pre-existed any form of society."*

> ~ *Colin Morris*[4]

Elucidation:

---

[3] Spengler, op. cit., p. 450.

[4] Colin Morris, *The Discovery of the Individual: 1050-1200* (New York: Harper, 1972), pp. 2-3.

4

The reader may wonder at this starting point, but it is useful, when approaching our difficult subject, to identify certain *causes* and how they might contribute to our present way of thinking. When we do this, the first thing we notice is that we are *inescapably self-centered beings*. Of course, man has always been taught by world religions that he has a tendency toward egoism, from Buddhism to Christianity, but these mere warned him of danger, assuming also that there was a part of him through which he identified with the world and those personal being around him, whether those personal beings were living or dead.[5] We differ in that it is no longer possible to make such an assumption: our self-centeredness is almost complete. Because the growth of this new, more comprehensive "self-centeredness" can be seen to have immediately preceded the birth of Liberalism, and in a way prepared the soil for its establishment, it is useful to pause on it before tackling Liberalism specifically.

Roughly speaking, the process in question—the "discovery of the self"—took place during the Middle Ages, specifically the 11th and 12th centuries. It was expressed in every area of life, not only in politics, but also in art and literature as well.

Take, for example, the fact that our modern literature is always based on the individual and his relationships, whereas the Greek forms seem to care very little for these aspects of a narrative. As Morris explains in his excellent work, *The Discovery of the Individual*: "Greek tragedy was a drama of circumstance, whereas the Western tragedy is essentially a drama of character."[6]

Compare the style and development of the plot in Oedipus with that of Shakespeare's Hamlet, Macbeth, and Othello. In the latter we hear constantly of inner and relational turmoil; in the former, the concern

---

[5] This is why Paul could speak so easily of a "cloud of witnesses" while contemporary Protestantism has absolutely no idea what to do with this notion.
[6] Morris, op. cit., p. 4.

is mainly with *destiny* and cosmic irony. The ancient themes were universal rather than personal.

During the same period we see the rise of autobiography.[7] We see also, in the church, new developments in the practice of confession. Until the 11th century we did not see the emphasis on self-examination and sincere contrition that would come to predominate during that period. Confession had been a more external and public sacrament. During the Middle Ages, it was to transform from a public exercise to a more private and internal affair, which is to say, its focus migrated from the collective aspects of sin to the individual. This transition can be clearly marked by observing the attacks of Peter Abelard on the system of public confession. He does not complain that the practice was too severe or embarrassing to the penitent, as we might imagine, but that *it was not deep enough*, it was too ceremonial and neglected the sincerity of the individual in his remorse. Intimately connected to this development, we see the first interests in what would become the field of psychology.

So thoroughgoing was this transition that a theological giant such as Abelard could title one of his most original works: *Ethics: or, Know Thyself* (1135). The title reflects the transforming emphasis on the self, and it inevitably led its author to try and make *intention* the foundation and criterion of morality itself. For Abelard it was a man's intent that mattered when it came to moral culpability, even going so far as to suggest that the men who crucified Christ were not sinning, since they believed that what they were doing was just, and this despite the fact that, were it true, it would immediately render Christ's words at that moment pointless. "Father, forgive them, for they know not what they do" has no meaning if their ignorance in itself absolves them.

---

[7] Augustine's *Confessions* was an exceptional work for its time, and the form did not become in any way "popular" until much later.

In this way, man's experience of life was becoming subjective. In fact, it was not until Pope St. John Paul II condemned this sort of morality, labeling it "consequentialism" in the 1993 document *Veritatis Splendor,* that the Church officially and specifically rejected *intention* as the sole criterion of moral culpability.

But this is not to say that the Church of the Middle Ages followed Abelard on this point. We only mention his error because it manifests the tendency we are studying; his ideas were in fact opposed in his own time. For it was at this point in history that the *tide of the self* crashed against the mountain that was St. Thomas Aquinas.

The philosophical weaponry that Aquinas contributed to the West will perhaps never be appreciated in its proper magnitude. By synthesizing Aristotle's objectivity with Christian subjectivity, he successfully fused and harmonized what at that moment threatened to dismantle Christian philosophy altogether. His fusion enabled man to be both subject and object, in the proper relationships and at the proper time, to be vincibly or invincibly ignorant of acts which were right or wrong. He reconciled Abelard's insistence that *intention counts* with the objective nature of good and evil. In St. Thomas we find man and Man, we find the individual both as *person* and as *member of a human community.* Finally, he showed us through his development of law—eternal, natural, and human—how man could be both material and spiritual, natural and supernatural.

But it was not to last, and in the end the Thomist synthesis decomposed back into its constituent elements and became a dichotomy: man is either individual or collective, animal or angel. It was when Thomism crashed to the ground that the possibility of a "religious life" separate from "ordinary life" first became possible in the minds of political philosophers, and with this conception was born the possibility of a secular state—the first seeds of the "wall of separation" which all moderns attempt to straddle.

Let us now step back to observe the long-term results of the process in its two extremes, which can be identified as egoism (man's personal aspect) and nationalism (man's collective aspect):

On a personal level, the victory of the self has led to acute self-consciousness of a negative sort. In the words of John Updike, writing of Franz Kafka, who exemplified this condition through his writing and life:

> "The century...has been marked by the idea of 'modernism'—a self-consciousness new among centuries, a consciousness of being new...a sensation of anxiety and shame whose center cannot be located and therefore cannot be placated; a sense of an infinite difficulty within things, impeding every step; a sensitivity acute beyond usefulness, as if the nervous system, flayed of its old hide of social usage and religious belief, must record every touch as pain."[8]

The experience of life as a *social* affair had its comforts. A man was, in a healthy community that acknowledged its bonds, never existentially alone. Even in his religious life, his sin was in part a social sin—he was *fallen* but the world was with him—and his relationship with Christ was not a 1-to-1 exchange but an intermingling of the two in such a way that the individual disappeared and the two were "one body."

With the onset of selfhood, this social perception of reality could not persist. Today, the best the Christian can hope for is the "personal savior." He takes the full weight of life on himself, stripping himself of the insulation that a co-experience of life could have offered, and he suffers for it.

In the opposite extreme, this cocooning of the self enveloped the collective aspect of man's psyche. Even what was left of his social

---

[8] John Updike, Foreword to *Franz Kafka: The Complete Stories* (New York: Schocken Books, 1971), ix.

awareness became prone to an insecure self-consciousness. Once this happened, the new hypersensitivity of one's separateness was made manifest in what would become *nationalism*.

As the formation of the "national self" occurred, the unity of the Christendom fractured and gave way to "nation-states," each attempting to satisfy the lust for a social self-consciousness in the collective sphere, a need that previous societies had apparently never felt. Just as the self-conscious man becomes automatically insecure, and therefore combative, in the presence of his peers, so the self-conscious nation becomes suspicious of everyone around it. In this way, the seeds of alienation and strife were planted in the soil of the West. They had only to germinate and flourish.

SECULARISM

Argument:

> *"As regards the Liberal school, I will merely say of it, that in its profound ignorance it despises theology, and not because it is not theological in its way, but because, though it is, it does not know it. This school has not yet comprehended, and probably will never comprehend, the close link that unites divine and human things, the great relationship which political, have with social and religious, questions, and the dependence which all problems relative to government, have on those others which refer to God, the Supreme Legislator of all human associations."*

> ~ *Juan Donoso Cortés*[9]

Elucidation:

---

[9] Juan Donoso Cortés, *Essays*, 60.

Without anticipating what we will have to say in a later installment, which will be devoted exclusively to the relationship between Church and State, we cannot avoid mentioning it here because it is central to Liberal theory. As the dichotomy of natural and supernatural was born, so was the notion that religious life could be separated from so-called "ordinary life." As difficult as it is for us, who have been formed from our cradles in the mold of Liberalism, to comprehend, the concept of religion had to be invented, and this creation is a very recent one.

In previous times, there was simply *life*, and life was theological: all questions were in some way religious questions. If you followed any line of thought far enough, it terminated in the divine. There was no purely economic life, for every craft had its own patron saint. There was a *theology of work* through which every industrious activity from saddle-making to glassblowing could be seen as an expression of the *true*, and on that basis could be judged as either good or bad, human or inhuman.

Liberalism, having attempted to rationalize and naturalize itself, severed this tie and from that moment on the sacred became excluded from all areas of life beyond that which was officially labeled *religious*, and this religious partition was inevitably very small in proportion to that claimed by "ordinary life," and which fell conveniently under the purview of the secular authorities of the new nation-states.

But as Cortés observed above, the exclusion of the sacred from public life proved impossible even for those who willed it. Rather than be excluded, the sacred simply migrated to the new secular arenas, and these became the temples of Liberal worship. But first the foundations of a new mythology had to be laid, and then a set of rigid ideologies constructed in order to direct the people in this new way of life. Ideologies like capitalism, socialism, nationalism, etc. These were the new doctrines with new rituals, new dogmas, and new answers to the perennial problems of life, no less demanding than the old, only less satisfying to the pilgrim.

LIBERALISM AND MYTH

Argument:

> *"The myth expresses the deep inclinations of a society. Without it, the masses would not cling to a certain civilization or its process of development and crisis. It is a vigorous impulse, strongly colored, irrational, and charged with all of man's power to believe. It contains a religious element. In our society the two great fundamental myths on which all other myths rest are Science and History."*

> ~ *Jacques Ellul*[10]

Elucidation:

Having delineated the gradual discovery of the self, we can isolate another process which was necessary to more firmly plant Liberalism in the Western soul. This was the adoption of a new mythology which would form the unconscious faith of the new order.

Every civilization has its mythology, even, and perhaps especially, our own; we differ from the ancients only in the style of the presentation. They, being personalist in their outlooks, chose gods, demigods, and detailed narratives in order to explain themselves to themselves (for this is the function of the myth). We moderns, however, prefer abstractions, and so we turn to ideas and processes rather than divine beings. As Jacques Ellul remarked, our foundational ideas—our guiding myths—may be reduced to two: Science and History.

Science, because we look to it as the guardian of and guide to the truth, the director of all our endeavors. If something is not *scientific*, it has no business claiming to be *true*. This development can be attributed in part to the scientific developments of the 18th century. These,

---

[10] Jacques Ellul, *Propaganda*, p. 40. See also pages 116-117 of the same work.

combined with the material progress they enabled, fostered an unprecedented degree of optimism about man and his earthly destiny. Hence, along with a materialistic scientism there came a reversal of the old view of history.

No age before our own looked forward to a Golden Age and backward to a Dark Age. Every people previous to us looked to back to Eden and forward to Apocalypse—the Golden Age was the first, and the Dark Age was the last. In this sense, we represent the reversal of all traditional wisdom regarding historical development.[11] And so, whatever the causes that led to this reversal, we now firmly accept the myths of Science and History, which is to say, Materialism and Progress. But these only form a basis, and in the style of the Greeks, we build many sub-myths on this foundation. Ellul continues:

> "And based on [the myths of Science and History] are the collective myths that are man's principal orientations: the myth of Work, the myth of Happiness (which is not the same thing as the presupposition of happiness), the myth of the Nation, the myth of Youth, the myth of the Hero."[12]

The myth of Work is that through which productive work of any kind is an unquestionable good. This should be seen as a natural outgrowth of the primary belief in Materialistic Progress. The myth of the Nation, likewise, is but the materialization of social consciousness. In various ways, each separate myth combines in the self-centered man to become an,

> "all-encompassing, activating image: a sort of vision of desirable objectives that have lost their material, practical character and have become strongly colored, over-whelming, all-encompassing, and which displace from the conscious all

---

[11] It is interesting that the Hindu scriptures predict just such a reversal of views as an indicator of the Dark Age.

[12] Jacques Ellul, *Propaganda*, p. 40. See also pages 116-117 of the same work.

that is not related to it. Such an image pushes man to action precisely because it includes all that he feels is good, just, and true...Eventually the myth takes possession of a man's mind so completely that his life is consecrated to it."[13]

Ellul does not exaggerate when he says that the modern man is religiously *consecrated* to his mythology. Secularism is, in the end, merely a new faith. As we've already said, there can be only a migration of the scared—never an elimination of it. And for us the sacred has migrated to these material myths, and these are further interpreted within the framework of Progress, a view of history that promises future Utopia, if only we keep treading blindly forward, because in a pure materialism more is always better.

LIBERALISM AND IDEOLOGY

Argument:

> "Ideologies were invented so that men who do not think can give their opinions."
>
> ~ Nicolás Gómez Dávila[14]

Elucidation:

By the time all of these subtle elements congeal in the social consciousness, they have settled into a collection of premises—certain patterns of thought—which go to form the preconceptions of the modern man. These prejudices, because they are so deep-seated and because they are shared with everyone around us, take on a guise of false obviousness. We even call them "common sense," even though they would have seemed utterly alien and even absurd to our ancestors.

---

[13] Jacques Ellul, *Propaganda*, p. 31.
[14] Dávila, 2001 edition, aphorism 1219.

These prejudices are uniform across a given society, which is a necessary result of the atomization that follows individualism. The atomized man becomes at the same time simpler in his thought and more open to suggestion. Today everyone in modern society takes it for granted that he thinks for himself, while nonetheless and without noticing it, he always thinks exactly like the man next to him.

Modern man is an island, in a historical sense. Every society born of revolution is an island, and it is an island that floats, like a thin film on the surface of history. He is always moving, disconnected from all that came before him, and never holding still long enough to strike the roots necessary to pass something on to those who will come after.

Such a man becomes incapable of appreciating supra-individual forms of knowledge, which is to say he becomes incapable of utilizing Tradition. His tie to the wisdom of the ages is severed, and he must cope with even the most commonplace things of life, from marriage to childrearing to prayer, as if he were Adam. Tocqueville observed this in America:

> "Amid the continuous shifts which prevail in the heart of a democratic society, the bond which unites generations to each other becomes slack or breaks down; each person easily loses the trail of ideas coming from his forbears or hardly bothers himself about them...As for the effect which one man's intelligence can have upon another's, it is of necessity much curtailed in a country where its citizens, having become almost like each other, scrutinize each other carefully and, perceiving in not a single person in their midst any signs of undeniable greatness or superiority, constantly return to their own rationality as to the most obvious and immediate source of truth. So, it is not merely trust in any particular individual which is destroyed, but also the predilection to take the word

of any man at all. Each man thus retreats into himself from where he claims to judge the world."[15]

What a sorry state indeed! And so, in this wretched position, he adopts a new way of dealing with the problems of life: He begins to turn to *general ideas*. Again, Tocqueville can teach us about the process. He begins by discussing the nature of omniscience, which is perfect knowledge:

> "God gives no thought at all to human kind in general. He casts a single and separate glance upon all the beings that form the human race, observing in each of them similarities which link him to them and differences which separate him from them. So God has no need for general ideas; that is to say, he never experiences the necessity of grouping a great number of similar objects under one heading so as to think more comfortably."[16]

Man does not have this power. Again, he is profoundly limited in his reach and where his reach was once supplemented by thousands of years of social tradition, he must now find a different means of arriving at judgments about the world. To do this he haphazardly gathers a few similarities between events and circumstances as they occur, and on these loose correspondences he formulates general rules which, although not very accurate, serve his purpose and allow him to "get by." This way of reasoning becomes his habit, and he mistakes for mental progress what is actually a progressive decay of knowledge:

> "General ideas do not bear witness to the strength of human intelligence but rather to its inadequacy for, in nature, beings are not exactly alike; there are no identical facts, no rules which can be applied loosely and in a similar manner to several objects at the same time. General ideas have the wondrous

---

[15] Tocqueville, op. cit., p. 494.

[16] Ibid., p. 503.

attribute of allowing the human mind to reach swift judgments on a great number of ideas at the same time. On the other hand, they only ever provide the mind with half-baked notions which lose as much in accuracy as they gain in range."[17]

This collection of "half-baked notions" is called an *ideology*. An ideology is an assortment of "common sense" answers to complex problems, forcibly pressed into a contradictory reality.

Liberalism, clearly, is the arch-ideology of the modern world. Its precepts, each of them complete with pre-packed rhetorical justifications, each requiring no study and no actual experience of life, are: equality, freedom, free markets, progress, productivity, growth, universal education, democracy, universal suffrage, patriotism, free speech, etc. This list is obviously not exhaustive, but it hangs together by the fact that each element is distilled from the underlying mythology of the modern era, and where the myth impels man to action, the Liberal ideology channels it into those pursuits that accord with its values. All of these values are accepted and pursued without question and without any real study of the relevant subjects—and most certainly without reference to history.

This leads us to a final observation about the formation of ideology in Liberal regimes, which is that it reinforces man's inherent mental laziness. By providing him the pre-packaged answers to the mysteries of the universe, it convinces him that he can become wise without the effort traditionally needed to acquire wisdom:

"One of the distinctive features of democratic ages is the taste shared by every man for easy success and immediate enjoyment—a trait evident as much in the pursuits of the intellect as in any other. The majority of those who live in times of equality are filled with ambition both vigorous and

---

[17] Ibid.

mild. They wish for immediate success without expending great effort. These contradictory elements lead them to search for general ideas with whose help they congratulate themselves on being able to depict huge objects at little expense and drawing the public's attention with no effort."[18]

Ideology, like ignorance, has from the beginning been a characteristic of Liberal democratic societies. Just as gravity is imbedded as a law in our physical reality, so the tendency toward ignorance is imbedded in the mental physics of the modern condition.

LOST CORRELATION BETWEEN RIGHT AND DUTY

Argument:

> *"The natural rights of which We have so far been speaking are inextricably bound up with as many duties, all applying to one and the same person. These rights and duties derive their origin, their sustenance, and their indestructibility from the natural law, which in conferring the one imposes the other...it follows that in human society one man's natural right gives rise to a corresponding duty in other men; the duty, that is, of recognizing and respecting that right. Every basic human right draws its authoritative force from the natural law, which confers it and attaches to it its respective duty. Hence, to claim one's rights and ignore one's duties, or only half fulfill them, is like building a house with one hand and tearing it down with the other."*
>
> *~ Pope St. John XXIII*[19]

Elucidation:

---

[18] Ibid., p. 507.

[19] *Pacem in Terris,* sections 28 and 30.

If we were to create a timeline tracing the relationship between rights and duties, as well as their corresponding prominence in the minds of men, we could say that for ancient man duties were predominant. Sensing the immanence of the divine order, which is essentially supra-individual, the ancients stressed the obligations which recognition of divine reality always implies. We can also relate this difference by referring to the discovery of the self, and saying that it is very difficult to emphasize rights when you have not yet emphasized the individual to whom the rights must belong. Rights, as we know them, are *individual* things. And so in the ancient world, dominated by a sense of the transcendent, man was dominated by a sense of duty. He spoke of obligations owed first to God, and then, by proxy, to king, community, and neighbor.

Having established this, we may proceed forward on our imaginary timeline. We will then come upon the discovery of the self and the rising tide of egoism. We will recall how this tide was temporarily stalled by the Dumb Ox, St. Thomas, who, through his synthesis, created a harmonious fusion of right and duty, acknowledging both the outward and inward demands of divine justice. In Thomism there is a hierarchy of the demands of justice, each taking care to acknowledge the various aspects of reality. By doing this, it was possible for Aquinas to speak of "right," but although he acknowledged the concept he was a far cry from what we mean by it today. He only spoke of right as "the object of justice."[20] A right was always "a work that is adjusted to another person."[21] In short, the rights of Thomism acknowledged individuality without becoming egoistic.

Unfortunately, Thomism proved unflattering in comparison to the humanism of the Enlightenment, with its optimistic promises and praises; Thomism was also difficult for the common man who, having begun to perceive any form of subordination as a species of injustice,

---

[20] *Summa*, II-II, q. 57, a. 1.
[21] *Summa*, II-II, q. 57, a. 2.

began to crave the security and respect that humanistic rights theory promised to deliver. And so, as the old way of imagining social justice fell out of favor, he turned away from the old authorities—first from the Church (Reformation), and then from the traditional political authorities as a whole (Revolution), and eventually turned away from the concept of objective law altogether.

In a way we could say that the history of the concept of right is a story of revolt against objectivity, for duty is the objective expression of that which the right attempts to achieve from a subjective point of view. When duty fell and right rose victorious, it should not have been surprising that this accompanied a disdain for all external authority, anything that dared make claims to universality and objective truth, anything that smacked of the supra-individual order of things.

The traditional world saw hierarchies everywhere, including within good itself. There were higher and lower goods, and then there was the Absolute Good, which was God. This is the result of seeing all things in relationship to one another, because such a view instills a sense of proper order to reality. When hierarchy is denied, what follows is not a levelling, but more often a reversal of the proper relationship. Thus, when it is pretended that the lower good is not subordinate to the higher, the lower inevitably subordinates the higher. It had always been said that man had duties, and it was from these duties that he drew his rights. Aquinas had considered right as a thing oriented outward, not something claimed for oneself. He would have agreed with Dávila's saying that a man "has no more right than that which he derives from another's duty."[22]

When Liberalism denied the correlation between right and duty, it ended by emphasizing right to the exclusion of duty. The led inevitably to the present situation, where no one can coherently speak of duties at all, for the only duty left is to respect another man's rights.

---

[22] Dávila, 2001 edition, aphorism 2979.

Daniel Schwindt

UNDERMINING THE CONCEPT OF RIGHT

Argument:

> "The tissues of society become cancerous when the duties of some are transformed into the rights of others."

> ~ Nicolás Gómez Dávila[23]

Elucidation:

We should notice now that the reversal in priority between right and duty is closely linked with the rejection of hierarchy in favor of equality. Liberalism's inherent egalitarianism renders it incapable of treating properly of the right.

As we have already said, according to the traditional view the right derived from the duty, and it is clear that duty is always different for every man depending on his station in life (family, vocation, etc.). If men varied in their rights, it was as a normal consequence of their varying duties. A man with a family would have rights differing slightly from those of a man without, for the simple reason that his duties were not comparable. In this way rights were "tethered" to duties and so they varied not so much because the "nature" of the man differed but for the plain and obvious reason that his obligations could be so diverse as to require varying degrees of latitude.

This is why the traditional wisdom abhors Liberal equality: it has little to do with a disdain for the dignity of the person, but stems from an insistence on realism—an actual taking into account of the demands circumstance. When the connection between right and duty becomes tethered and rights are dealt out to a theoretically homogenous mass of individuals, there will immediately arise a situation where some men do not have the proper rights to meet their obligations, while at the

---

[23] Dávila, 2001 edition, aphorism 1190.

same time other persons will have rights that they do not require and the exercise of which amounts to an injustice and becomes an undeserved privilege.

Davila's warning was not vain condescension. As he said elsewhere: "It has become customary to proclaim rights in order to be able to violate duties."[24]

Liberals can only complain of "violated rights," rights for which they never provided any real concrete justification in the first place. Nietzsche himself may have been hitting on man's best interests when said "never to think of lowering our duties to the rank of duties for everybody; to be unwilling to renounce or to share our responsibilities; to count our prerogatives, and the exercise of them, among our *duties.*"[25]

The inability to see one's right—one's prerogative—as something separate from one's duty is a hallmark of the traditional mind; the inability to see anything but the prerogative, absolute and "inalienable," is a hallmark of Liberalism.

EGOISM AND THE LOSS OF POLITICAL PURPOSE

Argument:

> *"Through the shift of emphasis from natural duties or obligations to natural rights, the individual, the ego, had become the center and origin of the moral world, since man— as distinguished from man's end—had become that center or origin."*

> ~ *Leo Strauss*[26]

---

[24] Dávila, 2001 edition, aphorism 2587.
[25] Friedrich Nietzsche, *Beyond Good and Evil*, 272.
[26] Leo Strauss, *Natural Right and History* (University of Chicago, 1953), p. 248.

Elucidation:

We've already spoken of Abelard's moral ego-centrism through which the "discovery of the self" almost became the "discovery of the self to the exclusion of all other realities." We also acknowledged that the discovery of the self did not have to become a negative development, that through men like Aquinas it was accepted and transfigured, becoming in Thomism what could be considered the apotheosis of Western philosophy. But by the Enlightenment, however, and with the downfall of Christendom, the Catholic edifice was destroyed and the Thomist fusion destroyed—ego-centrism was then released from all constraints. Finally, we acknowledged that this undermined the relationship between right and duty, emphasizing rights above all else.

Here are the two fundamentals of the Liberal mentality: egoism (man as the center of reality), and, as a natural consequence, a total loss of teleology (a purposeful orientation toward an end). This is a point that is not properly acknowledged in many criticisms of modernism and liberal regimes. When man becomes the origin of morality, the external moral imperative, which traditionally tethered his actions to a standard outside himself, giving him an external and objective aim, evaporates into thin air. He has freedom, yes, but it is like being liberated from one's natural atmosphere, like being flung into space, or into a desert. You are free, you have become the autonomous source and measure of the good, and you may go whatever direction you like—but you find yourself in empty space, in an infinite vacuum: you can go anywhere, but there is nowhere to go, and so you are not really free.

LIBERALISM PROMISES RIGHTS BUT DELIVERS HEAVIER DUTIES

Argument:

"As war has followed war, the burden of conscription has grown heavier. Like a slow contagion it has spread from State to State until now the whole of continental Europe is in its grip. There it holds court along with the friend of its youth, its twin brother, that comes always just before or after it—with universal suffrage; both of them brought to birth at about the same time, the one bringing in its train, more or less openly and completely, the other, both of them the blind and terrible guides or masters of the future, the one placing in the hands of every adult person a voting paper, the other putting on his back a soldier's knapsack. The promise which they hold for the twentieth century of slaughter and bankruptcy, the exacerbation of hatred and suspicion between nations, the wastage of the work of men's hands, the perversion to base uses of the beneficent discoveries of science, the return to the low and debased shapes of primitive societies on the warpath, the retrograde movement towards a barbarous and instinctual egotism, towards the feelings, manners and morals of ancient cities and savage tribes—all this we know too well!"

~ *Hippolyte Taine*[27]

Elucidation:

Universal suffrage is a very educational subject of study because it illustrates so well the Liberal sleight-of-hand: By holding out to the people a new right—the right to vote—it becomes possible set on them a radically new duty, a duty that no peasant population would have so readily accepted: the duty to wage war. This was always the justification of the nobility's privilege: they ruled because they fought, and they fought because they ruled.

With the rise of democracy the people were told that they too could rule like to nobility of old. And so flattered were they at the idea of

---

[27] Hippolyte Taine, *The Origins of Contemporary France*.

participating in government that they hardly noticed the cost. Men of today go when their government calls, kill whom it calls them to kill, and die in whatever country happens to have warranted their deployment. But if we are to judge by the words and actions of the common voter in today's democracy, we would have to say that he is beginning to see how he was swindled: The promise of "self-government" seems unfulfilled. At every turn he feels commanded by "them": "they" tell him what to do and demand his taxes; "they" start wars; "they" make unfair laws. It is becoming blatantly clear to him that the ballot sheet he is allowed to sign every four years was not worth the knapsack on his back—if it was worth anything at all. He does not feel that, in the end, his vote even matters; but he certainly feels the bullet in his belly.

Consider the fact that universal suffrage has always accompanied conscription. All through the days of kingship, it is true that men could not vote, but neither could they be pressed into service. I say to a peasant: You may now govern your fellows and yourself, like the aristocrat of old, but you must therefore also fight, like the aristocrat of old. And before long the deception becomes clear: I allow him to fight and to die, like the aristocrat of old—but he dies wondering whether or not he ever really got to govern himself, much less anyone else. The truth is that it is impossible to bestow a right. Only duties can be placed on a man, and anyone pretending to offer you a right is trying to smuggle "the last of all oppressions"[28] right under your nose. But this is how it has always gone, for Liberalism is a flatterer.

THREE FACES AND THREE FORMS OF LIBERALISM

Argument:

---

[28] This was the phrase Thomas Jefferson used to describe conscription.

"Who cannot see that Luther, Descartes, and Voltaire used the same method and that they differed from each other only in the greater and lesser use they claimed to make of it?"

~ Alexis de Tocqueville[29]

Elucidation:

We've already hinted that Liberalism universalizes itself, spreading through all areas of thought. Thus, it is dangerously naïve to entertain a view of Liberalism that recognizes it only as a limited set of *political* ideas. The movement invaded political philosophy, to be sure, but at the same time it reached both above and below that level, disturbing not only the mind of man, but also his body and soul. With its withering touch it dictated anew, not only how he would earn his daily bread, but even how he would relate to the sacred.

As Pope Paul VI was to say, "at the very root of philosophical liberalism is an erroneous affirmation of the autonomy of the individual in his activity, his motivation and the exercise of his liberty,"[30] which always carries with it, usually unconsciously, an unprecedented optimism about the mental aptitudes of the individual. With this in mind, if we pause and survey the last several centuries, do we find corresponding movements within the religious, economic, and political spheres which all manifest this same mentality?

Indeed, the task is too easy: The Reformation was nothing more than individualism of religion, transferring to the judgment the individual the weightiest of all tasks—the interpretation of both Scripture and Tradition. In the economic sphere, it is obviously Capitalism that represents an unrestrained embrace of individualism and liberty through the doctrines of sanctioned self-interest and "free markets." And we have just finished describing precepts which, through the

---

[29] Tocqueville, op. cit., p. 495.
[30] Pope Paul VI, *Octogesima Adveniens*, 35.

Enlightenment, expressed the same symptoms in the political realm: free speech, absolute rights, and secularism.

REFORMATION: OR, RELIGIOUS LIBERALISM

Argument:

> *"Liberalism is the dogmatic affirmation of the absolute independence of the individual and of the social reason. Catholicity is the dogma of absolute subjection of the individual and of the social order to the revealed law of God. One doctrine is the exact antithesis of the other."*

> ~ *Fr. Felix Sarda y Salvany*[31]

Elucidation:

That Liberalism is anti-authoritarian and individualistic we take as obvious. If we understand it to be also an error of *reductio ad absurdum*, severing branch from vine,[32] then it does not take extensive argument to show that Luther's three *solas* unquestionably fit the bill. How else can we interpret *sola fide* ("faith alone"), *sola scriptura* ("scripture alone"), and *sola gratia* ("grace alone") than as partial selections of a pre-existent whole? The atomized nature of these doctrines is itself implicit in the term, *sola*. They are the tenets of *nothing-but-ness*. Add to this doctrinal oversimplification the principle of private interpretation, and the concept of authority evaporates taking all hopes of traditional unity along with it.

Here we may draw benefit from a small work by Fr. Felix Sarda y Salvany, published in 1886 under the title *El Liberalismo es Pecado*, or

---

[31] *Liberalism is a Sin*, ch. 6.
[32] John 15:5.

"Liberalism is a Sin." This thin volume meticulously refutes the errors associated with religious Liberalism.

But first, in case the bluntness of its title and the relative obscurity of its author give pause to the cautious reader, making him suspicious that these are the ramblings of a radical, unsupported by the Catholic Church itself, we should mention that it was initially intercepted by a Bishop of Liberal opinions. This bishop submitted it to the Sacred Congregation of the Index, in hopes that the work would be put under ban. The Sacred Congregation reviewed the submission and responded on January 10, 1887 as follows:

> "…not only is nothing found contrary to sound doctrine, but its author, D. Felix Sarda, merits great praise for his exposition and defense of the sound doctrine therein set forth with solidity, order and lucidity, and without personal offense to anyone."

Thus reassured that the book is a truly Catholic one, we may cite from its pages and hear what case it brings against Luther's movement:

> "Rejecting the principle of authority in religion, [Protestantism] has neither criterion nor definition of faith. On the principle that every individual or sect may interpret the deposit of Revelation according to the dictates of private judgment, it gives birth to endless differences and contradictions. Impelled by the law of its own impotence, through lack of any decisive voice of authority in matters of faith, it is forced to recognize as valid and orthodox any belief that springs from the exercise of private judgment. Therefore does it finally arrive, by force of its own premises, at the conclusion that one creed is as good as another; it then seeks to shelter its inconsistency under the false plea of liberty of conscience. Belief is not imposed by a legitimately and divinely constituted authority, but springs directly and freely from the unrestricted exercise of the individual's reason or caprice upon

Daniel Schwindt

the subject matter of Revelation. The individual or sect interprets as it pleases—rejecting or accepting what it chooses. This is popularly called liberty of conscience. Accepting this principle, Infidelity, on the same plea, rejects all Revelation, and Protestantism, which handed over the premise, is powerless to protest against the conclusion; for it is clear that one who, under the plea of rational liberty, has the right to repudiate any part of Revelation that may displease him, cannot logically quarrel with one who, on the same ground, repudiates the whole. If one creed is as good as another, on the plea of rational liberty, on the same plea, no creed is as good as any. Taking the field with this fatal weapon of Rationalism, Infidelity has stormed and taken the very citadel of Protestantism, helpless against the foe of its own making."[33]

If we were to characterize the gist of this reasoning, it is that a process which begins in disintegration must proceed toward disorder and terminate in death. Neither can this argument be called a "slippery slope," for he was not conjecturing wildly about what *might happen*, but was observing what *already had.* He was merely connecting dots.

"Such is the mainspring of the heresy constantly dinned into our ears, flooding our current literature and our press. It is against this that we have to be perpetually vigilant, the more so because it insidiously attacks us on the grounds of *a false charity and in the name of a false liberty...*

"The principle ramifies in many directions, striking root into our domestic, civil, and political life, whose vigor and health depend upon the nourishing and sustaining power of religion. For religion is the bond which unites us to God, the Source and End of all good; and Infidelity, whether virtual, as in Protestantism, or explicit, as in Agnosticism, severs the bond

---

[33] *Liberalism is a Sin*, ch. 2.

which binds men to God and *seeks to build human society on the foundations of man's absolute independence."*[34]

Nothing else need be said at this point regarding Liberalism in its specifically religious manifestation, because a future installment will address the question of religion in a more comprehensive fashion.

ENLIGHTENMENT: OR, POLITICAL LIBERALISM

Argument:

> *"...these followers of liberalism deny the existence of any divine authority to which obedience is due, and proclaim that every man is the law to himself; from which arises that ethical system which they style independent morality, and which, under the guise of liberty, exonerates man from any obedience to the commands of God, and substitutes a boundless license. The end of all this it is not difficult to foresee, especially when society is in question. For, when once man is firmly persuaded that he is subject to no one, it follows that the efficient cause of the unity of civil society is not to be sought in any principle external to man, or superior to him, but simply in the free will of individuals; that the authority in the State comes from the people only; and that, just as every man's individual reason is his only rule of life, so the collective reason of the community should be the supreme guide in the management of all public affairs. Hence the doctrine of the supremacy of the greater number, and that all right and all duty reside in the majority."*

> ~ *Pope Leo XIII*[35]

Elucidation:

---

[34] Ibid., emphasis mine.
[35] *Libertas,* 15.

Daniel Schwindt

In much the same way that Luther could be considered the father of the Reformation, John Locke (1632-1704) has been considered the father of political Liberalism.[36] He was the most influential thinker to come from the Enlightenment, and was the philosopher of choice for revolutionaries such as the American Founding Fathers.

For our purposes here we will adopt Christopher Ferrara's summary, which concisely presents Locke's political legacy:[37]

> *A hypothetical "social compact" or contract as the foundation of the State.*
>
> *The origin of political sovereignty in the "consent" of the governed (invariably presumed to have been given by those who happen to be wielding power).*
>
> *"Government by the people" according to the "sovereignty of the people," meaning strict majority rule on all questions, including the most profound moral ones.*
>
> *Church-State separation and the non-"interference" of religion in politics.*
>
> *The confinement of religion, above all the revealed truths of Christianity, to the realm of "private" opinions and practices one is free to adopt (or to denounce) if it pleases him, but which are to have no controlling effect on law or public policy.*

---

[36] Delaney, Tim. *The march of unreason: science, democracy, and the new fundamentalism*. Oxford University Press, New York, 2005. p. 18.

[37] Christopher A. Ferrara, *Liberty, the god that failed: policing the sacred and constructing the myths of the secular state from Locke to Obama*. Angelico Press, Tacoma, 2012. p. 15.

The unlimited pursuit of gain, including the freedom to buy, sell and advertise anything whatsoever the majority deems permissible by law.

Total liberty of thought and action, both private and public, within the limits of a merely external "public peace" essentially reduced to the protection of persons and property from invasion by others—in sum, a "free-market society."

The dissolubility of marriage, and thus the family, as a mere civil contract founded on a revocable consent.

These principles found their most absolute expression in the French Revolution. The American Revolution, however, suffices as another clear example, and the Declaration of Independence acts as a neat summary of Locke's ideas. This should come as no surprise, since the Declaration was penned by Jefferson who was so enamored with Locke that he added his bust to a special canvas alongside Francis Bacon and Isaac Newton. These, he wrote, were "the three greatest men that have ever lived, without any exception…having laid the foundation of those superstructures which have been raised."[38]

CAPITALISM: OR, ECONOMIC LIBERALISM

Argument:

> *"The conviction that man is self-sufficient and can successfully eliminate the evil present in history by his own action alone has led him to confuse happiness and salvation with immanent forms of material prosperity and social action. Then, the conviction that the economy must be autonomous, that it must be shielded from "influences" of a moral character, has led man to abuse the economic process in a thoroughly destructive way.*

---

[38] Letter to John Trumbull, Thomas Jefferson: Writings, 939.

In the long term, these convictions have led to economic, social and political systems that trample upon personal and social freedom, and are therefore unable to deliver the justice that they promise."

~*Pope Benedict XVI*[39]

Elucidation:

That Capitalism is an expression of Liberalism should be painfully obvious, even though the American conservatives who today espouse it have no idea of the fact. To illustrate the point to such individuals, then, we might take Milton Friedman, economic advisor to Ronald Reagan and internationally known proponent of laissez-faire economic policy. In his 1962 book titled *Capitalism and Freedom,* he wrote that "the intellectual movement that went under the name of Liberalism emphasized freedom as the ultimate goal and the individual as the ultimate entity in the society."[40] This movement "supported laissez-faire at home as a means of reducing the role of the state in economic affairs and thereby enlarging the role of the individual."[41] Friedman thus considered himself a thoroughgoing Liberal, as much as this might dismay his contemporary disciples. But the only reason for this dismay is that Friedman was consistent; our contemporaries are not.

At this point I do not intend to examine the policies or problems associated with Capitalism. Here is will suffice to show what philosophical wellspring fed Capitalism in its beginnings, because that source has since been veiled by our confused American political terminology. Having cleared this up, we are able to understand the phrasing used in many Catholic encyclicals and documents which condemn Capitalism using the term Liberalism. For example, when Pope Pius XI applauds "boldly breaking through the confines imposed

---

[39] *Caritas in Veritate*, 34.
[40] Milton Friedman, *Capitalism and Freedom*.
[41] Ibid.

by Liberalism,"[42] and John XXIII condemns "unrestricted competition in the Liberal sense,"[43] they are speaking with a unified voice of Capitalism.[44]

Oswald Spengler had seen the connection between the money Liberalism of our capitalists and the more progressive moral Liberalism of their enemies, saying that Liberalism consists in "freedom of the intellect for every kind of criticism, freedom of money for every kind of business."[45]

LIBERALISM AND COWARDICE

Argument:

> *"A decline in courage may be the most striking feature which an outside observer notices in the West in our days. The Western world has lost its civil courage, both as a whole and separately, in each country, each government, each political party and of course in the United Nations. Such a decline in courage is particularly noticeable among the ruling groups and the intellectual elite, causing an impression of loss of courage by the entire society. Of course there are many courageous individuals but they have no determining influence on public life...Should one point out that from ancient times decline in courage has been considered the beginning of the end?"*

> ~ *Aleksander Solzhenitsyn*[46]

---

[42] *Quadragesimo Anno*, 25.

[43] *Mater et Magistra*, 23.

[44] See also: *Sollicitudo rei Socialis*, 20, 21, and 41.

[45] Oswald Spengler, *Decline of the West: Perspectives on World History*, p. 403-404.

[46] Aleksander Solzhenitsyn, Harvard Commencement Address delivered on June 8, 1978.

Daniel Schwindt

Elucidation:

There is an old parable regarding some servants who, being trusted by their master with varying quantities of money, each acted in a different fashion. Two of the three invested it, and then surrendered the profit to their master. The third man, however, buried his portion, and returned precisely the amount that he was given. When he does this, his master condemns him as a coward, and has him thrown out into the darkness. From this parable we can assume two things, one about the master, and the other about the servant. About the master, we can say that he obviously prefers courageous error to cowardly omission, and that this fact ought to have been clear to everyone who knew him. About the servant, we can assume that his fear drove him to an act of the second kind, which explains why it was inexcusable. This, then, is a parable about loyalty, yes, but also, and more important for our study, about courage, and it seems to us that it is a perfect representation of the modern world.

As Carl Schmitt said in his *Political Theology*:

> "The essence of Liberalism is negotiation, a cautious half measure, in the hope that the definitive dispute, the decisive bloody battle, can be transformed into a parliamentary debate and permit the decision to be suspended forever in an everlasting discussion."

In this he identified the paradox of Liberalism: it is jealous and therefore aggressive, but it is cowardly and therefore timid in its aggression.

Liberalism fosters the behavior of Hitler in C.S. Lewis's *The Great Divorce*, who spends his eternity building and re-building his cottage further and further away from the community of the damned. Each time he completes construction, he discovers that he has not gotten far enough away from the other individualists.

Fear is also paralyzing, particularly in the mental sphere. This is perhaps why general ignorance has increased since the rise of liberalism, despite whatever scientific achievements have also occurred. As Frank Herbert, the master of science fiction, once put it: "fear is the mind-killer." And this is the precise truth, because a person acting in fear loses his capacity for judgment precisely insofar as he is affected by his fear. In fear, he does things that, in a peaceful frame of mind, he'd have found ridiculous. This is why we would expect that, if fear were to become a generalized condition in a civilization, knowledge itself would begin to deteriorate.

Knowledge has a character of command. If something is true, and if we know it is true, we must act in accordance with it. Men across all various creeds agree at least on that, and this is why the immoralist does not claim the right to ignore morality, but rather denies its existence. No one acknowledges a truth and at the same time denies the obligation—the duty—it imposes. And so again, in ages of fear, truth, because of its imperious character, is the most despised of things.

It is like small child who chooses not to ask his mother a question because he knows he isn't going to like the answer. The modern man is just such a figure—the questions every man in history was ready to ask, are by him denied as valid. He wants nothing to do with them.

Cowardice says: "Only this—and only if I must."

One has to completely ignore the past in order to worship the future.

When Spengler famously wrote that "optimism is cowardice," it was just this sort of thing that he was describing. He was not so much condemning a "positive attitude" as he was condemning a very specific kind of positive attitude, the one adopted in order to avoid the severe realities of life, because it is only through these realities that courage and honor can be teased out of existence:

"We are born into this time and must bravely follow the path to the destined end. There is no other way. Our duty is to hold on to the lost position, without hope, without rescue, like that Roman soldier whose bones were found in front of a door in Pompeii, who, during the eruption of Vesuvius, died at his post because they forgot to relieve him. That is greatness. That is what it means to be a thoroughbred. The honorable end is the one thing that cannot be taken from a man."[47]

He was summarizing the effects of Liberalism, with its contradictory attempt to combine perpetual strife with promises of Progress and Happiness. Through this new myth, called Competition, it taught that by waging perpetual war with our neighbor for the means of self-indulgence, Happiness will be forthcoming, and that the longer we wage this war, the more wealth we will have and the happier we'll become.

We could proceed through a number of examples, familiar to all, to illustrate this omnipresent and enslaving fear which creates animosity: Think of the man who stockpiles weaponry in his basement, and rages in the streets about his "rights," and who imagines the day when he will have to do battle with his government—which, as likely as not, will actually be one of his neighbors—when they come to steal these "rights" from him. Clearly this behavior is an expression of paranoia, an extreme and enslaving condition of fear. But it is also inertia. Without courage nothing happens, and culture withers into nothing. Nietzsche's unique definition of Liberalism is then proven accurate:

"The honourable term for mediocre is, of course, the word 'Liberal'."[48]

REDUCTIONISM

Argument:

---

[47] Oswald Spengler, *Man and Technics* (Arktos, 2015), p. 77.
[48] Friedrich Nietzsche, *Will to Power*, paragraph 864.

"The present danger does not really lie in the loss of universality on the part of the scientist, but rather on his pretence and claim of totality...What we have to deplore therefore is not so much the fact that scientists are specializing, but rather the fact that specialists are generalizing. The true nihilism of today is reductionism...Contemporary nihilism no longer brandishes the word nothingness; today nihilism is camouflaged as nothing-but-ness. Human phenomena are thus turned into mere epiphenomena."

~ *Viktor Frankl*[49]

Elucidation:

Cowardice manifest in the intellectual sphere is reductionism. Here I wish merely to isolate the results of ideological Liberalism, with its fearful minimalism and mental slackness, in the sphere of knowledge, which, if we can see beyond the façade of industrialism, has rapidly decayed in the modern period.

We will examine the contributions to this decay of Rene Descartes, Isaac Newton, Martin Luther, Adam Smith, John Locke, Charles Darwin, and Sigmund Freud. These figures are chosen for the diversity of the fields they represent. If some of this recapitulates what has been said above, the reader is asked to excuse the repetition as a matter of necessary emphasis.

Rene Descartes (Philosophy): Descartes put a ceiling on man's knowledge which limited "truth" to rational concepts. This rejected the traditional conception of the self and of our ability to know God through the superior faculty, "the eye of the heart," which sees things beyond "the eye of the mind". Thus, rooting his own existence in his

---

[49] Cited in E.F. Schumacher, *A Guide for the Perplexed*, pp. 5-6.

mind, he also rooted God in the mind. Everything becomes rational, and therefore impoverished.

Isaac Newton (Physics): Joining with Descartes, Newton reduced his science to mathematics and therefore deterministic mechanism. "According to the mechanical philosophy and its theory of 'atomism,' the operations of material beings are owing entirely to movements of units of matter (atoms) governed by physical laws rather than the constitutive forms of the Aristotelian-Thomistic system lying beyond the matter of which things are composed."[50] This rejected any "metaphysical" considerations in regard to matter, and effectively severed this science from transcendence.

Martin Luther (Religion): We have already discussed Luther's work in this field. Suffice it to repeat here that he did not reform—he reduced. He took sections of traditional doctrine, such as the teachings about grace, faith, and scripture, and elevated them to absolutes. He simplified all theology into the "nothing-but-ness" of the three solas: *sola scripture, sola fida, sola gratia.*

Adam Smith (Economics): The well-known treatise *Wealth of Nations* contained not a single new idea. Great minds from Aristotle to St. Augustine to St. Thomas Aquinas had spent the last two-thousand years developing the science which they called "Political Economy," such that when Smith found it they had already taken into consideration the totality of economic action. They had separated it into four categories: production, exchange, distribution, and consumption. All Smith did was destroy the edifice by dropping the last two categories (distribution and consumption), and by rejecting any moral or metaphysical considerations. In this he made the same error as Newton, reducing a sacred science to a profane one, and in the

---

[50] Christopher Ferrara, *Liberty: The God that Failed*, p. 40.

process destroying it (it became considered a mechanical and mathematical science called just "Economics").[51]

Charles Darwin (Biology): It was said by C.S. Lewis that "evolution is as old as Epictetus," and he was right. Just as the Greeks knew the world was not flat,[52] they also conceived of the idea that life originated in the sea, in some primordial sludge, and then migrated onto land and eventually became man. What Darwin did, which the Greeks refused to do, was take this out of a metaphysical context which could not be proven. Darwin eliminated the transcendent from biology, as Newton had eliminated it from physics. Man is then a result of mechanism, and all of his complexity and subtlety can therefore be accounted for by this mechanism, given enough time.

Sigmund Freud (Psychology): Working from the combined reductions of Descartes, Newton, and Darwin, Freud formulated his ideas, which were perhaps the most reductionistic to date. Man's mind is here reduced to a shaky and entirely predetermined product of its environment. All man's passions and beliefs are the result of subterranean influences of the unconscious. Through this process we see that the Cartesian prison of the mind eventually—and necessarily—gave way to man becoming a prisoner of instinct and animal "drives."

John Locke (Politics): The reader may not be familiar with Locke by name, but everyone in America is intimately familiar with his political theory. He was one of the famous and influential liberals of the Enlightenment. He is responsible for the radically reductionistic political doctrines on which liberal democracies like America now operate. Like all of the previous characters, his claim to fame is the severing of transcendence from his area of science. We know this as the doctrine of "separation of church and state," which today both

---

[51] John Mueller makes this case in *Redeeming Economics: Rediscovering the Missing Element*.

[52] They observed the spherical shadow of the earth on the moon during eclipses.

Christians and pagans embrace as a wonderful advance, although they justify it in different ways. He completed this reduction by placing all authority in "the people," the government drawing its sovereignty from the bottom up. This is the opposite of the traditional teachings, traced out by Paul, showing that political leaders must acknowledge and remain attached to God, because their authority comes *from the top down*. Based on Locke's liberal principles, and with God unmentioned in the American Constitution, whatever the people desire is law. This holds true even if the people wish to reinstate child sacrifice—as they have so recently done.

UNIVOCITY FETISH AND THE COMMON GOOD

Argument:

> "*Due to their fetish of univocity, the men of the Enlightenment were largely unable to comprehend the idea of the common good. The atoms of Democritus and Newton's particles of light / made philosophes think they could ground the common good in private right.*
>
> "*Since all people discover themselves within a society, and discover within themselves an impulse towards sociability, it was necessary to come up with some other justification for the existence of community, even if the common good was not acceptable as an explanation. This is the origin of social contract theories.*"
>
> ~ *Coëmgenus*[53]

Elucidation:

---

[53] Coëmgenus, *The Josiahs,* "Theses and Responses on Antiamericanism", http://thejosias.com/2014/11/01/theses-and-responses-on-antiamericanism/.

One last hallmark of Enlightenment thought needs to be addressed, as it will assist the reader in subjects taken up in later installments of this series, and that is its obstinate, unrelenting insistence on errors of univocity: It was assumed that if there was such a thing as the individual good, then the only human good that could be considered was this limited one, and that the traditional concept of the common good could be nothing other than the sum total of individual good. Thus, even when Enlightenment thinkers acknowledge the duty of the State to seek serve the common good, they interpret this to mean that the State ought to limit itself to the protection of individual rights, since the common good can mean this and nothing more. We notice here again the inability to identify hierarchies of any kind, which ends each and every time by subordinating the higher to the lower.

This could also be described as the inability to make distinctions. Look through the *Summa* of St. Thomas, for example, or any work of Aristotle's. On almost every question these men were concerned with making the proper distinctions between orders and meanings for each term, allowing for a diversity of interpretations that nonetheless combine to form a coherent philosophy. Thus in the traditional conception, the common good a good of a higher order, complementing the individual good but at the very same time superior to it. Thus, a State which does nothing but protect individual right is doing nothing to seek the common good, but is limiting itself to an inferior, even if necessary, function. State action which does not go beyond individual right does not approach the common good, which is supra-individual. The common good is only one of the many concepts rendered incomprehensible through the univocity fetish of the Liberals.

STRIFE AS THE BASIS OF CIVILIZATION

Argument:

> *"All things desire peace."*

Daniel Schwindt

~ St. Augustine[54]

Elucidation:

If the Christian tradition is indeed correct in identifying man's highest desire as peace, then it is by thwarting this thirst for peace that Liberalism has done man the most violence. Ours is in fact the first civilization to attempt to base itself on strife. So engrained in our mentality has this become that at first we don't even see that it is there. It had always been said that the end of activity, even war, was peace; today peace is an evil. Peace is not productive.

While Augustine and Aquinas taught that we must seek not only the absence of war but the harmony of wills, Liberalism teaches that "if you desire peace, prepare for war"—thus, war is the engine of peace, and whatever peace, progress, or happiness exists, is credited to the perpetual interplay of various forms of combat.

Human life, for example, is a result of the "survival of the fittest," a doctrine which finds its economic expression in the Liberal ideas of capitalism and *laissez-faire* competition. Here not only material prosperity but even man himself is the outcome of the great battle for survival, whether that battle be for genetic superiority or natural resources. We can follow this line of thinking even through politics, where we see that the foundations of Liberal regimes such as the United States are a conceived as a "balance of powers," a balance which could more properly be termed a "battle" between powers. These powers are designed in such a way that they are always and everywhere trying to check each other's progress. This aspect of political Liberalism has fused itself ever so naturally onto the economic version in such a way that the former is now steered by almost entirely by the interests. As far as the people are concerned (which is always in a decreasing degree), this process is embodied by two parties vying for control over the machine. Peace, then, is not an ideal—it is a

---

[54] Augustine, *De Civ. Dei* xix, 12,14; Dionysius, *Div. Nom.* xi.

byproduct of the chaos, a byproduct which is, ironically, becoming more scarce every day as the process becomes more efficient, for if competition is good, then the system which maximizes the sort of "controlled discord" required by capitalism will be the best.

The most unexpected outcome of this confused situation is, first, a perpetually agitated human race, but also a strange timidity toward conflict. It is as if the undercurrents of conflict instill a fear of open war while also preventing true restfulness. In this state of mediocre warfare everyone loses, and even the winners are degraded. It is "the struggle for supremacy amidst conditions that are worth nothing: this civilization of great cities, newspapers, fever, uselessness."[55]

THE LIBERAL AND THE REACTIONARY

Argument:

> "The pure reactionary is not a dreamer of abolished pasts, but a hunter of sacred shades on the eternal hills... The reactionary does not aspire to turn back, but rather to change direction. The past that he admires is not a goal but an exemplification of his dreams."
>
> ~ Nicolás Gómez Dávila[56]

Elucidation:

In our study on democracy we used monarchy as a counterpoint for study. It is time we adopted another device here, identify some alternative as a useful contrast to the Liberal mentality, since until this point we've given the impression that everyone is a Liberal.

---

[55] Friedrich Nietzsche, *Will to Power*, 748.
[56] Dávila, 2001 edition, aphorism 2253.

This is true, of course: nearly everyone today *is a Liberal*. Yet there have been characters who rejected the modern consensus. Some of the more notable figures in this group are: Nicolás Gómez Dávila, Bertrand de Jouvenel, Joseph de Maistre, Julius Evola, Rene Guénon, Ivan Illich, various popes of the Catholic Church, and many others. These I will term the *Reactionaries*.

All such labels are admittedly imprecise. No doubt some of these men would reject outright the label I've chosen for them. But a label is necessary and useful so long as we acknowledge its limits.

I might have used instead the term "Traditionalist," and that would have perhaps been truer. Unfortunately, due to an omnipresent misunderstanding about the nature of Tradition, leading some to imagine that the Traditionalist argues for a rigid set of forms long-dead, wishing to reincarnate these dead forms and force them upon the living, it has become necessary to offer an alternative "type" which is better able to speak to contemporary audiences and convey the proper meaning, even if still imperfect. Reactionary, then, is my term of choice, which I will describe in the last section of this work, but which I will simply define here by referring back to Davila's aphorism quoted above, and by providing a table of contrasting values to give the reader a more thorough starting point:

The Liberal	*The Reactionary*
Equality	Hierarchy
Right	Duty
Patriotism	*Fides*
Uniformity	Unity
Democracy	Monarchy and aristocracy
Accumulation	Subsistence
Competition	Cooperation
Economic sex	Vernacular gender
Corporation	Guild
Anonymity	Personality
Revolution	Rebellion

Conflict	Order, peace
Legalism	Custom, tradition
Popular sovereignty	Divine sovereignty
Materialism, vague "spirituality"	Religious life
Worship of scientists, doctors	Worship of saints
Subjectivity	Objectivity
Majority opinion	Natural law
Agitation	Contemplation
Clinging to youth	Veneration for old age
Speed	Procrastination
Fear of mortality	Awareness of immortality
Education	Wisdom
Technical know-how	Art
Escapism	Confrontation
Novelty, "originality"	Beauty, truth
Worship of health, fitness	Indifference to fitness
Determinism	Free will
Security, safety	Adventure
Nationalism, internationalism	Empire, Supranationalism
The soldier, militarism	The knight, samurai, warrior
Industrial production	Craftsmanship
Individualism and collectivism	Personalism
The apartment, skyscraper, hotel	The castle, farm, hut
Anthropocentrism	Theocentrism
Homogeneity and the masses	Mosaic of families and villages
Monotony	Harmony
Courage	Cowardice
Centralism	Federalism
Horizontal order	Vertical order
Contractual society	Service, patriarchal authority
The city, the megalopolis	The village, chalet, rural community

With these values in mind, we have hopefully provided sufficient analysis to call into question the soundness of Liberal philosophy, while identifying a type which we will, throughout the remaining installments of this series, have reason to refer back to. For now, we can close by observing that the American Right and the Left fight endlessly for the controls of a hideous machine which the reactionary would not cheapen himself by controlling even if he could, nor would he degrade his fellows by lording its control over them if he were ever forced to assume it. The moderns join together to fight for a victory that the reactionary understands as a suicide.

PART 2: DEMOCRACY

The cause of democracy's stupidities is confidence in the anonymous citizen; and the cause of its crimes is the anonymous citizen's confidence in himself.

˜ Nicolás Gómez Dávila

INTRODUCTORY

What you have before you is the first in a series of works calling into question the unconscious and therefore unquestionable assumptions of the modern world. These preconceptions—these prejudices—are today treated as dogma, not in an official sense, but in a practical one, since all that is beyond question automatically enters the sphere of the sacred. Because of this, any flaws in the ideas, any weaknesses inherent in them, are able to operate and wreak havoc unnoticed. Or, perhaps more commonly, if the weaknesses are noticed, the blame is misplaced, and the great problem solvers of our era are then led to apply cures that having nothing to do with the diseases that afflict us.

Our purpose here is to exercise the modern mind, and hopefully to break down the barriers against thought which have been erected by our unacknowledged ideological prejudices. To do this we will call into question notions such as equality, liberty, liberalism, natural rights, progress, and war, and many others. The first we will bring to trial, because it is perhaps most mentioned and most familiar to us, is *democracy*.

Tell a man that political parties do more harm than good, and you may find some degree of agreement. Suggest that voter misinformation is a serious impediment to functional government, and you may again find some common ground. But if you then suggest that these problems are rooted in the nature of democracy itself, then you will meet, and best, a confused stare and the sound of crickets.

Here in our freethinking regime no traditional doctrine is beyond question and no person beyond criticism. Even in the most "patriotic" of circles, amongst the "good ole boys," we hear talk about shooting the President, if he is not the one these patriots voted for. In our democracy, then, we are willing to call everything into question—except democracy itself. That we treat as dogma—one of the only ones we have.

The purpose of this essay is not to paint a picture of democracy as always, everywhere, and in every form an evil. It is rather to offer criticism of it, because if we cannot mark the weaknesses of our own system then we render ourselves incapable of facing any problems that might be rooted in the system itself; and indeed it turns out that, after some honest reflection, most of our contemporary problems are of just that nature.

Democracy is only bad, or only became bad, when it escaped all forms of critical reflection. At that point it became what we should properly call a superstition, because a superstition is an activity or belief that continues even when those who practice it no longer understand its nature, purpose, beginning, or limits.

The traditional world was not necessarily set against democracy. It simply believed that such a system did not provide the most effective means for achieving peace, providing personal autonomy, and fostering the good life. They preferred monarchy, but did not exclude aristocracy and some forms of democracy.

Modern regimes, on the other hand, are much less open-minded than their ancestors. They hold democracy in highest regard, and hold every other possibility in disgust. Thus, if we single out democracy for critique, it is not so much because the traditional world had no room for it, or because we consider it an unqualified evil, but because the

Liberal world where we live today seems to have room for it and nothing else. The modern Liberal-Democratic world is intolerant to an unprecedented degree, and this narrowness is disturbing. If we can figure out why, then we will have learned something.

A second reason to engage in a study such as this, even though the first alone is sufficient justification, is for the simple reason that if you cannot take seriously any alternative point of view than your own, then you are a bigot. A Western Christian who cannot imagine a sincere Hindu, a Hindu who takes his own religion as seriously as any saint, a Hindu who loves truth and who is therefore deserving of respect as a pilgrim—this Christian is a bigot. In the same way, the Westerner who cannot imagine a monarchy without automatically inferring backwardness, tyranny, ignorance, and injustice, is blind both to the insufficiencies of his beloved democracy and to the strengths of the alternative.

With these justifications and purposes in mind, we may begin.

A HISTORICAL FALLACY

Argument:

> *"It has been attempted to give ancestors to modern democracy: ancient democracies, the urban or peasant democracies of the Middle Ages. These are only pictures acquired by a newly rich to adorn his chateau; he may take on the name but he is not of the same house."*

> ~ *Gonzague de Reynold*[57]

Elucidation:

---

[57] Gonzague de Reynold, *L'Europe Tragique*.

First we must place our modern notion of democracy in its proper historical significance by acknowledging it as the novelty that it is. What we call democracy has no precedent in terms of Western civilization. The common references to Athens and Rome are ridiculously inappropriate. Yes, the government was in some cases carried out by the citizens, and the citizens participated in the courts and legislation. But these were slave societies and so whatever freedom and participatory powers were exercised by the citizens were of a very exclusive nature. The citizenry was in fact a minority, and so what they called democracy was really nothing but the belief in the self-government of the elite. Majority rule for them meant the majority of a small minority.

Only if we limited political power to a small percentage of economically powerful individuals in America, and allowed only those few to vote, and then called the result the majority opinion, then perhaps we could begin to draw parallels. What's more, we must keep in mind that the ancients were conscious of this fact: they would have never preached a kind of democracy that included everyone, for they believed that slavery was a condition for the kind of government they were attempting. They believed that the only way men could be capable of giving the amount of time necessary for government, as well as achieving the knowledge necessary for judgment of such affairs, was only made possible by the fact that slavery exempted the citizenry from physical toil.

THE PATRICIDAL OFFSPRING OF LIBERALISM

Argument:

> *"Democracy...will devour liberalism, whose child it is. Liberalism from the beginning on felt that it would have to be the victim. Liberalism is generous and therefore weak. Democracy is jealous and therefore strong."*

~ Gonzague de Reynold[58]

Elucidation:

Although we must reserve our discussion of Liberalism for the next installment in this series, we must give brief attention to it in order to understand the rise of democracy, for the most important democracies of our day, America for example, are properly classified as *Liberal democracies.*

We must first be careful to separate the contemporary use of the word "Liberal" from its actual philosophical and historical meaning. Liberalism is *not* an American political party, and it only partially corresponds to the set of ideas proffered by that party. Instead it represents ideals shared by both American parties, for if these two acknowledged their roots accurately, they would have to call themselves "Right liberals" and "Left liberals." But so confused has our rhetoric become that we see these two siblings acting as if they were completely alien to one another, when in fact they are but branches of the same creed.

Liberalism properly considered is represented by the collection of ideals formulated by the Enlightenment philosophers: free speech, equality, liberty, representative government, universal suffrage, rights, free markets, etc. With this clarified, we can interpret modern democracy as the offspring of Enlightenment Liberalism, for although democracy is only one possible realization of the Liberal ideals, democratism is the inevitable manifestation of these with respect to the popular mind which, unable to effect the moderation and limits within which the original Liberals hoped to circumscribe their principles (the American Founders, for example, spoke of a Republic and not a democracy), carries them with blind acceleration to their extreme ends. We may live in a Republic, but the modern man thinks

---

[58] Gonzague de Reynold, *L'Europe Tragique.*

51

and feels and acts in terms of democracy. Thus, we can speak of a deep-seated *democratism* regardless of any originally intended *republicanism*.

Democratism is at the same time Liberalism's caricature and conclusion. It exaggerates and brings to completion the aforementioned principles which the Founders would, through a prudent inconsistency, carry only so far. Where Jefferson thought that all men could be educated men, and that all educated men would be disciplined enough to vote rationally, it was only when Liberal-democratism had matured in the common mind that America actually attempted to educate all those men and give them all a vote. Jefferson was willing to do neither, for although his principles seemed to dictate this, he was an aristocrat at heart. He had no intention of giving votes to his own slaves.

It is clear by the way in which those early Liberals shunned democratism that they feared it; it is as though they sensed that it would be their undoing. Gouverneur Morris, Founding Father and so-called "Penman of the Constitution" wrote to Robert Walsh in 1811: "History, the parent of political science, had told them [the framers of America's Constitution] that it was almost as vain to expect permanency from democracy as to construct a palace on the surface of the sea."[59]

There is, in truth, not too much danger in having Liberal sentiments, and in the past there was many a nobleman and monarch who had them. What doomed modern civilization was the extension of these sentiments to all men everywhere, not only as an optimistic view entertained by a superior about his inferiors, which could be healthy in a nobleman, but as an opinion of every man, however inferior, about himself.

---

[59] Jared Sparks, *The Life of Gouverneur Morris with Selections of His Correspondence* (Boston: Gray and Bowen, 1832), III, 263.

From the moment Liberal sentiments became the preconceived notion of every man about his own nobility, goodness, and intelligence, there was born Liberalism, which could not but produce the mentality of democratism, and which could only end in the death of the original, healthy liberal sentiment. Liberalism was originally generous, but it could remain generous only so long as it was directed from the nobility toward the world. When it became the attitude of all of humanity toward itself it became suicidal.

DEMOCRACY AS THE MOST PRIMITIVE FORM OF GOVERNMENT

Argument:

> *"Democracy or the democratic state is the natural state for a primitive society where the diversity of conditions is not very distinct; or maybe in an arbitrary state of cells where social conditions are considered having no report to political functions. . . . We therefore find democracy sometimes at the origins of a society or in their decline but rarely at the height of their historic development."*

> *~ François-René*[60]

Elucidation:

Benjamin Disraeli called monarchy a government which "requires a high degree of civilization." "It needs the support of the free laws and manners, and of a widely diffused intelligence. . . . An educated nation recoils from the imperfect vicariate of what is called a representative government."[61] Even children naturally adopt democratic methods in

---

[60] Le Marquis de la Tour-du-Pin la Charce, *Aphorismes de politique sociale.*
[61] Coningsby, Book V, Ch. 8.

their play when there are more than two in the group. It is no advanced form of reasoning to follow the will of the assembly and to occasionally surrender one's own desires to the desires of the mob. Many animal species do just this, allowing themselves to be guided instinctually, falling in line with the surrounding members of the group, de-individuating and melting into one body.

Of course, this point of view also implies something else: that the "evolution" of society in the direction of democracy is actually a devolution—a regression back to a more unsophisticated state. And again we find confirmation of this view in traditional writings, such as those of the Christian Father Hyppolytus of 3ʳᵈ century Rome, who wrote in his commentaries on the book of Daniel that the "toes mingled with iron and clay" which represent the fourth kingdom are to be understood to represent democracies, the weakest and most inferior of all the substances.[62]

DEMOCRACY IMPLIES THE USE OF FORCE

Argument:

> *"One could well imagine that if seven out of ten cavemen wanted to do a thing collectively in one way and the three others decided differently, the majority of these cavemen (assuming that they are of about equal bodily strength) could force the rest to accept their decision. The rule of majorities, in combination with the employment of brutal force, is likely to be the most primitive form of government in the development of mankind."*

---

[62] *On Daniel,* Second and Third Fragments. Available online at New Advent: http://www.newadvent.org/fathers/0502.htm.

~ Erik von Kuehnelt-Leddihn[63]

Elucidation:

As a further illustration of the primitive nature of democracy, it is worth noting that even though in theory the proponents of democracy picture their system as a highly advanced form of social cooperation, this is never the case in the concrete political reality. Taking the contemporary United State as an example, there seems at any given time to be at least half the population which is dissatisfied by the operation and decisions of the governing authority, and in no way feels that the decisions being made by it are an expression of their own will. This amounts to saying that they feel they are being governed by an unwelcome authority, and the only reason they put up with the oppression is because they entertain hopes of someday becoming oppressors themselves.[64] Democracy, then, differs not in the degree of force required to carry out the wishes of the government, but in the condition of passivity it has been able to maintain in its people by doing nothing else but "letting them drive" every so often—or, even if not actually allowing them to drive, at least giving them a tour of the cockpit.

All this goes to show that government by force is alive and well in the democratic system, as it always has been; and insofar as it is alive and well, democracy cannot be said to represent an advance, but instead only mirrors the earliest of possible arrangements. It is the arrangement of the caveman.

---

[63] Erik von Kuehnelt-Leddihn, *Menace of the Herd* (Milwaukee: Bruce, 1943), p. 103.

[64] "Universal suffrage in the end does not recognize any of the individual's rights except the 'right' to be alternately oppressor or oppressed" (Nicolás Gómez Dávila, *Scholia to an Implicit Text*. 2013, Bilingual Edition. p. 181. Since this edition does not offer numbers with aphorisms, they will be referenced by page number for this edition.)

Daniel Schwindt

DEMOCRACY AS THE DEPERSONALIZATION OF POWER

Argument:

> *"Modern man accepts any yoke, as long as the hand imposing it is impersonal."*
>
> *~ Nicolás Gómez Dávila*[65]

Elucidation:

Bertrand de Jouvenel, who demonstrated in his treatise *On Power* that the rise of Liberal democracy has only aided the growth of power, said that it owed its continued expansion to the impersonal nature that such regimes are able to assume. He says of State power:

> "Formerly it could be seen, manifest in the person of the king, who did not disclaim being the master he was, and in whom human passions were discernible. Now, masked in anonymity, it claims to have no existence of its own, and to be but the impersonal and passionless instrument of the general will."[66]

Do you detest the encroachments of the state? Well then it is your own will that you detest, since you live in a regime of self-government. You govern yourself, do you not? And if you have come to the conclusion that you do not, and that you are ruled, who is ruling you? What name can you really identify? Certainly not the President who, although he has more power than the British monarch, makes only a few laws in comparison to Congress. And who drives Congress?—it is impossible to tell.

---

[65] Dávila, 2001 edition, aphorism 1345.
[66] Bertrand de Jouvenel, *On Power* (Boston: Beacon, 1962), p. 9.

You eventually realize that to choose any one man is to miss the point and to have nothing but a scapegoat. You also cannot choose to blame no one at all, for where there is blame there must also be personal responsibility, and so you are left again with yourself, which is absurd. This difficulty which stems from the impersonal nature of democracy is the modern State's greatest asset, and is responsible for the fact that today the common man must cope with more burdens, whether in terms of taxation or liberty plain and simple, than any man before him.

THE DEPERSONALIZATION OF THE STATESMAN HIMSELF

Argument:

> *"Politics, under a democracy, reduces itself to a mere struggle for office by flatterers of the proletariat; even when a superior man prevails at that disgusting game he must prevail at the cost of his self-respect. Not many superior men make the attempt. The average great captain of the rabble, when he is not simply a weeper over irremediable wrongs, is a hypocrite so far gone that he is unconscious of his own hypocrisy—a slimy fellow, offensive to the nose."*

> *~ H.L. Mencken*[67]

Elucidation:

We select a candidate for any office we are not selecting a leader—in fact we are not looking at character traits at all—we are merely selecting a mirror, and the man who can best function in that reflective capacity is the victor.

---

[67] H.L. Mencken, Introduction to Nietzsche's *The Antichrist*.

Unfortunately, since this requires the politician not only to try to "mirror" my desires, but also a thousand others, the one who wins is not simply a mirror, but a complex "prism" of sorts, attempting to "represent" a thousand wills at once. The last person he is actually allowed to be is himself. Needless to say, no authentic man—much less a great leader—would subject himself to such degradation. And yet we demand it of all politicians.

THE RISE OF THE POLITICIAN

Argument:

> *"And this hypocrisy found I worst amongst them, that even those who command feign the virtues of those who serve...'I serve, thou servest, we serve'—so chanteth here even the hypocrisy of the rulers—and alas! if the first lord be only the first servant!"*

> ~ *Friedrich Nietzsche*[68]

Elucidation:

What disgusted Nietzsche so much about the operations of democracy was the effect that it had on men whose role was traditionally one of a superior character. The leader of a people had always been selected because he was presumably of man of exceptional wisdom, virtue, ability, or birth. In short, he received his exceptional position on the basis of his exceptional character. Whatever the area of exceptionality, it was assumed that he was in some way "better" than those he was to lead. If he were not better, then it would have made no sense to appoint him. With the adoption of democratic modes of thought, with the emphasis on "representation" as the utmost, if not the only,

---

[68]Friedrich Nietzsche, *Thus Spake Zarathusra*, "The Bedwarfing Virtue".

qualification for an office, all of the highest attributes of a man, and therefore all of the highest types of men, because automatically excluded from consideration. Only the man who could present himself as most "representative" of his constituency was considered a valid choice. And so, while it would neither have been expected nor proper for the most important leader of a society to feign a likeness to those he was to lead, it now became the single factor determining whether or not a man would hold an office. Because great leaders are differentiated—that is to say, they are inherently *unlike* the common man, in that they surpass him in wisdom and virtue and boldness—democratic societies immediately run up against a conundrum: either they demand that these differentiated men pretend they are not what they are, that is to say, they demand hypocrisy; or else they drive these men out of their midst and choose "leaders" who are not leaders but are simple experts in mediocrity.

This leads us to a second point: It is possible, and in fact very useful, to draw a distinction between the sphere of "politics" and the sphere of "statesmanship": the former can then be said to pertain to those activities by which a candidate seeks and maintains his office, which in democratic regimes involves campaigns, speeches, promises, and expensive PR experts; the latter pertains instead to the actual activities proper to a head of State in his strictly administrative role. These two activities, it has been observed, are mutually exclusive. So long as a man is concerned with "politicking" or, as we say, "campaigning," he cannot begin to concern himself with actual statesmanship; and, likewise, insofar as he is acting in his proper role as statesman, he cannot allow himself to be influenced by the fluctuations of public opinion. If we separate these two roles or spheres of activity, we can see immediately that in democracies or "representative republics" where the officials are perpetually insecure and dependent on the voters, they never actually are able to enter into the role of statesmen. No doubt they made administrative decisions—and important ones at that—but they do so as politicians, which is to say they do so under improper conditions and therefore badly. Thus, we can say that Nietzsche's complaint was that he saw the active exclusion of

Daniel Schwindt

statesmen in preference of politicians whose activity consisted primarily in pretending that they were not even that.

HONORABLE MEN ARE AVERSE TO DEMOCRACY

Argument:

> *"Democratic republics place the spirit of a court within the reach of a great number of citizens and allow it to spread through all social classes at once. That is one of the most serious criticisms that can be made against them...Among the huge throng of those pursuing a political career in the United States, I saw very few men who displayed that manly openness, that male independence of thought, which has often distinguished Americans in previous times and which, wherever it is found, is virtually the most marked characteristic of great men...It is true that American courtiers never say: 'Sire,' or 'Your Majesty,' as if this difference was of great importance, but they do constantly speak of the natural enlightenment of their master. They do not seek to question which is the most admirable of the prince's virtues for they convince him that he has every virtue without his having acquired them and without, so to speak, desiring them. They do not give him their wives or daughters for him kingly to raise them to the position of his mistresses but, in sacrificing their opinions to him, they prostitute themselves."*

> *~Alexis de Tocqueville*[69]

Elucidation:

---

[69] Tocqueville, op. cit., p. 301.

For those who still cannot see how we demand the hypocrites and flatterers that we complain of so often, for those who still believe that we do in fact prefer authentic men in our American offices, perhaps a comparison between two men of different nations and different times will suffice. I choose them not for their faith, but for the types of character they illustrate.

Take first the famous historian, Hilaire Belloc. In 1906 he ran for a seat in the English parliament. His opponent, knowing that Belloc was a devout Catholic and of French blood, made his slogan "Don't vote for a Frenchman and a Catholic." Belloc responded by standing up amidst his Protestant audience and saying:

> Gentlemen, I am a Catholic. As far as possible, I go to Mass every day. This [taking a rosary out of his pocket] is a rosary. As far as possible, I kneel down and tell these beads every day. If you reject me on account of my religion, I shall thank God that He has spared me the indignity of being your representative.

The audience erupted in applause, and Belloc won the seat. He overwhelmed the prejudices of his audience with his manly authenticity, and the people decided they would rather have a leader in office than a mirror.

Turn now to John F. Kennedy, also a Catholic, who found himself in an identical situation, speaking before a Protestant audience amidst a presidential campaign. His words, however, are somewhat different:

> I believe in an America where the separation of church and state is absolute...I am not the Catholic candidate for president. I am the Democratic Party's candidate for president, who happens also to be a Catholic. I do not speak for my church on public matters, and the church does not speak for me...Whatever issue may come before me as president—on birth control, divorce, censorship, gambling or any other

subject—I will make my decision...in accordance with what my conscience tells me to be the national interest, and without regard to outside religious pressures or dictates.[70]

Between these two men we see a profound difference of attitude, which we may assume reflects the attitudes of the voters to whom they were speaking. Belloc would not compromise his honor to win a vote, and his voters loved him for it. Kennedy, on the other hand, apparently felt that he could not enter office at all without first swearing an "oath of inauthenticity," pretending to leave his faith on the White House lawn.

This should tell us something about our politicians, but it should also tell us much about ourselves and what we must come to demand of our so-called leaders. We have, in a very real sense, created a special breed of hypocrite. We have systemically excluded the possibility of any real leader winning an office, because a real leader could never transform himself into the representative "prism" of pretence and hypocrisy that the office now requires.

The result? In the words of C.S. Lewis: "We make men without chests and expect of them virtue and enterprise. We laugh at honour and are shocked to find traitors in our midst. We castrate and bid the geldings be fruitful."[71]

Or, to turn to Gomez Davila: "Democracy is the political regime in which the citizen entrusts the public interests to those men to whom he would never entrust his private interests."[72]

---

[70] *Address to the Greater Houston Ministerial Association* delivered on September 12, 1960 in Houston, TX.
[71] C.S. Lewis, *The Abolition of Man*.
[72] Dávila, 2001 edition, aphorism 1088.

THE DEMOCRATIC TENDENCY TOWARD MATERIALISM

Argument:

> *"As for the effect which one man's intelligence can have upon another's, it is of necessity much curtailed in a country where its citizens, having become almost like each other, scrutinize each other carefully and, perceiving in not a single person in their midst any signs of undeniable greatness or superiority, constantly return to their own rationality as to the most obvious and immediate source of truth. So, it is not merely trust in any particular individual which is destroyed, but also the predilection to take the word of any man at all. Each man thus retreats into himself from where he claims to judge the world...As they realize that, without help, they successfully resolve all the small problems they meet in their practical lives, they easily reach the conclusion that there is an explanation for everything in the world and that nothing is beyond the limits of intelligence. So it is that they willingly deny what they cannot understand; that gives them little faith in the extraordinary and an almost invincible distaste for the supernatural."*

> *~Alexis de Tocqueville*[73]

Elucidation:

Tocqueville comments on the tendency toward baser pleasures and also the call for government to lift men's minds.

QUANTITY OVER QUALITY

---

[73] Tocqueville, op. cit. p. 494.

Daniel Schwindt

Argument:

> *"[W]hat is this law of the greatest number which modern governments invoke and in which they claim to find their sole justification? It is simply the law of matter and brute force, the same law by which a mass, carried down by its weight, crushes everything that lies in its track. It is precisely here that we find the point of junction of the democratic conception and materialism..."*
>
> *~ René Guénon*[74]

Elucidation:

That democracy automatically implies force, we've already acknowledged. That this implication is directly connected with materialism, we've also mentioned. That this also creates a poisonous preference for quantity over quality, we will speak of now.

In this sense, we can say that democracy is anti-rational since it prefers "victory by numbers." It is no coincidence that mass warfare became the norm alongside the rise of democracy, and that the army of career warriors came to be replaced by the armed horde and universal suffrage. But close to the operation of democracy, we can see this in the way political activity, even in the most noble of cases, is carried out.

If is deemed important, or one's position needs to be justified in a democracy, how does one proceed? In many famous cases a "demonstration" is organized in the form of a protest or a march, whether the cause is civil rights, gay pride or the March for Life. The obvious assumption is that the greater the number of participants, the more the proponents of that agenda feel justified in their position,

---

[74] René Guénon, *Crisis of the Modern World* (Hillsdale: Sophia Perennis, 1996), p. 76.

and—so the thinking goes—the more convinced the general population ought to be of the validity of the cause. The congregation of a mass is interpreted as an argument in itself—as a proof of truth.

But clearly it doesn't matter how many people take part in such "demonstrations" if they do not have a basis in justice, and no quantity of participants can prove the justice or rationality of an opinion. In fact, it proves nothing except a general desire amongst the participants. For St. Thomas Aquinas, on the other hand, a "demonstration" could only have been conceived as a well-constructed argument that proves the truth of a certain proposition. If this rational "demonstration" of the point was properly made, then the truth of the statement was shown, hence the term "demonstration." Quantity had nothing to do with it: if the point was shown to be true, then it mattered very little how many citizens agreed with its conclusions, or how many participated in its construction. This is the difference between quality and quantity, and it demonstrates (in the non-democratic sense) the underlying mentality of a democratic people.

EQUALITY, NOT LIBERTY, IS THE RULING PASSION OF DEMOCRACY

Argument:

> "Freedom has appeared in the world at different times and under various forms; it has not been exclusively bound to any social condition, and it is not confined to democracies. Freedom cannot, therefore, form the distinguishing characteristic of democratic ages. The peculiar and preponderant fact that marks those ages as its own is the equality of condition; the ruling passion of men in those periods is the love of this equality. Do not ask what singular charm the men of democratic ages find in being equal, or what special reasons they may have for clinging so tenaciously to equality rather than to the other advantages that society holds

> *out to them: equality is the distinguishing characteristic of the age they live in; that of itself is enough to explain that they prefer it to all the rest."*

> ~ *Alexis de Tocqueville*[75]

Elucidation:

This point is not merely an interesting bit of sociological trivia, but becomes extremely important when we enter a discussion of equality and its relationship to liberty. Without getting too far ahead of ourselves, we can simply say that liberty and equality cannot both be sought at the same time and to the same degree, because at a certain point they become mutually exclusive. Equality cannot be sought except at the expense of liberty, and vice versa. Thus, a social preference for equality will inevitably demand the sacrifice of liberty.

PREFERENCE FOR EQUALITY LEADS TO THE CULT OF INCOMPETENCE

Argument:

> *"I have often wondered what principle democrats have adopted for the form of government which they favour, and it has not required a great effort on my part to arrive at the conclusion that the principle in question is the worship and cultivation, or, briefly 'the cult' of incompetence or inefficiency."*

> *Émile Faguet*[76]

---

[75] Tocqueville, op. cit., p. 584.
[76] Emile Faguet, *Cult of Incompetence*, p. 15.

Elucidation:

This citation comes from Émile Faguet's *Cult of Incompetence*. After some consideration, it became obvious to me that the best commentary on the notion came from Faguet himself a bit further on into the work:

> "What is the people's one desire, when once it has been stung by the democratic tarantula? It is that all men should be equal, and in consequence that all inequalities natural as well as artificial should disappear. It will not have artificial inequalities, nobility of birth, royal favours, inherited wealth, and so it is ready to abolish nobility, royalty, and inheritance. Nor does it like natural inequalities, that is to say a man more intelligent, more active, more courageous, more skilful than his neighbours. It cannot destroy these inequalities, for they are natural, but it can neutralise them, strike them with impotence by excluding them from the employments under its control. Democracy is thus led quite naturally, irresistibly one may say, to exclude the competent precisely because they are competent, or if the phrase pleases better and as the popular advocate would put it, not because they are competent but because they are unequal, or, as he would probably go on to say, if he wished to excuse such action, not because they are unequal, but because being unequal they are suspected of being opponents of equality. So it all comes to the same thing. This it is that made Aristotle say that where merit is despised, there is democracy. He does not say so in so many words, but he wrote: "Where merit is not esteemed before everything else, it is not possible to have a firmly established aristocracy," and that amounts to saying that where merit is not esteemed, we enter at once on a democratic regime and never escape from it."[77]

---

[77] Emile Faguet, *Cult of Incompetence*, pp. 30-31.

Daniel Schwindt

MONARCHY AS A COUNTERPOINT FOR THE AMERICAN MIND

Argument:

> *"Every teacher of comparative political science will discover what enormous effort it requires to impart a clear notion of European monarchical institutions to even quite mature students. A Napoleonic tyranny, a dictatorship— this is easily within the realm of their comprehension. But a legitimate monarchy seems to the American a simple absurdity, and he cannot understand how otherwise quite intelligent people can have faith in such a thing."*

> *~ Ernst Bruncken[78]*

To put the problem in concise Chestertonian terms, Americans are political bigots. That is to say, when it comes to political arrangements, Americans display "the incapacity to conceive seriously the alternative to a proposition,"[79] which was Chesterton's own definition of bigotry. It seems that Americans, regardless of how dissatisfied they are with their political circumstances, cannot or will not (it matter little which, at this point) imagine any concrete alternative. And they apply this not only to their own situation, which would be somewhat understandable, but even to their view of history. They seem unable to picture a functional and just monarchy anywhere else at any point in time, regardless of the frequent appearance of such regimes. It is thus rendered nearly impossible to speak to Americans of any political arrangement *other than* liberal democracy.[80]

---

[78] Ernst Bruncken, *Die amerikanische Volksseele* (Gotha: Perthes, 1911).

[79] G.K. Chesterton, *Lunacy and Letters.*

[80] See also D. W. Brogan, *The American Character* (New York: Knopf, 1944), p. 146: "In the same way, the word 'republic' has an almost magical significance for Americans...whatever the origin of the belief, it is now part of the American credo that only citizens of a republic can be free. And no matter what romantic

It was for this reason that we delayed our discussion of monarchy until a thorough critique of democracy as such had been completed. It is my hope that this exploration would, in itself, prepare and enable the earnest reader to appreciate the beneficial aspects of monarchical government, whether we are speaking of a constitutional monarchy or otherwise. Regardless of whether or not my hopes are realized, it is necessary to make the effort, because the plain fact is that no real analysis of our own system is possible if we cannot at least historically understand alternatives. Even if the reader still remains convinced of the superiority of democracy after reading this section, he will at least have a more realistic and, therefore, challenging notion of monarchy with which he can contrast his preferred system. In this way, a general enumeration of the strengths of monarchy will be of great benefit as a *counterpoint* to what, for most Americans, is an opinion justified by nothing, a philosophy floating in a void.

MONARCHY AS THE EMERGENCE FROM SAVAGERY

Argument:

> "[T]he rise of monarchy appears to be an essential condition of the emergence of mankind from savagery. No human being is so hide-bound by custom and tradition as your democratic savage; in no state of society consequently is progress so slow and difficult. The old notion that the savage is the freest of mankind is the reverse of the truth. He is a slave, not indeed to a visible master, but to the past, to the spirits of his dead forefathers, who haunt his steps from birth to death, and rule him with a rod of iron. What they did is the pattern of right, the unwritten law to which he yields a blind unquestioning obedience. The least possible scope is thus afforded to superior

interest Americans may display in the human side of monarchy, it should never be forgotten that politically they regard it as a childish institution."

talent to change old customs for the better. The ablest man is dragged down by the weakest and dullest, who necessarily sets the standard, since he cannot rise, while the other can fall. The surface of such a society presents a uniform dead level, so far as it is humanly possible to reduce the natural inequalities, the immeasurable real differences of inborn capacity and temper, to a false superficial appearance of equality."

~James George Frazer[81]

Elucidation:

This passage is taken from *The Golden Bough*, a massive work of twelve volumes by James George Frazer, a man considered by many as the father of modern anthropology. Although the documentary value of the work will quite possibly never be surpassed, Frazer's value as a philosopher is limited. We say this because, for one so passionate about his work, he refused at every step to take the people he studied seriously. He condescends at the outset and on every page thereafter, toward the customs and actions he spent so much effort gathering together. However, it is for this very reason that we can somewhat appreciate his observation regarding primitive democracy and the rise of the king: that because he proved himself willing to interpret his data according to preconceived notions, he has no reason to favor kingship, but would probably be considered something of a liberal himself. Thus, his statements can be taken at their face value since they do not coincide with his typical prejudices and thus do not fall in the category of his philosophical interpretations, but rather within the category of his valid sociological observations.

---

[81] James George Frazer, *The Golden Bough*, Vol. 3.

THREE ARGUMENTS FOR MONARCHY FROM ST. THOMAS AQUINAS

Argument:

> *"[We] must now inquire what is better for a province or a city: whether to be ruled by one man or by many...*
>
> *Now it is manifest that what is itself one can more efficaciously bring about unity than several... several men, for instance, could not pull a ship in one direction unless joined together in some fashion. Now several are said to be united according as they come closer to being one. So one man rules better than several who come near being one.*
>
> *Again, whatever is in accord with nature is best, for in all things nature does what is best. Now, every natural governance is governance by one...Wherefore, if artificial things are an imitation of natural things and a work of art is better according as it attains a closer likeness to what is in nature, it follows that it is best for a human multitude to be ruled by one person.*
>
> *This is also evident from experience. For provinces or cities which are not ruled by one person are torn with dissensions and tossed about without peace, so that the complaint seems to be fulfilled which the Lord uttered through the Prophet [Jer 12:10]: "Many pastors have destroyed my vineyard." On the other hand, provinces and cities which are ruled under one king enjoy peace, flourish in justice, and delight in prosperity."*
>
> ~ *St. Thomas Aquinas*[82]

Elucidation:

---

[82] *De Regno*, Book 1, paragraph 3.

Daniel Schwindt

The arguments of St. Thomas are helpful not only because of their simplicity (anyone could memorize them in a minute) and cogency (they would be difficult to directly refute) but because they convey very well the traditional modes of reasoning. For example, the common doctor bases his arguments on nature, which is to say, *concrete reality* as it is. He does not begin in an abstract ideal which he then attempts to realize, as must be done with democracy. He also insists on rationality, and then follows with historical experience. Also, to get a further idea of the medieval mind, he stresses the need for *unity*, which is a specifically traditional principle, as opposed to the liberal belief in "progress by competition." Furthermore, he argues from nature and its mode of governance. His he does because natural laws are derived from the eternal law, which is nothing but the mind of God. Therefore, it can be assumed that nature has educational value. If natural things are governed by one, then the artificial things of man can be considered better if they follow this example. Statesmanship is an art, and "Art is the imitation of Nature in her manner of operation."[83]

SECURITY OF STATION AND DISPASSIONATE JUDGMENT

Argument:

> "*Constitutional monarchy offers us...that neutral power so indispensable for all regular liberty. In a free country the king is a being apart, superior to differences of opinion, having no other interest than the maintenance of order and liberty. He can never return to the common condition, and is consequently inaccessible to all the passions that such a condition generates, and to all those that the perspective of*

---

[83] *Summa Theologica,* 1.117.1.

finding oneself once again within it necessarily creates in those agents who are invested with temporary power."

Benjamin Constant[84]

Elucidation:

I am tempted to think that King Solomon, when faced with the famous dispute between two mothers, would have actually cut the baby in half, had he been a democratically elected official. I say this because all elected officials seem to be, at most, half-acceptable specimens. They always split the people down the middle, and in like fashion the justice that emanates from their offices always has an abortive character to it. If a good law enters, it comes out maimed and disfigured beyond recognition because they are bound, by the nature of their position, to always tend toward the "happy middle," the "reasonable compromise." Objectivity for such men is completely impossible: not only can they not access objective judgment; they cannot access their own judgment at all. Their decisions rest entirely on the will of their constituency, whether that means votes or the moneyed interests responsible for their successful campaigning. An official whose job is on the line (and an elected official's job is perpetually on the line) can never detach himself from concern for his own self-preservation, and in fact the quicker and more tumultuous the electoral process, the less he is able to turn his mind away from himself and toward the demands of justice. A king, even a foolish or mediocre one, can at least apply whatever wisdom he has to the task before him; the elected official, on the other hand, even if he is wise, is too busy preserving his job to ever begin doing it.

"SELF-GOVERNMENT" IS BY DEFINITION AN IMPOSSIBILITY

---

[84] Benjamin Constant, *Constant: Political Writings*, pp. 186-187.

Daniel Schwindt

Argument:

> *"It is possible, with the help of prudently balanced institutions, to provide everyone with effective safeguards against Power. But there are no institutions on earth which enable each separate person to have a hand in the exercise of Power, for Power is command, and everyone cannot command. Sovereignty of the people is, therefore, nothing but a fiction, and one which must in the long run prove destructive of individual liberties."*
>
> ~ *Bertrand de Jouvenel*[85]

Elucidation:

Anyone who promises the people the power of self-government must be immediately suspect as either a conscious or an unconscious propagandist, for he promises a pleasant notion that is sounds plausible and even laudable as an ideal, but which is utterly impossible in practice. To employ a more thoroughly reasoned argument, one might turn to Rene Guénon:

> "If the word 'democracy' is defined as the government of the people by themselves, it expresses an absolute impossibility and cannot even have a mere *de facto* existence—in our time or in any other. One must guard against being misled by words: it is contradictory to say that the same persons can be at the same time rulers and ruled, because, to use Aristotelian terminology, the same being cannot be 'in act' and 'in potency' at the same time and in the same relationship. The relationship of ruler and ruled necessitates the presence of two terms: there can be no ruled if there are not also rulers, even though these be illegitimate and have no other title to power than their own pretensions; but the great ability of those who are in control in

---

[85] Jouvenel, op. cit., p. 257.

the modern world lies in making the people believe that they are governing themselves; and the people are the more inclined to believe this as they are flattered by it, and as, in any case, they are incapable of sufficient reflection to see its impossibility."[86]

By referring to Aristotle's terminology we can disband the illusion through simple reasoning: a man cannot *sit* and *not sit* at the same time. He has the power to sit, certainly, but at any given moment he is either *actually* sitting or he is *potentially* sitting. All men can both sit and not sit, but it is impossible for both to be done by the same man at the same time. For those who appreciate logic, this argument suffices to disqualify the notion of self-government automatically. Nor is this limited to high-minded political philosophers, as it could be heard in the American colonies from Protestant preachers the likes of John Cotton:

> "Democracy, I do not conceyve, that God did ever ordeyne as a fitt government either for church or commonwealth. If the people be governors, who shall be governed?"[87]

If the people govern then there is no one to be governed, and this is equivalent to anarchy. The fact that men who claim to be self-governed do not live in actual anarchy is simply proof of the illusion under which they live, that they have only escaped subjection by becoming subjects-in-denial.

SELF-GOVERNMENT AS EXPERIENCED BY THE INDIVIDUAL

Argument:

---

[86] Rene Guénon, op.cit., p. 74.
[87] Larzer Ziff, *The Career of John Cotton: Puritanism and the American Experience* (New Jersey: Princeton University Press. 1962). p. 28.

> *"You have, it is true, a twenty-millionth share in the government of others, but only a twenty-millionth share in the government of yourself. You are therefore much more conscious of being governed than of governing."*

> ~ *Bertrand Russell*[88]

Elucidation:

The theory of self-government is much more pleasing than the reality, because it does not take into account the psychological experience of the individual participant, but rather concerns itself only with its lovely abstractions. In actual practice, the abstraction becomes a sort of Promethean agony, which is that specific type of suffering that results from man attempting, in hubris, the impossible.

"Self-government" is a marriage of two terms, expressible mathematically as a ratio (self-government). The first thing we should observe about this relationship is that the first term is always static while the second is potentially infinite. The smaller the second term, which is to say, the fewer are the "others" that go to make up the apparatus of government, which within democracy is theoretically everyone, the more tolerable we find the arrangement. But as the second term approaches infinity, the more we feel our isolated "self" dissolving into insignificance. The wider the circumference of the "self-government," the smaller the share of each self in the governing of the selves which comprise it. We begin to understand that what was flattering in theory can become terrifying in practice.

Thus, universal suffrage enfranchised everyone and, in doing so, reduced everyone's power to the smallest share possible. While this was acceptable when it was conceived as impotence over others, it becomes intolerable when we realize that our power over ourselves in

---

[88] Bertrand Russell, "Authority and the Individual," *The First Reith Lectures* (London: Allen and Unwin, 1949).

included in the bargain. The individual in a regime of universal suffrage has an absolute minimum of influence.

Now the apologists of modernism may retort that, in the *ancien regime*, the individual did not have even the nominal power that we are arguing against presently. This is due to their prejudice toward Liberal arrangements which excludes from their comprehension any alternative means of political effectiveness.

To point to one such empowering institution that is quite incomprehensible today, we can mention patriarchy. To begin, we might consider the family unit as it remains today, which occasionally has characteristics of traditional patriarchy even if we've driven them out of every other area of social life. In a family where the father is considered the "head" and actually functions in that role, the mother technically does not have any "rights" explicitly stated, much less do the children have any sort of "suffrage." However, although the child does not have a vote, he has his father's ear. He knows his father, and his father knows him and is intimately familiar with the life and situation of the realm where he so governs. In this patriarchal arrangement, the "subjects" do not have any of the rights and safeguards of the modern citizen, but they have infinitely more sway within that patriarchal sphere. It is an "organic" political power and is therefore far more reliable that any abstract legal measure.

Now we may extend this to its broader expression in the traditional world, which was thoroughly patriarchal in attitude and operation. Instead of a President whom he'd never see and or representatives he'd never meet, the peasant had a single lord. This lord was a local master whom he knew by sight even though he had no television or newspaper. This proximity allowed for an organic familiarity between ruler and ruled. They were not "on a first name basis," of course, but they were acquainted in the sense that they could be rightly considered "neighbors," even if they were not equals. This organic familiarity meant that the peasant paid his taxes in person, complained in person, and if need be he hung the lord from a local tree in person.

Keep in mind that we are speaking of the local nobility, because this was the only ruler of the land whose "rule" was actually felt by the peasant. The common man was aware of the king, or the emperor, but the more distant the ruler the further removed was he from the peasant's own life. In short, his relationship to his authorities was the inverse of what ours is today, where those who impact our lives the most are those furthest from us. The peasant and his patriarch formed a more or less autonomous sphere, although this sphere existed in conjunction with concentric or intersecting circles. Because of this *subsidiarity*, what little sway the peasant had in the eye of his superior had more in common with that of a son to his father, and it would be anachronistic to imagine him to be as impotent as a modern American would be if deprived of voting rights. The peasant's voice was incomparably louder because the ratio of ruler to ruled was so much smaller within in the jurisdiction where he fell.

ONLY THE PATRIARCH CAN IDENTIFY WITH THE GENERAL INTEREST OF THE PEOPLE

Argument:

> *"[S]ince it is human nature for habit to engender affection, the king, though acting at first only from concern for authority, comes to act with affection as well and in the end to be motivated by affection."*

> ~*Bertrand de Jouvenel*[89]

Elucidation:

Theodore Roosevelt once asked Francis Joseph, Emperor of Austria, what the role of a monarch in this modern age could possibly be, and the Emperor answered: "To protect my nations from their

---

[89] Jouvenel, op. cit., p. 118.

governments!" This attitude paints a true picture of monarchy in most periods: he is not "the government," but is rather the advocate of his people in the government, or at least has the capacity of functioning as such. For in medieval period the monarch met with nobility, and by his ever-so-slight functional superiority over his peers, he was able to in some way transcend their particular interests for the sake of the general interest—the interest of the people. Today it is much the same: while the seats in Congress are manipulated by special interests, the president himself largely captive to those who provide the millions required for his victory, the monarch whose position is secure can withdraw and contemplate the needs of the common man, and the population at large—something it is almost impossible for everyone else to do. Thus, only a monarch can effectively protect his people from their government when such a necessity arises.

This process molds well with the nature of man. A man invested with power will inevitably feel it in his ego. This is unavoidable and is no less present in socialist and democratic regimes than it is in any monarchy. The task, then, if we must deal with men who are always prone to egoism, which form of government is most conducive to that process of sublimation by which the egoism of the empowered is converted into an authentic sense of duty and care toward one's subordinates. In short, which regime is more likely to produce power-hungry, self-centered beings who view their subjects as footstools, and which encourages the egoist to instead view them as children under his care, family members under his protection?

While it is possible to conceive of a king who cares for his people out of this familial affection, it is utterly impossible to conceive of a bureaucracy caring for its people for any other reason than efficiency. We say this for two reasons: first because a bureaucracy is too impersonal to "feel" anything whatsoever, regardless of the humanity of the fact that it may be composed of men. Second, because all such bureaucracies, particularly electoral bureaucracies of democracy, are by nature positions of insecurity. A man concerned always for himself does not have the opportunity to escape from self-concern and to allow his ego to fully identity the people with itself—a necessary condition in order for him to *love them as himself.* This requires security and time, and he has neither. The king, on the other hand, may achieve this identification:

> "And in this way the institution of monarchy, so far from merely subsuming the interests of the mass into those of one man, became sensitive to every wound received by every little cell. A secure hold on Power and its descent in a regular line assured the maximum of identification of egoism with the general advantage. Whereas, contrariwise, a transient or precarious hold on Power tends to make of the nation merely the instrument of a personal destiny, of an egoism which resists absorption in the whole."[90]

Here we may be tempted to recoil in horror as we imagine the king viewing his people as an extension of himself, depersonalizing them into so many objects to be moved about on a playing board. Yet a cursory study of the psychology of *identification*, combined with a character study of great monarchs, would show us that the process is actually quite the opposite: it is the ego of the king who becomes subsumed by the people, rather than the people subsumed by the king. It is he who begins finally to feel their pain as his, and their good as his, at least as much as this is possible. The former assumption, which degrades the people into objects to be moved to the advantage of their superiors, while admittedly possible in a monarchy, is virtually guaranteed in the framework of democracy where the healthy form of identification is simply not possible:

> The more quickly the holders of Power succeed each other, the less completely can their egoism be extended to a body which is but their mount of a day. Their ego stands more apart and takes its enjoyments in more vulgar fashion. Or else, if their egoism can be projected outwards at all, it stops at a formation,

---

[90] Ibid., p. 135.

such as a party, with which it can stay in long association. So that the nation gets ruled by a succession of men who have identified their egos not with it but with parties in it.[91]

And so we see that in America if the president does manage to identify with the ruled it is only a portion, and a very specific portion at that, while he is likely to view the remainder not with the indifference of a negligent monarch, but with outright hostility, for they are truly his enemies.

PATRIARCHY OR THE POLICE STATE

Argument:

> *"The full realization that the Catholic world is faced by the simple alternative of the patriarch or the policeman would have spared millions of lives."*

> ~ *Erik von Kuehnelt-Leddihn*[92]

Elucidation:

The idea that a man can live in a functional society, can participate in its government, and at the same time not feel himself governed at any time, is one of the more frustrating contradictions that must be endured when hyper-individualism becomes the norm. This attitude is reinforced, albeit irrationally, by the myth of self-government, for reasons we've already examined. In such a situation the individual comes to believe that no exercise of authority is necessary so long as everyone "looks out for themselves." If any authority is felt, it is automatically perceived as an injustice. This injustice is either the result of an overreaching government (the paternal state), or else it is

---

[91] Ibid.

[92] Erik von Kuehnelt-Leddihn, *Liberty or Equality* (Caldwell: Caxton, 1952), p. 204.

the fault of some external group of persons who have either failed or refused to "look out for themselves." Because of the anti-social tendencies brought on by the promises of hyper-individualism, all acts in favor of social justice must be realized by force, and are met with utmost hostility and cries that "that government governs best which governs least." The result is what we see in America today: an unprecedented realization of the police state in which the police officers, which congeal into a privileged social class of their own, wield a power hitherto unheard of. This is a specific fruit of egalitarian regimes, and was not possible in the present of social hierarchies:

> "[I]n a stratified society the police agent is afraid to attack anyone of importance. He is never free of the fear that he will come off second best in such a conflict, and that fear keeps him down and renders him inactive. It is only in an egalitarian society that the nature of his activities elevates him above everyone else, and this inflation of the man contributes to the inflation of the office."[93]

And so the downfall of the institution of patriarchy and the establishment of equality historically accompanies the increase of police forces. And as hard as this is for the modern man to imagine, the offenses of which policemen are constantly acquitted in today's news are ones that would likely have cost government officials of the Middle Ages their lives.

MONARCHY IS MORE CONDUCIVE TO SUBSIDIARITY THAN DEMOCRACY

Argument:

> "The state, in feudalism, was merely the King's estate."

---

[93] Jouvenel, op. cit., p. 384n21.

~ Will Durant[94]

Elucidation:

The complaint that our government are prone to gigantism are evidence of a lack of understand regarding the nature of our own regimes. An informed look at previous periods would quickly abate the shock of moderns at any government overreach, because the shock they feel is a result of having been reassured, repeatedly and without any historical basis, that democracy would result in a minimum of government interference. Had they looked toward experience instead of theory, this idea would have been seen as preposterous.

Thus, while Durant's statement is not surprising to a student of the Middle Ages, it sounds strange to anyone who has been taught to imagine the king as a man of relative omnipotence while presidents are men of moderate influence. But it is a fact of history that no king could push his people into war as rapidly and as fluidly as George Bush or Barack Obama. And this cannot be dismissed as a technological issue brought about by progress. It stems directly from the configuration of power structures. Here we must emphasize the difference between a stratified society and the modern egalitarian regime. In the latter, the state has direct authority over each individual or group, and this is true primarily because all have been reduced to one dead level. Access to one member on any single level implies access to all. In the stratified framework, however, the authority of a man at the uppermost level *does not* imply access to any other level beyond that which happens to be immediately adjacent to his own. He does not subsume command of all that falls below him in the vast hierarchy. He sits on the top rung, indeed, but his arms aren't any longer than yours or mine, and so he can only grasp at the next rung down from his own. The medieval king could command his dukes, but he could not command their knights. He could draw taxes from the peasants who lived on his own estate

---

[94] Will Durant, *The Age of Faith* (New York: Simon & Schuster, 2011), p. 565.

(which was not much larger than a duke's), but he could not draw taxes from the peasants who lived on his dukes' estates. In this way the monarch had no effective way of exercising direct dominion over anyone but the dukes themselves. Any influence on the peasantry was indirect, as a result of convincing the nobility of the justness of his cause. It was open to them to refuse in a way that no American governor can refuse mobilization of his population for a military engagement.

POWER CORRUPTS?—ABSOLUTELY NOT

Argument:

> *"Power tends to corrupt and absolute power corrupts absolutely. Great men are almost always bad men, even when they exercise influence and not authority: still more when you superadd the tendency or the certainty of corruption by authority."*

> ~*Lord Acton*[95]

Elucidation:

Lord Acton's famous statement, quoted above, brings us to one of those slogans which moderns use to comfort themselves in their mediocrity, and with regard to the timidity of their institutions. Power corrupts, certainly, but the frequency and degree of the corruption depends entirely on the man. Power corrupts, but it only corrupts certain men in certain ways and under certain conditions. Since power is unavoidable even in democracy, then it would be much wiser to learn what conditions lead to corruption, and, more importantly, what type

---

[95] Lord Acton in a letter to Mandell Creighton (5 April 1887).

of men are most prone to this kind of corruption. This would have better results than our pretending that we can avoid it altogether.

And what do we find when we analyze the conditions that lead to the corruption of those invested with power—those men which every society must allow to exist if it wishes to live?

First, we find that power is most likely to corrupt the man who has no training for its vicissitudes. That is to say, if two men are to be placed in a situation that makes great demands on their character, the man who has been prepared specifically for this role is more likely to be able to stand the strain than the man who, as a matter of whim or as the result of popular enthusiasm, rode to the heights of his station on a wave of electoral sentiment.

Second, the rule of St. Thomas More in his *Utopia*, although openly utopian, had a rationale which anyone can admit as sound: Anyone who campaigned for a public office became disqualified from holding any office at all. The obvious reasoning here is that men who seek most fervently after a public office are often of precisely that character most prone to corruption by power; that is to say, the man whose desire is strongest for wine is probably the man with whom you'd least want to drink it. A man who so passionately believes himself worthy of an office that he is willing vie for it in the shameless fashion that we see in every electoral campaign, is a man in whom the virtue of humility is only tenuously active. By allowing the holding of offices to become the prizes of popular competition, those men of moderate temper whose constitutions will not allow them to participate are automatically excluded, and in their place a category of most undesirable candidates is ushered in.

Third, even for a man somewhat prepared for the weight of power is apt to be crushed under it when its pressure is applied too rapidly. Human virtue holds up the best under natural, which is to say gradual, adjustments and transitions. From this particular point of view, a man groomed for statesmanship, able to observe at close range the pressures it entails from his earliest moments, would be the ideal candidate for the position—one who steps into the role as he would his natural adulthood, rather than as the result of some "victory" in popular combat after which he is thrust into the midst of conditions entirely foreign to any of his experience.

Offering a sort of summary of these points, Erik von Kuehnelt-Leddihn:

> "Even a monarch of mediocre talents and natural gifts has the advantage of having received an education for his profession. A democratic leader can only have the hasty technical training of those with a 'late vocation'...The education which the ideal monarch can enjoy is not only intellectual, but also moral and spiritual. The democratic leader coming into power is always 'unprepared'...corruption through power, naturally, is worse in a plebiscitarian dictatorship, where popularity combined with autocracy and lack of humility show the most devastating results...On the other hand, the continuous preparation for the exercise of power which, with a king, begins practically at the cradle, usually prevents this loss of all sense of proportion."[96]

It seems that in all three of these cases we find that democracy would be the natural incubator of the tyrant, and that it was the hierarchical and hereditary systems of old that precluded the possibility of the Hitler.

The truth is that, if the maxim "power corrupts!" is a reliable one, then we would expect the papacy to be always and everywhere the most corrupt institution in the world. But instead we find that in majority of cases—with a few glaring exceptions which rather prove the rule—the office of the pope is most often held by a man of very high intelligence, virtue, and devotion. Even if he is simply mediocre or simple or incompetent, it is quite rare that he is "corrupt," which is the requirement we must demand if we are to give the saying any

---

[96] Erik von Kuehnelt-Leddihn, *Liberty or Equality*, pp. 151-152.

credibility. Yes, the king could be a Nebuchadnezzar; but he could also be a David. And whatever else is true, he could never have been a Hitler or a Lenin. This brings us to our next point.

POWER AS A NECESSARY CONDITION FOR HUMANE GOVERNANCE

Argument:

> *"The absolute ruler may be a Nero, but he is sometimes Titus or Marcus Aurelius; the people is often Nero, and never Marcus Aurelius."*
>
> ~ *Antoine de Rivarol*

Elucidation:

That democratic movements tend to show more animalistic and violent tendencies is a point given far too little attention, and which could be easily proven by a study of persecutions carried out since the modern liberal regimes came into existence. Connecting the two significant examples of American history and the French Revolution, A.J. Nock observed:

> "The American mob's grim reputation for sheer anthropoid savagery is equaled only by that of the revolutionary mobs of Paris. At the outset of the German Government's movement against the Jews, an American visitor asked Herr Hitler why he was making it so ruthless. The *Reichskanzler* replied that he had got the idea from us. Americans, he said, are the great rope and lamppost artists of the world, known of all men as such. He was using the same methods against the Jews that we used against the loyalists of '76, the Indians, the Chinese on the

Western coast, the Negroes, the Mexicans, the—every helpless people in fact whom we had ever chanced to find underfoot."[97]

And so it seems that Rivarol's point was simply that, while it has been proven that the mob can do at least as much irrational violence as any absolute monarchy, often more, it remains to be proven that the mob can, through universal suffrage or any other means, produce figures such as St. Louis, Charlemagne, or Empress Maria Teresa—all products of hierarchical and authoritative institutions. Likewise, if we turn to the religious realm and apply the principle, we can see that the democratism of the Protestant movement has resulted in quite a few Christian leaders of mediocre influence (if we judge not by their momentary popularity but by their historical significance), but has produced no theologian or political character of the stature of Leo the Great, a Pius XII, or a John Paul II. Men will continue to speak of the great popes for hundreds of years—yet in a generation no one will care about Joel Osteen. Always and everywhere we are reminded that the answer to evil is not the prideful denial of hierarchy or the cowardly attempt to deny the exercise of any worldly power, for both are necessities for higher human development and can only be denied at the cost of retarding human possibilities, limiting them to their lowest level; and we must remember always that at the lowest level the greatest evils are still possible.

DEMOCRACY NECESSITATES PROPAGANDA

Argument:

> *"[I]n a democracy, a government that is honest, serious, benevolent, and respects the voter cannot follow public opinion. But it cannot escape it either. The masses are there; they are interested in politics. The government cannot act*

---

[97] A. J. Nock, "The Jewish Problem in America," *Atlantic Monthly*, June, 1941.

without them. So, what can it do?...Only one solution is possible: as the government cannot follow opinion, opinion must follow the government."

~Jacques Ellul[98]

Elucidation:

Propaganda is the subject of a later installment of this series, because it is a very modern phenomenon and because it shapes the minds of our people and determines their fates. And so, while avoiding too much depth at this moment, we must explain how and why democracy requires the existence of propaganda, both for the operation of the state and for the peace of mind of the people.

It is an inescapable rule of democracy that any public operation, however complex, must be addressable to all of the citizenry, regardless of whether or not this populace has the experience or perspective to assess the information they receive. If it is not actually addressable to the entire population, it must at least *appear* addressable to them. The populace who believes itself the engine of democracy will not have it any other way. As a consequence, the operations of democracy must be simplified, either in *reality* or in *presentation.*

If they are simplified in reality, then we immediately see that democracy will only be able to address those problems that even the most ignorant of its citizenry would be able to understand. We then come to understand why democracy has been called the most primitive of systems, because in this case any sort of action would be reduced to the level of comprehension of the lowest elements in society. Such a mode of operation will prevent the government from ever rising to meet any significant issue, such as the formulation of a coherent foreign policy, for it is evident from experience that the general population has no possible way of achieving this.

---

[98] Jacques Ellul, *Propaganda* (New York: Vintage, 1973), p. 126.

However, we find that democracies do indeed carry out foreign policy, and that they do so in a very complex and coordinated fashion, along with many other vast projects on the national and local level. Therefore, we must assume that the simplification chosen was not the simplification of problems in reality but only in *presentation*. In short, the issue remains incredibly complicated, but the solutions proposed to the populace are ultra-simplified so that it can respond yay or nay. This should be expected, because it is much easier to oversimplify the statement of a problem than it is to simplify the problem..

This is why the social authorities in democracy, unable to honestly present the problems with which they, as government official, must cope, must resort to propaganda, the main purpose of which is to offer artificial simplifications of reality to an audience incapable or unwilling to acknowledge reality as it actually is. Propaganda, and the ideologies it develops and encourages in order to further its ends, is the life-blood of democratic operations. These elements combine to distill a beverage that the average man can drink, and which will intoxicate him so that he applauds actions he does not understand fills out ballot sheets covered with names of men he does not know. We recognize the fruits of this distillation in various forms: political slogans, catchphrases, party platforms, and most of all ideologies which are by definition over-simplifications of reality. All of these represent pre-packaged sets of opinions, most of them meaningless or at least too vague to present any specific and useful meaning, which serve to comfort the consumer, telling him that he comprehends the actions of the State agrees with them—nay, that they are *his* actions. The program offered is the program *he himself wanted*. This function—the manufacturing of certainty for the individual—is one of the primary functions of propaganda. The individual thirsts for it; and the government cannot do without it. It satisfies both, and so both collude to keep the intoxicating beverage flowing.

THE RISING COSTS OF DEMOCRACY

Argument:

> *"Money, money, always money—that is the essence of democracy. Democracy is more expensive than monarchy; it is incompatible with liberty."*

> ~ *P.J. Proudhon*[99]

Elucidation:

It was Oswald Spengler who first developed the intimate connection with the democratic mentality and plutocracy:

> "…it must be concluded that democracy and plutocracy are the same thing under the two aspects of wish and actuality, theory and practice, knowing and doing. It is the tragic comedy of the world-improvers' and freedom-teachers' desperate fight against money that they are ipso facto assisting money to be effective. Respect for the big number—expressed in the principles of equality for all, natural rights, and universal suffrage—is just as much a class-ideal of the unclassed as freedom of public opinion (and 'more particularly freedom of the press) is so. These are ideals, but in actuality the freedom of public opinion involves the preparation of public opinion, which costs money; and the freedom of the press brings with it the question of possession of the press, which again is a matter of money; and with the franchise comes electioneering, in which he who pays the piper calls the tune. The representatives of the ideas look at one side only, while the representatives of money operate with the other. The concepts of Liberalism and Socialism are set in effective motion only by money."[100]

---

[99] P. J. Proudhon, *Solution Du Problême Social*.
[100] Oswald Spengler, *Decline of the West: Perspectives of World History* (New York: Knopf, 1928), pp. 401-402.

Various other massive expenditures that accompany the establishment of democracy are not difficult to identity: since conscription always accompanies universal suffrage, armies become gigantic hordes of men who must be paid out of the state's coffers since, unlike the nobility who traditionally waged the wars, they cannot afford to sustain themselves away from their crafts. The United States military is now the largest "employer" in the world, and the "defense" portion of the budget reflects this reality.

Further, if we look at the tax burden on the common man, we see that it has increased profoundly with democracy. The same man who must leave his craft to fight ends up paying himself for the trouble. The American of the 1940's paid more in taxes that the typical peasant of the Middle Ages paid in dues, and we must also note that the peasant labored about half the amount of his over-worked modern counterpart. It is of course a commonplace that government operations are inefficient, that campaigning costs a fortune,[101] but it is rarely acknowledged that these expenditures are necessitated by the nature of democracy itself and are not some sort of "aberration" due to negligent officials, as is commonly implied by those who would fault the government for being what it must necessarily be.

HONOR WHERE HONOR IS DUE—AND NOWHERE ELSE

Argument:

> *"A man's reaction to Monarchy is a kind of test. Monarchy can easily be 'debunked;' but watch the faces, mark the accents of*

---

[101] We ought to carefully note the relation of campaign costs to those of democratic warfare itself. They are, in a way, expensive for the same reasons, because they are both expressions of popular conflict: "Every change of regime and, to a lesser extent, every change of government is, as it were, a reproduction, on a more or less reduced scale, of a barbarian invasion" (Jouvenel, op. cit., p. 119).

the debunkers. These are the men whose tap-root in Eden has been cut: whom no rumour of the polyphony, the dance, can reach - men to whom pebbles laid in a row are more beautiful than an arch. Yet even if they desire equality, they cannot reach it. Where men are forbidden to honour a king they honour millionaires, athletes or film-stars instead: even famous prostitutes or gangsters. For spiritual nature, like bodily nature, will be served; deny it food and it will gobble poison."

~ *C.S. Lewis*[102]

Elucidation:

C.S. Lewis was not one to argue for monarchy, but he was at least honest in his observations. He knew that, whatever man thinks he wants, his actions reveal an insatiable impulse to show honor to persons of honor—to engage in that healthy worship of greatness where it is found. This impulse is a completely healthy one because it corresponds to reality: that which is superior deserves respect from that which is inferior.

Hierarchical societies were the result of an acknowledgment of this principle. Egalitarian societies are the result of its denial, and because this denial is unnatural it has one of two results: either it frustrates the impulse or else it directs honor toward that which is not honorable, or is only honorable in a perverse sense. For example, the man who really believes in egalitarianism will wind up honoring himself, refusing to see in his betters (which are always many) anything that outstrips his own self-image. If he does not do this and chooses to express the impulse externally, he will worship, as Lewis wrote, money or fame or some other surrogate-nobility. That is, after all, what happens in capitalist societies such as America: they worshipers of capitalism deny that any man is better than any other, but they also speak and act as if they rich man is automatically—simply because of his wealthy—a

---

[102] C.S. Lewis, "Equality", *Present Concerns* (Orlando: Harcourt, 1986), p. 20.

superior specimen, both in morals and in aptitudes, than those with less. In short, they project the class assumptions of old regarding the stratification of human virtue, with the difference that they project it in purely economic terms, which is perhaps the lowest possible measure of a man's worth. The aristocracy of money is the material aristocracy. Further, by allowing these surrogate-aristocracies to thrive (which they always do when traditional aristocracies are denied), new models of virtue are erected for imitation. Where the wealthy are the most noble of citizens, and where wealth is the very mark of this nobility, then men seek after money rather than nobility. In short, greed replaces the good life—*becomes* the good life. The same happens regarding celebrity and fame.

IT REMAINS FOR DEMOCRACY TO PROVE ITSELF IN THINGS THAT TRULY MATTER

Argument:

> *"I say that democracy can never prove itself beyond cavil, until it founds and luxuriantly grows its own forms of art, poems, schools, theology, displacing all that exists, or that has been produced in the past, under the opposite influences...For know you not, dear, earnest reader, that the people of our land may all read and write, and may all possess the right to vote—and yet the main things may be entirely lacking?"*

> ~ *Walt Whitman[103]*

Elucidation:

What the poet is saying is that if democracy cannot manage to produce a culture, then it is not a valid or desirable system, whatever else it may produce, be that wealth, power, or leisure. This is in fact one of

---

[103] Walt Whitman, *Democratic Vistas* (1871).

the most powerful arguments against the rule of the people and the modern democratic regimes: that they are bland. And in fact it is true of the free peoples of the past in some significant cases. Rome, it has been said, merely copied its art and culture from the Greeks—it even borrowed their mythology. And what philosophical heritage did the Egyptians leave? Their constructions boast in nothing else but enormity, which is not often taken to be an aspect of beauty. We can mention the Greeks, of course, but the comparison is, in the end, absurd. The "free men" of Greece were a small elite compared to the slaves and the non-free that made that freedom possible. And so Whitman's challenge stood and still stands: that democracy can begin to make an argument for itself when it proves conducive to the higher realizations of human potentiality. Until then, we consider it on trial, and failing.

Part 3: KNOWLEDGE

"When a candidate for public office faces the voters he does not face men of sense; he faces a mob of men whose chief distinguishing mark is the fact that they are quite incapable of weighing ideas, or even of comprehending any save the most elemental—men whose whole thinking is done in terms of emotion, and whose dominant emotion is dread of what they cannot understand. So confronted, the candidate must either bark with the pack or be lost...All the odds are on the man who is, intrinsically, the most devious and mediocre—the man who can most adeptly disperse the notion that his mind is a virtual vacuum. The Presidency tends, year by year, to go to such men. As democracy is perfected, the office represents, more and more closely, the inner soul of the people. We move toward a lofty ideal. On some great and glorious day the plain folks of the land will reach their heart's desire at last, and the White House will be adorned by a downright moron."

~H.L. Mencken

Introductory

No one contests the fact that knowledge ought to play a decisive role in determining political decisions. Differences of opinion only come about with regard to the best way to put knowledge in the political driver's seat.

Most of our contemporaries, being naturally suspicious of far-removed bureaucrats, believe the best way to achieve this is to place decision-making powers directly in the hands of the people, giving their opinion precise expression to the fullest degree possible: aka, *democracy*. This seems reasonable—at least as a "lesser evil"—if we imagine that the only alternative is to hand over totalitarian powers to the State.

But what if this choice—the common man or the bureaucrat—is in fact a false-dichotomy? After all, we've just admitted that neither of them is an ideal, for the neither the bureaucrat nor the man on the street is the best candidate to direct complex political and economic affairs. Nonetheless, the contemporary democratic citizen automatically accepts the dichotomy and inevitably chooses the vote as the best means of political direction.

Our purpose here, then, is to show that the decision has proven to be a disastrous one, and this for two reasons: First, because the attempt to place government controls in the hands of amateurs (democracy) has not, in fact, driven the bureaucrat into extinction or even slowed the centralization of powers in the national bureaucracy. Second, it is false because, for reasons the early proponents of democracy were not able to foresee, the mere extension of suffrage to the common people does not, in itself, either liberate or empower them.

The reason for this can be found in the ancient saying that *the truth will set you free*—the obvious implication being that, if one is not in possession of the truth, then no matter what other conditions are present—whether it be the right to vote or the absence of external political interference—freedom is precluded, and the slavery of ignorance must ensue. What we plan to demonstrate below is that ignorance has in fact ensued, and is today the driving force of modern nations.

We will make heavy use of Alexis de Tocqueville in this discussion, for the simple reason that, in the opinion of the author, Tocqueville's meticulous style and insightful observations regarding the American mind are unsurpassed even to this day. If Americans were ever to take up the study of political philosophy, then *Democracy in America* would be the indispensable starting-point.

*I*NDIVIDUALISM + EGALITARIANISM = IGNORANCE

Daniel Schwindt

Argument:

> *"I discover that, in the majority of mental processes, each American has but recourse to the individual effort of his own reason...perceiving in not a single person in their midst any signs of undeniable greatness or superiority, [Americans] constantly return to their own rationality as to the most obvious and immediate source of truth...Each man thus retreats into himself from where he claims to judge the world."*

> *~Alexis de Tocqueville[104]*

Elucidation:

To return continuously and exclusively to oneself as the "source of truth," is not simply to risk ignorance, but to chase after it full speed. For the self is "the arch-flatterer, with whom all the petty flatterers have intelligence,"[105] and I believe it was Samuel Johnson who said that the self-taught man has had the worst of all possible teachers.

There is no real excuse or justification for this mentality, although the explanation of its rise and popularity is not hard to surmise. Having once adopted the individualist mindset, everything else naturally follows: for if all knowledge can be reduced to the effort of the individual's reason, if all truths are in the reach of each of us in isolation and without need for that collective body of truth once called Tradition, then there is no need to seek the counsel of a friend, a master, or a priest. Indeed, Luther's *solas* were but the application in the religious field of what Descartes had done in philosophy. These two reduced truth to the individual—told him that he was "the most obvious and immediate source of truth." The rest is history whether

---

[104] Tocqueville, op. cit., p. 494.

[105] From Bacon's essay *On Praise*. He returns to this same subject in *On Friendship*, saying that "a man were better relate himself to a statue or picture...for there is no such flatterer as is a man's self."

we are looking at the handful of platitudes to which Protestantism has been reduced, or the great waste that has been post-modernist philosophy.

Equality aggravates the issue, of course, but individualism is its root, for equality always accompanies it in one way or another, even if we are speaking of socialism, because the view of man as an isolated and autonomous molecule (individualism) or as one atom in mass of like atoms (collectivism) are both examples of having reduced man to homogeneity.

The effect of this process on knowledge has been that, while it was once perhaps true to say that "we stand on the shoulders of giants," it is not true any longer. We've severed our connection, and we are free-floating in history, alone.

R ATIONALISM AS INDIVIDUALISM IN THE INTELLECTUAL SPHERE

Argument:

> *"America is thus one of the countries in the world where the precepts of Descartes are least studied and most widely applied. We need not be surprised by that. Americans do not read the works of Descartes because the state of their society diverts them from speculative study and they follow his maxims because it is this very social state which naturally disposes their minds to adopt them."*

> ~*Alexis de Tocqueville*[106]

Elucidation:

---

[106] Tocqueville, op. cit., pp. 494-495.

In the ancient world the higher forms of knowledge were supra-individual: the sacred books of the Hindus, for example, have no author, are not expected to have had an author, and this fact is not considered to present any problems for the Hindu mind. In the West, this simply would not do—we must know the author, and it must be demonstrably proven that authorship is correctly attributed. There is no better illustration than this of the difference between an individualist, rationalist approach to knowledge and one that is supra-individual and supra-rational one. The East has retained the latter, while the West has settled inflexibly into the former.

While it is possible, and in fact it is popular, to place all of the blame for our "truncated epistemology" at the feet of Descartes, it is important to remember that this is only true to a certain degree, and he could not have instigated the revolution that he did if individualism has not already prepared the soil: individualism is the prerequisite and substrate of rationalism. Keeping this in mind, we can discuss rationalism specifically, since it pertains directly to knowledge, which is the concern of this study.

The rationalist method was the overthrow of the ancient view of knowledge as something which, in the form of Tradition, was degree supra-rational and supra-individual. The first outcome of this was a new attitude toward hierarchy. In societies that centered on Tradition, it was self-evident that one ought not expect the higher parts of knowledge to be within the grasp of his individual reason. Those truths at which he could arrive by himself and on his own efforts were in fact quite few, and of the lowest order. To sit down alone with his scriptures and try to discern their meaning in isolation would have been unthinkable. This ancient mentality was simply the acknowledgement of a universal truth: knowledge is not and cannot be brought within the reach of all people at all times. If you want it, you must engage in a trans-historical project of cooperation.

But after Descartes, Luther, and in many ways after Adam Smith, the collective side of knowledge evaporated, and the individual was left with no other option than to become a rationalist. Tocqueville observed that America in particular manifested this phenomenon almost automatically, as a natural consequence of its development and without any exposure to the Cartesian precepts. America, being a post-revolutionary society, was born detached from Tradition, and so the individualist substrate was almost inborn with the nation. Individualistic rationalism is, we might say, a genetic trait. Another way of saying it is that individualistic rationalism is America's *origin-al* sin. Much of the present mental condition of our country can be easily understood once we admit this.

UNREALISM AND ABSTRACTION

Argument:

> "It is characteristic, however, of the course of democracy, that the authors of popular constitutions have never had any idea of the actual workings of their schemes...Since these forms of theirs are not, like feudalism, the result of growth, but of thought (and based, moreover, not on deep knowledge of men and things, but on abstract ideas of right and justice), a gulf opens between the intellectual side of the laws and the practical habits that silently form under the pressure of them, and either adapt them to, or fend them off from, the rhythm of actual life."

> ~ *Oswald Spengler*[107]

Elucidation:

---

[107] Oswald Spengler, *Decline of the West: Perspectives of World History* (New York: Knopf, 1928), p. 455.

Daniel Schwindt

Rationalism also divorces man from reality, as Descartes did through the mind-body antithesis, or Protestantism through the dichotomizing of body and soul. This is why Julius Evola identified "unrealism" was the most conspicuous characteristic of modern civilization. It is difficult to disagree with his assessment. In every area of life man is further removed from the concrete reality of things than ever before. In his daily work he never sees a whole picture, but only a very specific part of a massive process that he neither understands nor experiences; in his politics he thinks and speaks in abstract about things he's never experienced or studies; in the news he watches he learns to internalize the concerns of the Middle East, which he then expresses in his own sphere of influence where they do not belong. He lives in a verbal universe. An unborn child, for example, is not what it looks like, what it feels like, what everyone previous to our society acknowledged it to be: a human child. No, for him it is or is not a "person," and a person is an abstract thing that can be believed or not depending on one's choice ideology, which is just a cheat-sheet used to handle easily all the abstractions.

Tocqueville said that "nothing is a greater waste of effort for the human mind than an abstraction."[108] He may have been right. Even the lofty thought of St. Thomas was thoroughly realist, perhaps the most realist of any philosophy to date.

Keep this in mind when considering the principles of Liberalism in general, which were the principles of the American Founding Fathers, and which have been integrated into the American psyche. The whole edifice was not born out of the ground but built in the air, out of pure abstraction—out of humanist optimism. The seeds of the Revolution and the New Order were not taken from a strong tree but conjured from the intellect; there was no need to test the soil or take into account history's lessons, so confident were the Liberals in their untried imaginings. Much more needs to be said on this point, but

---

[108] Tocqueville, op. cit., p. 716.

these problems will be discussed in more depth in our study on America in particular, which will be forthcoming.

GENERAL IDEAS AND IDEOLOGY

Argument:

> *"When I repudiate the traditions of rank, profession, and birth; when I escape from the authority of example, to seek out, by the single effort of my reason, the path to be followed, I am inclined to derive the motives of my opinions from human nature itself; which leads me necessarily, and almost unconsciously, to adopt a great number of very general notions."*
>
> *~Alexis de Tocqueville*[109]

Elucidation:

In the absence of custom and Tradition man has only himself, which is to say he does not have very much. Again we see how interwoven are the tendencies toward individualism, rationalism, and egalitarianism. They reinforce and perpetuate one another, and as one gains more footing the others come in its trail and soon make up the difference.

Here we come to the specific way of thinking adopted by men under such conditions, which Tocqueville describes as the adoption of "general ideas":

> "Men who live in ages of equality have a great deal of curiosity and very little leisure; their life is so practical, so confused, so excited, so active, that but little time remains to them for

---

[109] DIA, 2.1.3.

thought. Such men are prone to general ideas because they spare them the trouble of studying particulars...

"One of the distinguishing characteristics of a democratic period is the taste all men have at such times for easy success and present enjoyment. This occurs in the pursuits of the intellect as well as in all others. Most of those who live at a time of equality are full of an ambition at once aspiring and relaxed: they would fain succeed brilliantly and at once, but they would be dispensed from great efforts to obtain success. These conflicting tendencies lead straight to the research of general ideas, by aid of which they flatter themselves that they can figure very importantly at a small expense."[110]

Davila, of course, said all this in a single aphorism: "Every straight line leads right to a hell."[111] Adding elsewhere: "Generalizing enlarges our power and impoverishes our spirit."[112] These general ideas will, sooner or later, congeal into a semi-coherent, seemingly obvious, set of assumptions. This collection of assumptions is like a warm blanket for the mind—covering everything and concealing all of its own contradictions, hiding the uniqueness of every individual case by painting it over with the generality. If such a collection of general ideas are fitted together and popularized, it will become socially sanction and eventually unconscious set of preconceptions which allow men to answer every question without ever having to solve the problem it raised. This "master key" to life is called an ideology. Our present ideologies are several, but interconnected: liberalism, capitalism, socialism, nationalism, secularism, individualism, etc.

---

[110] *Democracy in America*, 2.1.3.

[111] *Scholia,* 133.

[112] *Scholia,* 141. He also says elsewhere: "Ideas tyrannize he who has but few."

Of course, as Tocqueville explained, the ideologies *never* correspond to reality, but rather reality is pressed into the ideologies by brute force, and is always badly mauled in the process. We must remember, however, that ideologies are not only flattering, but necessary to the modern man: he requires ideology, not just for the sense of empowerment, but in order to believe in the great idea of democracy. For if he did not have answer to all the Great Problems, he would at that moment cast a shadow of doubt on his competence as a voter; and then the modern world would collapse.

RETROACTIVE EFFECTS OF IDEOLOGY

Argument:

> *"Ideological entities have never been mere fictions rather, they are a distorted consciousness of reality, and, as such, real factors retroactively producing real distorting effects; which is all the more reason why that materialization of ideology, in the form of the spectacle, which is precipitated by the concrete success of an autonomous economic system of production, results in the virtual identification with social reality itself of an ideology that manages to remold the whole of the real to its own specifications."*

> ~ *Guy Debord*[113]

Elucidation:

In the same work, Guy Debord speaks of ideology as "the abstract will to universality and the illusion thereof."[114] A better definition would not be found. Modern man's mania for generalization, which ends in the assembly of various ideological systems, is nothing else but the

---

[113] Guy Debord, *The Society of the Spectacle*, 212.
[114] Ibid., 213.

wish to explain with a few universal formulas the mysteries of the universe. And any apparent success in this endeavor must be purely illusory, because reality simply cannot be reduced in such a way.

But the more important point made by Debord here is that, just because the truth of the ideology is illusory, does not mean that it does not have real effects. Men act, and acting men have the ability to transform patterns of development, modify interpretations of history, and reinvent culture. Thus, an ideology, although it may be more or less false, can and does lead men to remake reality in its image. Because it represents a distortion reality, then it is clear that reality can never truly be made to conform to it, but adherents of ideology expend massive efforts in the attempt, and this is the explanation of much frustration and conflict in the modern world.

If an ideology happens to achieve total domination in a civilization, as Liberalism has in our period, then a final transformation occurs:

> "Once ideology…finds itself legitimated in modern society by universal abstraction and by the effective dictatorship of illusion, then it is no longer the voluntaristic struggle of the fragmentary, but rather its triumph. The claims of ideology now take on a sort of flat, positivistic exactness: ideology is no longer a historical choice, but simply an assertion of the obvious."[115]

In short, while at the beginning the adherents may have been aware that they were fighting in favor of a theory, at the end, through universal acceptance, it ceases to be perceived as theory and takes on the appearance of common sense. It is obvious, and the discussion is officially closed.

---

[115] Ibid., 213.

THE ILLUSION OF "COMMON SENSE"

Argument:

> *"Explanations exist; they have existed for all time; there is always a well-known solution to every human problem — neat, plausible, and wrong."*

> ~*H.L. Mencken*

Elucidation:

Common sense, as we understand it, ceased to exist when good sense ceased to be common, for it was always a thing taught and never, as we tend to assume, inborn in all men at all times. For us, then, there are common mistakes, common confusions, and common prejudices, but there is no such thing as common sense. Many men could escape a great deal of vexation if they acknowledged this reality, for it seems that much anger and alienation is, at its source, the frustrated expectation that my neighbor ought to agree with my opinion on some matter because it appears to me that my opinion is "common sense." Well, it obviously isn't, or else your neighbor wouldn't be arguing with you now would he? In fact, if common sense is taken to mean "what most people consider to be obviously true," then we'd have to say that it is common sense in America unborn children and not children at all, and that a union between two men is the same as one between two opposite genders.

The passion for generalization combined with an education in abstraction results in the sort of mentality expressed by

ANTI-INTELLECTUALISM

Argument:

> *"There is a cult of ignorance in the United States, and there always has been. The strain of anti-intellectualism has been a constant thread winding its way through our political and cultural life, nurtured by the false notion that democracy means that 'my ignorance is just as good as your knowledge.' "*

> ~ *Isaac Asimov*[116]

Elucidation:

Thomas Carlyle once said that "Democracy prevails when men believe the vote of Judas as good as that of Jesus Christ." Although most democrats would not perhaps admit this degree of prejudice, Carlyle's words do capture the spirit of the democratic mind. So afraid are we of offending against the doctrine of equality—of implying that one man might actually be better, wiser, more virtuous than his neighbor—that we cannot bring ourselves to make any distinctions, however glaringly obvious they may be.

This sort of thing is implicit even in aristocrats like Thomas Jefferson, who said in a letter to Peter Carr:

> "State a moral case to a ploughman and a professor. The former will decide it as well, and often better than the latter, because he has not been led astray by artificial rules."

Well, moral cases have indeed been stated to the ploughman for many generations since Jefferson made the recommendation, and the truth has become evident: the professor may be prone to artificial rules, but the ploughman has no rules at all and must be led by intuition or, more commonly, fear. Thus, we now have to publicly discuss what is a human being and what isn't, whether torturing our enemies is becoming of a civilized nation (the denser ploughman can't even seem to figure out what torture even *is*).

---

[116] Isaac Asimov, "A Cult of Ignorance", *Newsweek*, 21 January 1980.

All of this by the denial of the fact that, if you must take a vote, then the votes ought to be *weighed* rather than *counted*, because it is plainly false that all ballots are of equal value. Some are worth a great deal; some are worth nothing at all.

THE TYRANNY OF PUBLIC OPINION

Argument:

> *"In the United States, the majority takes upon itself the task of supplying to the individual a mass of ready-made opinions, thus relieving him of the necessity to take the proper responsibility of arriving at his own."*

> *~ Alexis de Tocqueville*[117]

Elucidation:

Here Tocqueville identifies the *passivity* of the American citizen. The justification for such a claim is provided in the surrounding text, which I feel justified in quoting at length:

> "When conditions are unequal and men have dissimilar outlooks, there are a few very enlightened, learned, powerfully intelligent individuals while the masses are very ignorant and extremely limited. People who live under this aristocratic rule are naturally inclined to take as a guide for their opinions the superior reason of one man or one class, whereas they are not persuaded to recognize the infallibility of the masses. In times of equality, the opposite prevails.

---

[117] *Democracy in America*, 2.1.2.

"Gradually, as citizens become more equal and similar, the inclination for each man to have a blind belief in one particular man or class lessens. The predisposition to believe in mass opinion increases and becomes progressively the opinion which commands the world.

"Not only is commonly held opinion the only guide to the reason of the individual in democracies but this opinion has, in these nations, an infinitely greater power than in any other. In times of equality, men have no confidence in each other because of their similarities but this very similarity gives them an almost limitless trust in the judgment of the public as a whole. For it appears likely, in their view, that, since they all have similar ideas, truth will reside with the greatest number...

"This very equality which makes him independent of each of his fellow men delivers him alone and defenseless into the hands of the majority.

"In democratic nations, the general public possesses an unusual power which aristocracies could not imagine. It does not impose its beliefs by persuasion but inserts them in men's souls by the immense pressure of corporate thinking upon the intelligence of each single man."[118]

De-individuation would be the proper sociological term for this process, and it is a much-overlooked effect of the successful imposition of equality. Inequality by its nature diversifies the mental climate of a society, while equality homogenizes it.

---

[118] Ibid.

IS MAN MOSTLY EVIL OR MOSTLY IGNORANT?

Argument:

> *"In contradiction to St. Thomas (and to Luther, after all) the Church often seemed to take the position that man is rather stupid than wicked. Protestantism, though rather pessimistic about the spiritual qualities of the 'sin-cripple,' nevertheless gave him the Bible without explanatory footnotes, trusting in his intelligence (or 'inspiration'). Catholicism, on the other hand, frequently tended to adopt the view that a superficial half-education was much worse than no education at all, and thus in Catholic countries we saw (and sometimes still see) a large number of illiterates side by side with an intellectual elite of high standards. The Protestant goal of education is usually one of good averages—the optimum for democracy. In democracies there will always be resentment and contempt for the 'highbrow' and the illiterate, the intellectual and the 'peasant.'"*

> *~ Erik von Kuehnelt-Leddihn*[119]

Elucidation:

Here Kuehnelt-Leddihn touches on one of the principal divisions between the traditional and the modern way of thinking about man. When Protestantism overthrew the Church, it proclaimed at the same time an unprecedented pessimism about man's *moral* capabilities combined with a bizarre optimism about his *mental* aptitudes. In short, the Christian, ever since the birth of the humanistic age, is a totally depraved Einstein. The traditional outlook, on the contrary, is better embodied in the words of Prince Metternich: that the people tend to

---

[119] Erik von Kuehnelt-Leddihn, *Liberty or Equality.*

111

be "good but childish,"[120] seeking after good ends but inevitably by the wrong means.

Now it is not the purpose of this work to approach theological issues. Such a task is reserved for a later project where the author intends to affirm the traditional outlook, whereas the present work is intended as a critique of the modern one. Thus, we are more concerned with the socio-political reality that corresponds to each of these two ways of viewing man. We are concerned here with the effect that the liberal-humanistic view has had on man's view of himself and the civilization that this view has led him to construct. With all purely theological concerns aside for the present, which of these views can we say is more "realistic," in the sense that it corresponds to what we actually know about ourselves and our neighbors?

Obviously if we begin with an honest appraisal of our own personal competence, we'll find that it does not go very far at all. If we imagine the personal range of competence of each individual as a sphere emanating from his person, we can say that this sphere does not often go very far. It usually extends to himself, to his family, to his home. Sometimes it extends further. Sometimes it does not. But the point is that there are very few men whose range extends to a national or supra-national level, and these must be considered men not only of exceptional aptitude but also of special experience. And yet we know that the average voter in a democracy believes himself competent to pronounce on scientific issues such as global warming (although he has never studied ecology), economic ones such as monetary policy (although he does not know what money is), and foreign policy (although he couldn't find Benghazi on an unlabeled map). Turning to the religious sphere, he believes that he can choose the best translation and then interpret that translation, choosing and verifying proper doctrine based on his own interpretations of his chosen interpretation. This he believes despite the fact that he knows no Greek, knows little of the history of the Bible, and has no idea that his interpretations

---

[120] *Memoirs of Prince Metternich: 1773[-1835]*, vol. 3, p. 511.

inevitably wind up conforming to whatever his "like-minded" friends think.

After any honest study of the practical results of the Liberal view of man, we find that it has done little more than disconnect the individual from any long-term stabilizing structures (political or religious) that may have led him out of the prejudices of his own age. He was liberated from tradition, which embraced several thousand years, to become trapped in the 50-60 years that go to form his generational epoch.

What can we say then of this the new mentality? First, we can say that it cannot have won out by its practical results, which are absurd. It must have won for some other reason. Or, to look at it another way: was the Liberal revolution a result of the Lutherian-Lockean "discovery" of man's intelligence, or were these new claims about man adopted because they served the ends of the revolution.

We find in the end that what we normally imagine to have been the significance of these ideas is in fact a confusion of proper order. The new view was not so much a new discovery but rather served as a self-justification in the name of "Liberty." The new views about human intelligence were *necessitated* by the Liberal revolution, because if they were not true then the various revolutions, whether we are concerned with secular democracy or the private interpretation of scripture, would have been defeated from the start. Their inner logic depends on the truth of the premise that man is rationally self-sufficient, because the alternative would automatically necessitate an interdependent hierarchical arrangement in the corresponding spheres (political and religious). In short, the alternative would necessitate the return to a traditional-Catholic worldview.

The political Liberals were more consistent than the Protestants in this case, for the simple reason that the Liberals had no need for God after their humanistic revolution. The Protestants, however, still needed to convince man that he needed God. Since they'd rejected the idea of man's dependence on the Church and Tradition, which had been the social expression of man's need for God, they had to find some other need for God which could be proclaimed but which would not necessitate any concrete religious institution. In short, it had to be personal, and so they latched onto morality. Morality would now epitomize man's "fallen-ness."

Here we are reminded of the famous Taoist teaching:

> *When goodness is lost, there is morality.*
> *When morality is lost, there is law.*[121]

In the downward progression, the Protestant form of Liberalism still holds to the first step, while the political Liberals moved on to the second, and live by the law alone.

IRRATIONALITY AND MAJORITY RULE

Argument:

> *"The combined ignorance of ten millions is not the equivalent of one man's wisdom."*
>
> *Hippolyte Taine*[122]

Elucidation:

Some errors are so simple that the mind is repelled, as if they were so obvious as to be impossible to perceive. This is the only explanation for the persistent belief in the justness of majority rule. Those who adhere to it seem to reason thusly: if I know half a truth, and my neighbor

---

[121] Tao Te Ching, 38. It is significant that in the same chapter another connection is made: "The moral man does something, and when no one responds he rolls up his sleeves and uses force."

[122] Taine, Origins of Contemporary France, v. 1.

knows half a truth, then our combined opinions will amount to the whole truth. Obviously this is not a reasonable expectation, and the outcome will most likely be that both of us happened to have achieved the same half truth—the simplest half—and in combination we will be no better off than when we started.

For example, if we imagined the problem as an algebraic equation required a number of operations, properly ordered, in order to reach the solution, what is most likely is that my friend and I, if we even have half the solution, which is unlikely, will inevitably have the first half only, for if either of us had the last half then we'd have the first half too, and we'd be in full possession of the solution. Thus, if we imagine a problem in this way, then two men, each with half the truth, will never combine to achieve the whole truth.

H.L. Mencken put it in similar terms, saying: "If x is the population of the United States and y is the degree of imbecility of the average American, then democracy is the theory that $x \times y$ is less than y."[123]

Even the sciences, as we now have them, will tell us the same thing—that the average opinion of a mass is not, in fact, even on par with the average intelligence of that mass, but is a measure of the floor. In the words of Rene Guénon:

> "This now leads us to elucidate more precisely the error of the idea that the majority should make the law...the opinion of the majority cannot be anything but an expression of incompetence, whether this be due to lack of intelligence or to ignorance pure and simple; certain observations of 'mass psychology' might be quoted here, in particular the widely known fact that the aggregate of mental reactions aroused among the component individuals of a crowd crystallizes into a sort of general psychosis whose level is not merely not that of

---

[123] H.L. Mencken, *Sententiæ: The Citizen and the State*.

the average, but actually that of the lowest elements present."[124]

And as Guénon was speaking of this problem as it relates to legislation, we are led to our next point.

DEMOCRATIZATION OF LAW

Argument:

> "It is a besetting vice of democracies to substitute public opinion for law. This is the usual form in which masses of men exhibit their tyranny...Although the political liberty of this country is greater than that of nearly every other civilized nation, its personal liberty is said to be less. In other words, men are thought to be more under the control of extra-legal authorities and to defer more to those around them, in pursuing even their lawful and innocent occupations, than in almost every other country...It is not difficult to trace the causes of such a state of things, but the evil is none the less because it is satisfactorily explained."
>
> ~ James Fenimore Cooper[125]

Elucidation:

Enamored with the idea that majority opinion will be right a majority of the time about the majority of the issues—or else how could anyone consciously adhere to majority rule?—the social mind tends, consciously or not, to start to associate truth and justice themselves with the opinion of the majority.

---

[124] Rene Guénon, *Crisis of the Modern World*, 75.
[125] James Fenimore Cooper, *The American Democrat* (New York: Knopf, 1931), pp. 64, 141-42.

Thomas Jefferson is sometimes falsely quoted as having said "I would rather be judged by twelve farmers than twelve scholars."[126] Even though this quote is spurious, it does accurately express the present sentiments of many Americans. In fact, what else could explain the construction of that most insane of all institutions—*trial by peers?*

What madness would lead men to try and solve the most difficult criminal cases by pulling twelve amateurs—mechanics, grocers, carpenters, and housewives—off the street and forcing them to present the verdict? We now live in an age where it is unacceptable for one to suggest that judgments ought to be carried out by a man whose vocation is specifically *to judge*, while the admirable notion is that the judge ought sit quietly and wait to affirm whatever nonsense is produced by the proletariat, whom, out of necessity more than negligence, know little about the law. The idea of being tried by a jury of peers completely terrifies me.

DEMOCRATIZATION OF TRUTH ITSELF

Argument:

> *"Looking very closely, it can be seen that religion itself dominates less a revealed doctrine than a commonly held opinion."*
>
> ~ *Alexis de Tocqueville*

Elucidation:

The final outcome of the processes just explained is that all truth becomes seen as a matter of consensus: that opinion is true which is

---

[126] Glenn Beck made the reference on television, although it is uncertain who first invented the spurious quotation.

most popular. This is the unconscious premise of democratism and its gravest error. Knowledge is the most aristocratic—which is to say exclusive—of fields, and to imagine that the Gallup Poll is the most effective way of discovering it is to plummet into darkness at breakneck speed. This is best illustrated by the fact that, in American, the mentality has invaded even the sphere of religion itself, the last stronghold of the aristocratic tradition, where, even when men of knowledge were denied their say in every other area, the clergy was still respected as the authority in its own domain. But with the victory of democratism, even Christian doctrine became "less a revealed doctrine than a commonly held opinion." Religion itself went the way of quantity over quality.

AUTHORITY, IGNORANCE, AND THE COMMON GOOD

Argument:

> "...the superior makes use of his subjects for their own benefit and good; and this kind of subjection existed even before sin. For good order would have been wanting in the human family if some were not governed by others wiser than themselves...Nor is inequality among men excluded by the state of innocence."

> ~St. Thomas Aquinas[127]

Elucidation:

One of the most important questions for democratic societies to answer is this:

---

[127] *Summa Theologica*, I, q. 92, a. 1, ad. 2. See also: I, q. 96, a. 4.

"To what degree should ignorance be allowed to impact the common good?"

Now ignorance, as we've already suggested, is inevitable and is in no way a sin on the part of the ignorant. It is simply a reality we must live with: most of us are ignorant of all but a few things, namely those things that we've experienced, studied, contemplated, and to which we've committed our lives. If we haven't ever given time to a subject, we are probably ignorant of it, and this is usually *okay*.

But what occurs when those who are ignorant in a particular field begin to demand a say in it?—whether it is the science of medicine, technology, or politics, the answer ought to be the same: ignorance should not be allowed to short-circuit those pursuits necessary to the common good of society. Ignorance cannot be allowed to short-circuit political procedure and justice.

So where does this leave us? We return inevitably to one of the original sins of democratic regimes, which is the demand for imaginary equality, for equality despises the "exclusivity" aspect of knowledge. It cannot acknowledge that some men know what others do not. To say the same thing another way, we come again to the question of hierarchy. Hence, the reason we referred above to St. Thomas Aquinas, acknowledging that *Liberal equality never existed in the created world*.

So much for James Madison's famous nonsense: "If men were angels, no government would be necessary."[128] Angels in heaven, just as man in Eden and after, exist in a hierarchical reality. It cannot be explained, and it cannot be justified, it simply *is*, and to attempt to deny it is *chasing after the wind*.

Logically, we must assume that if there is a hierarchy to the social order, then the superior justly wields some sort of authority over the

---

[128] *The Federalist no. 51.*

inferior, and more than this, that because the hierarchy is real and no, as in Liberalism, abstract or imaginary, it corresponds to a real difference in the aptitudes of the individuals. The man on the superior level is, if justice has been satisfied, really a superior man, in one way or another.

This is why it was common sense to all traditional peoples that, on difficult questions, the man whose superiority lay in judgment, discernment, and the study of law, ought to make decisions on the subject, and that the ignorant ought to remain within their spheres of competence.

Thus, St. Thomas continues elsewhere, quoting Aristotle: "we ought to pay as much attention to the undemonstrated sayings and opinions of persons who surpass us in experience, age and prudence, as to their demonstrations."[129]

The implication here is that the inferior—the ignorant—individual will not understand the reasoning of the one who knows, just as the man who receives open heart surgery does not understand the procedure that is being carried out by the surgeon. And to demand that it be explained in its entirety would be death to the patient.

UNIVERSAL EDUCATION: OR, DENYING HUMAN NATURE

Argument:

> *"Whatever one does, it is impossible to raise the intelligence of a nation above a certain level. It will be quite useless to ease the access to human knowledge, improve teaching methods, or reduce the cost of education, for men will never become educated nor develop their intelligence without devoting time*

---

[129] *Summa Theologica*, I-II, q. 95, a. 2; Arisitotle, *Ethics*, bk. 6, ch. 11.

to the matter...Thus it is as difficult to imagine a society where all men are enlightened as a state where all the citizens are wealthy."

~Alexis de Tocqueville[130]

Elucidation:

Tocqueville's observation would have been common sense to anyone not imbued with Liberal humanism. And in these few words, he refutes the entire premise of the modern school system, and in fact of democracy itself as conceived by the products of that school system, which is that universal compulsory education, if properly funded and engineered, can alter human nature in such a way as to bring about the utopia of the equal enlightenment. A pleasant dream, to be sure, but a denial of the diversity inherent in the human species. And every system based upon a denial of human nature does violence to those passed through it.

This is what caused reactionaries like D.H. Lawrence to lash out so often and so violently against such a system:

> "The fact is, our process of universal education is to-day so uncouth, so psychologically barbaric, that it is the most terrible menace to the existence of our race. We seize hold of our children, and by parrot-compulsion we force into them a set of mental tricks. By unnatural and unhealthy compulsion we force them into a certain amount of cerebral activity. And then, after a few years, with a certain number of windmills in their heads, we turn them loose, like so many inferior Don Quixotes, to make a mess of life."[131]

And elsewhere in the same work, he elaborates:

---

[130] DiA, I.2.5. 229-230.
[131] D.H. Lawrence, *Fantasia of the Unconscious*, "First Steps in Education".

"The top and bottom of it is, that it is a crime to teach a child anything at all, school-wise. It is just evil to collect children together and teach them through the head. It causes absolute starvation in the dynamic centers, and sterile substitute of brain knowledge is all the gain. The children of the middle classes are so vitally impoverished, that the miracle is they continue to exist at all. The children of the lower classes do better, because they escape into the streets. But even the children of the proletariat are now infected...We don't want to educate children so that they may understand. Understanding is a fallacy and a vice in most people. I don't even want my child to know, much less to understand. I don't want my child to know that five fives are twenty-five, any more than I want my child to wear my hat or my boots. I don't want my child to know. If he wants five fives let him count them on his fingers. As for his little mind, give it a rest, and let his dynamic self be alert. He will ask "why" often enough. But he more often asks why the sun shines, or why men have mustaches, or why grass is green, than anything sensible. Most of a child's questions are, and should be, unanswerable. They are not questions at all. They are exclamations of wonder, they are remarks half-sceptically addressed. When a child says, "Why is grass green?" he half implies. "Is it really green, or is it just taking me in?" And we solemnly begin to prate about chlorophyll. Oh, imbeciles, idiots, inexcusable owls!"[132]

I quote Lawrence at length here because his words run so contrary to the contemporary mindset—I quote at length in hope that this language, by the power of its strangeness, pierce through our prejudices that have calloused us. But now, having used the colorful language of a literary figure—for Lawrence was a novelist before anything else—let us turn to those who would know even better the concrete situation of modern educational systems.

Dr. Caspar Kraemer, Professor of New York University, was quoted in the New York Times, Mar. 12, 1939 saying: "We spend more money than any other nation in the world to get an inferior product. The democracy of our education consists of the regimentation of all students, no matter what their degree of proficiency, upon a single level, which must of necessity be low if it concerns itself only with those needs of the best students which are common to the worst."

Professor Virginius Dabney (University of Virginia) wrote that: "The malady is doubtless due to numerous causes. But perhaps a certain conception of 'democracy' underlies more than one of them. The notion that one man is just as good as another and perhaps a little better has something to do with it...One curse of American life is the subordination of quality to quantity. Our educational system would be much better if there were fewer but better schools and colleges, fewer but better paid teachers in the schools, fewer but better paid professors in the universities with only half the number of students."[133]

President Robert Maynard Hutchins of the University of Chicago also writes: "Since our students have lived up to our expectations, we have succeeded in postponing maturity to a date undreamed of in the Middle Ages, or ever in Europe today. The American college senior is two or three years less grown up than his French or British contemporary. In ability to use his mother tongue and the other instruments of intellectual operation he does not at all compare with them."[134]

To avoid vagaries, we might do well to pause on one particular goal of the educational system, which is the wish for universal literacy. To examine the merits of this goal in itself will help us further understand the merits of the system into which it fits.

---

[133] From an essay titled "Spurious Democracy".
[134] "Education for Freedom," Harpers Magazine, October, 1941.

Daniel Schwindt

AGAINST LITERACY

Argument:

> *"...we really can make a move on our children's behalf. We really can refrain from thrusting our children any more into those hot-beds of the self-conscious disease, schools. We really can prevent their eating much more of the tissues of leprosy, newspapers and books. For a time, there should be no compulsory teaching to read and write at all. The great mass of humanity should never learn to read and write—never..."*

> *~ D.H. Lawrence*[135]

Elucidation:

Loud and clear we proclaim it: the ability to read does not, of itself, make a man any better off. A neutral, technical skill, literacy has been transformed into an ideal—almost a moral ideal, and perhaps even a pseudo-doctrine—of the modern world, such that attempts are now being made to apply it to all indiscriminately, as if it were an absolute good in itself, without respect to the individual aptitudes of the person, the idiosyncrasies of culture, or the real needs of civilization. Even insofar as this "war against illiteracy" has been successful, it has driven the illiterate into extinction only so that the ignorant could inherit the earth.

This new ideal is a product of two obsessions, which it is impossible to over-emphasize: one is the egalitarian mentality which demands that no differences between men be acknowledged; the second is the belief in progress, which attempts to carry each good to its extreme limit, transforming it into its opposite. The implication was that the only thing keeping men ignorant and oppressed was their inability to have

---

[135] D.H. Lawrence, *Fantasia of the Unconscious* (Rockville: Serenity, 2008), 70-71.

free access to information. Equipped with literacy and this coveted information, it was believed that truth would naturally follow and flourish in civilization. This, unfortunately, has never been the case.

Wilhelm Roepke reflected on these "high hopes which a progress-happy era had pinned on the fight against illiteracy. We can but marvel that those who cherished these naive hopes—some of them may still be about—never seem to have realized that what really counts is what all these people are to read once they have learned how to read. Nor do they seem to have asked themselves whether the standardized educational system by which illiteracy is eradicated was always favorable to a wise choice of reading matter."

He then quotes Russell Kirk: "The average Englishman reads nothing except a thin and vulgar daily newspaper, though he has been compelled to go to school for half a century; while in Portugal, the state with the highest rate of illiteracy in western Europe, the reading of serious books and journals per head of population, is much higher than in enlightened Britain. The broad nineteenth-century public for English literature, in short, has very nearly ceased to exist."[136]

In short, literacy is a means—good within a certain limited context, but not good, much less necessary, in every context and for every person. If this skill, once superfluous to most men, has become a necessity for us, we must ask what has changed that has made us needier than our fathers. Coomaraswamy offers us an answer: "For a proletariat, literacy is a practical and cultural necessity. We may remark in passing that necessities are not always goods in themselves, out of their context; some, like wooden legs, are advantageous only to men already maimed."[137]

---

[136] Humane Economy, 59.
[137] Coomaraswamy, Bugbear, 53

Having reduced the mass of humanity from craftsmen and artisans to a homogenous pool of technical laborers, literacy has indeed become vital for a man's usefulness in the labor market.

That is, in short, the economic result of the fight against illiteracy. The cultural result has, arguably, been worse. "Universal compulsory education, of the type introduced at the end of the last century, has not fulfilled expectations by producing happier and more effective citizens; on the contrary, it has created readers of the yellow press and cinemagoers." Men have not been enabled to raise themselves through the skill, but are rather through it subjected to more base forms of entertainment, not to mention subjection to relentless propaganda which is especially effective when delivered through that superficial and hasty medium, the newspaper.

The ideal of literacy is a result of the confusion of process and substance, which is to say, it is a confusion quantity and quality, knowledge and wisdom. "Learning and wisdom have often been divided; perhaps the clearest result of modern literacy has been to maintain and enlarge the gulf."[138]

It was against this that D.H. Lawrence reacted, and perhaps now we can understand his prescription:

> "Let all schools be closed at once. Keep only a few technical training establishments, nothing more. Let humanity lie fallow, for two generations at least. Let no child learn to read, unless it learns by itself, out of its own individual persistent desire."[139]

None of the most virile and colorful elements of culture would be lost by adopting Lawrence's attitude. He merely agrees with Whitman, who questioned his contemporaries:

---

[138] Karl Otten, Bugbear
[139] First Glimmerings of Mind

"For know you not, dear, earnest reader, that the people of our land may all read and write, and may all possess the right to vote -- and yet the main things may be entirely lacking?"[140]

On the contrary, it would open the way from the technical, process-based approach to education, back toward a more personalistic approach. Not only could the memory more than compensate for the information necessary for most tasks and trades, but, more importantly, where education existed it could once again take the form of a master who "forms" his pupils, which is a far different thing from the modern school where the teacher merely "administers" a curriculum. It is to this that Coomaraswamy further attests:

"There are hundreds of thousands of Indians even now who daily repeat from knowledge by heart either the whole or some large part of the *Bhagavad Gita*; others more learned can recite hundreds of thousands of verses of longer texts. From the earliest times, Indians have thought of the learned man, not as one who has read much, but as one who has been profoundly taught. It is much rather from a master than from any book that wisdom can be learned."

By ignoring all this we end with 6 million literates who lack most of the experience and all of the prudence of their illiterate grandparents. "The illiterate were eliminated, only to multiply the ignorant."[141]

For example, the modern man's illiterate 19th century American counterpart, lacking a television and unable to make use of any newspapers, would have engaged with and authentic, organic enthusiasm the pressing issues of his own neighborhood and village. He would have heard whispers, perhaps, of great wars and happenings 1000 miles away, but would have known that they are well beyond his

---

[140] Walt Whitman, *Democratic Vistas*.
[141] 179

ability to fix, and therefore he would not have allowed far-removed concerns to eat up his limited stock of worry and concern.

The modern man who reads his columnists and watches his evening news, does not know a single member of his own city council, but nonetheless feels compelled to speak his mind on global, regardless of his experience or knowledge. The illiterate man is protected from this peculiar brand of idiocy by the very deprivation that we like to blame for his ignorance—but it should be clear that the ignorance we attribute to him is actually ours.

THE MYTH OF UNIVERSAL SUFFRAGE

Argument:

> *"Only experience has ever taught the lesson, and only at the end of the whole development has it been assimilated, that the rights of the people and the influence of the people are two different things. The more nearly universal a franchise is, the less becomes the power of the electorate."*

> *~ Oswald Spengler*[142]

Elucidation:

Now, if there is a consensus on the failure of the ideal of universal education, and not only a consensus but masses of objective evidence pointing to it, then we must ask ourselves why this chimera is still pursued with such passion, as if our survival depended on its success. What is at stake? Well, it is not the survival of humanity, because humanity lived before widespread literacy and will live on after it. *It is*

---

[142] Decline of the West, v. 2, p. 455.

not humanity that is at risk, then, but an ideal that modern humanity has adopted—the ideal of universal suffrage.

Universal education is the result of the belief in universal suffrage: men have known for some time now that universal suffrage could not function with an ignorant populace, even if they only felt this unconsciously, and because this threatens to undermine the feasibility of the democratic idea, they fight feverishly to overcome it with the chimera of education. Let us, then, look at the ideal of suffrage that has fueled this project.

The term "suffrage" itself signifies the right to vote in political elections, and when we attach an adjective to this term, we specify the category of persons to whom this right will be extended. Women's suffrage, for example, concerns the voting rights of women, and a regime that accepts women's suffrage is one that allows women to vote. Universal suffrage, then, means *theoretically* unlimited extension of voting privileges to all regardless of class, gender, etc.

Yet our first point of discussion must be to admit that this idea is always and everywhere only theoretical—something embraced in the abstract and not in the concrete. Even in nations such as the United States, where we congratulate ourselves on our realization of universal suffrage, we can see immediately that the principle is applied only in part. For example, we know of no society, however democratic, that allows groups such as children to vote. No one even argues for it.

In addition to the discrepancy between theoretical and practical suffrage, we need to acknowledge that even the *desire* for universal suffrage is a very novel thing. The American Founders would not have dreamed of allowing their wives, their slaves, or their un-propertied neighbors to take part in an election. In fact, rarely do we see even the most avid proponents of democracy advocating the sort of universal suffrage that Americans today imagine that they accept.

Whether we are speaking of the philosophical history of the concept or the contemporary reality of its application, everyone stops somewhere. They all set a limit, even if that limit is the requirement of adulthood (a completely arbitrary classification if there ever was one). This unwillingness to apply the principle completely tells us something: First, it tells us that almost everyone knows that there ought to be some sort of qualification for electoral participation; and second, it tells us that no one knows exactly what this qualification ought to be. Because everyone agrees, even if unconsciously, on the first point—that qualifications there must be—then we can consider this an implicit acknowledgment that universal suffrage, even where it is preached, must be considered a purely sentimental notion which no one is actually willing to implement. We may then set about examining the second point, concerning the necessity and nature of the qualifications that ought to be set before the voting citizen.

CHILDHOOD SUFFRAGE?

Argument:

> "It is a melancholy but indubitable fact that in a democracy each social category can get what is due to it both in justice and in humanity only in so far as its voting power makes possible its extortion. No working-class vote, no laws protecting the worker. No women's vote, no laws protecting women...Democracy being a battle for Power, those who are not represented necessarily go under. Children, for instance, having no vote, get little attention, and what concerns their well-being tends to be neglected. For this to be remedied under the present system they would have to receive in their cradles the ballot papers which are the sole means of self-defence."

~*Bertrand de Jouvenel*[143]

Elucidation:

Perhaps we can be aided in this by taking up an obvious exception—one we can all agree upon. It seems obvious that children should not vote, but even those who agree with this fact are unable to enunciate the reasons why it is true based on their premises; and if they are able, they are yet unwilling because to do so would for upon them certain conclusions which would inevitably exclude other groups from the electoral process as well. Because this offends their sensibilities, they simply ignore the child's exclusion as a self-evident, albeit contradictory, true and move on. The conversation is in this way not decided one way or another. It is simply avoided. So let us not avoid the question any longer, and begin by asking why children should not vote.

The first possible objection to childhood suffrage might be the obvious lack of knowledge in the child-voter, whether that knowledge be acquired through experience or study. This objection is obviously valid, but it cannot be the objection that the proponents of democracy, as we hear them in the streets, have in mind. For if the problem was one of intelligence, then we'd be led down a very uncomfortable road since there are quite a few adults whose judgment and intelligence is arguably not much better than that of a boy of, say, 15-years-old—and in addition we can say that there are some young men of 15 whose judgment is quite sound, even without many years of experience to mold it. And so, if we accepted the qualification of intelligence, we'd be no better off, because we'd either have to admit that not all children ought to be disqualified, but we have to also admit that many adults ought to be. Let us, then, admit the difficulty here, and set the argument temporarily aside.

---

[143] Jouvenel, op. cit., p. 267.

The second objection is one of responsibility: we could say that the child cannot vote because the child is not responsible for himself. He is "dependent" upon another person for his basic needs. This objection is also valid, but here again we would be quickly led down an even more uncomfortable path, because

UNIVERSAL SUFFRAGE AS THE INSTITUTIONALIZATION INDIVIDUALISM

Argument:

> "In the beginning the legislator did not have to concern himself at all with the son, the daughter, and the salve, for these fell within the exclusive jurisdiction of the father. Step by step they all became subject to the law: the state had broken through into a world from which it was at first excluded, and had claimed as subject to its own jurisdiction those who had in former days been subjects of the father alone."

> ~ Bertrand de Jouvenel[144]

Elucidation:

The greatest victory of universal suffrage was to put into law the individualistic mentality from which it had sprung. It achieved in writing the final dissection of the last hierarchical barrier between the State and the individual, which was the family. For each voter is to the State a basic political unit, autonomous and ready to be set against every other unit in comparison to which it is theoretically identical. Thus, husband and wife could now be treated separately by the State, and although the child has not yet been given a ballot he is nonetheless absorbed through compulsory education. The family,

---

[144] *On Power*, 180.

which had always been the fundamental political unit, was no more, and from then on became something "artificial" rather than organic, which had to justify the customary protections it has always received, which now seemed like "privileges" (for, after all, why should two or three identical individuals receive benefits and supports that an individual does not?).

THE PROBLEM OF VOTER DEPENDENCY

Argument:

> *"The right to vote is the only test of citizenship; but this right presupposes the independence of him who wishes to be not only a part of the Republic but also a member of it—a part, in other words, that acts as it sees fit in conjunction with the others. Action in this capacity compels a distinction between the active citizen and the passive."*

> ~ *Immanuel Kant*[145]

Elucidation:

Even Immanuel Kant, an advocate of Enlightenment Liberalism, knew that Aristotle was right long ago when he observed that one of the most important qualifications for participation in government, and therefore citizenship, was independence, not only in mind or in law but also in concrete reality. Thus, Aristotle does not consider laborers to be citizens, although they may have rights and access to the court, since they do not have the leisure time or autonomy required to practice the intellectual virtues. Moreover, in agreement with Kant, such men are for their livelihood dependent on an employer, and so their interest is subordinate to his, which means that their vote is

---

[145] *Metaphysics of Morals*, part 1, xlvi.

really dictated by the employer's well-being rather than their own. In short, their autonomy is compromised.

Discussions regarding servants are especially enlightening on this subject, particularly those taken from the 17th, 18th, and even 19th centuries. This is because modern men might readily agree that a "servant-master" relationship is one of dependence, and therefore the vote of the servant could not really be considered an independent one. These men, however, will turn around and congratulate themselves on the fact that we no longer have "servants" or "masters" and that, therefore, we can all imagine ourselves as autonomous individuals. Yet how surprised they would be if they were to read the following excerpt from C.B. Macpherson's work:

> "The term servant in seventeenth-century England meant anyone who worked for an employer for wages, whether the wages were piece-rates or time-rates, and whether hired by the day or week or by the year."[146]

Thus, it seems that we can call the laboring man whatever we want—servant or the more flattering "employee"—we are still a society of servant-master relationships, and the same relationship of dependence holds true. The employee is beholden to his employer—his security, indeed his family's welfare, is wrapped up with and subordinate to the welfare of his employer. He does not vote as an independent member of the community, and so the worth of his vote is somewhat dubious.

THE TWOFOLD IGNORANCE OF THE VOTER

Argument:

---

[146] *The Political Theory of Possessive Individualism: Hobbes to Locke* (New York: Oxford, 1964), p. 282.

"Many people in Europe believe without saying so, or say so without believing it, that one of the great advantages of universal suffrage is to summon men worthy of public trust to the direction of public affairs...For my part, I am bound to say, what I have seen in America does not give me any reason to think that this is the case...It is a permanent feature of the present day that the most outstanding men in the United States are rarely summoned to public office...The race of American statesmen has strangely shrunk in size over the last half-century...I willingly accept that the bulk of the population very sincerely supports the welfare of the country...But what they always lack, more or less, is the skill to judge the means to achieve this sincerely desired end...I hold it proved that those who consider universal suffrage as a guarantee of the excellence of the choice made are under a complete delusion."

~ Alexis de Tocqueville[147]

Elucidation:

The typical voter requires two complex and very different areas of competence in order to assert himself honestly and effectively:

First, he must know the man for whom he is voting. If I do not know anything about you as a person, your strengths, weaknesses, experience, opinions, etc., then I am not competent to decide whether or not you can effectively govern, or do any other job for that matter. While I may conceivably achieve appropriate knowledge of this type about people who live down the street from me, it is nothing short of ludicrous to imagine that I can achieve that level of knowledge in regard to a presidential candidate whom I've never met and cannot meet, and about whom my only sources of information are a pair of warring tribes who either paint the candidate as a devil or a saint. The

---

problems here are fairly obvious, but remember this is only the first area of competence I must achieve.

Second, after I attain knowledge of the candidate, I must attain knowledge of the job itself. If I do not know how the job works or what it is like, what strengths and aptitudes it requires, then I can't select someone to do the job even if I know all of the candidates personally.

Now here again, I can conceivably fulfill this second requirement of competence if the candidate in question lives down the street and will decide whether or not the forest across town gets cleared for development. I know the man, I know the forest, and I know the town. However, the knowledge required to truly know what it takes to be a "good president" is astonishingly complex: here one needs not only knowledge of history, geography, rhetoric, military science, international law, and foreign languages, but he also needs *experience*. If I have neither knowledge nor experience, then I'm like a baker trying to judge the technique of a brain surgeon: the baker might have an opinion on the surgeon's technique, but his opinion is not valid—it is but the expression of ignorance.

Because the attainment of the level of competence described above is obviously impossible for the average man who works and maybe even has a family, and because democracies like the United States are predicated on the notion that this same man can and should choose the president anyway, then democracy itself can be said to be predicated on the reinforcement of Augustinian ignorance. It not only suggests but *demands* that a man pick and choose between a thousand things he knows nothing about, and which he may have never even considered.

Needless to say, such an atmosphere is fertile ground for the enthronement of ignorance. Consider again our typical voting citizen:

- *He thinks he knows* what's going on with global warming, whether the science is valid or not.

- *He thinks he knows* what sort of effect a tax adjustment would have on the national economy.
- *He thinks he knows* how immunizations work.
- *He thinks he knows* what "organic" means.
- *He thinks he knows* what sort of foreign policy is needed in the Middle East.

This list could go on and on, from Benghazi to the Big Bang, but I'm sure the point is clear: The voter cannot possibly have formed valid opinions about these things. Considered individually, the number of people who fully understand any one of the above points is undeniably very, very small. Considered as a whole and all at once, *no one could possibly have reached a level of understanding that could be termed "competent."*

SCITA AND SCIENDA

Argument:

> *"...we have pointed out before that the discrepancy between the things which are theoretically known, the* scita, *and those which ought to be known by the "politicized" masses, the* scienda, *is increasing by leaps and bounds. Even if it is true that general education is improving and that the general level of education is rising—which we sincerely doubt—the political and economical problems with their implications as well as the scientific answers for their solution are growing in number as well as in complexity. This is a race between an arithmetical and a geometrical progression."*

> ~ *Erik von Kuehnelt-Leddihn*[148]

---

[148] Erik von Kuehnelt-Leddihn, *Liberty or Equality*, p. 278.

Daniel Schwindt

Elucidation:

Above we examined the problem of knowledge as it pertains to the candidates and to specific political roles. Closely related to this point, but different in that it addresses human knowledge more generally, is Kuehnelt-Leddihn's problem of *scita* versus *scienda*.

By setting these two terms in opposition he is pointing to the intersection between the information that is theoretically available to the modern man, and that which actually makes it into his head. The distinction could also be described from a slightly different angle, as between *what is actually known* by the people, and *what should be known* in order to reach rational-moral conclusions about complex problems.

To use the problem of global warming, it seems clear that, with our sciences as developed as they are today, that those who work in this field probably know whether or not the problem is real or imaginary. Yet we find that, in the end, none of that really matters. All that matters is whether or not the accurate bits information, accompanied by the most appropriate interpretations, actually get absorbed into the popular mind; and at this point in the climate debate it is pretty clear that this is not happening with any efficiency.

This is the illusion of the so-called "information age." We do indeed live in an "information age," but we tend to forget that the sheer *availability* of information may or may not have any impact on whether or not that information can be distributed effectively, much less utilized properly. In fact, we could say that the greatest lie of the information age is that, just by piling up trillions of bits of data, we perpetually increase the intelligence of the human race as a collective whole. This optimistic assumption about the human mind has been almost universally accepted since the rise of humanism, and is completely false. There is a very rigid limit on the amount of knowledge that an individual can absorb and utilize, and it is never very much. We all live and die in ignorance of almost everything there is in the world to know. To say this is not pessimism, but is simply an honest acknowledgment of the vastness of our reality, its laws, and its mysteries.

If we begin with a proper view of man, then we are faced immediately with man as the limit. Only then may we turn our glance to the "information" heaped up in databases. We then see that this is in large part irrelevant to the average intelligence of a nation, since each individual still has his own limits. And neither can we cite the specialists, or those few individuals of incredible intelligence, for my neighbor's knowledge is not in any way mine, and it does not make my ballot sheet any more intelligently completed.

For example, there is an unprecedented amount of information available on the Internet. This gives the impression that everyone with access to the Internet, because they have such a wonderful resource before them, should be able to use this resource to evaluate and decide on any problem they face. But is this at all feasible?

In the end: No. The sheer availability of information does not in any way guarantee that the right bits of information will be discovered by the right people at the right time. The Internet holds an incomprehensible amount of data, and sifting through it to find information that is both timely and true can turn into an equally incomprehensible enterprise, even if the voter has the stamina to wade through the mountains of partial statistics, slanted reports, adware, and pornography that will interfere with his search.

THE CULT OF INCOMPETENCE

Argument:

> *"I have often wondered what principle democrats have adopted for the form of government which they favour, and it has not required a great effort on my part to arrive at the*

> *conclusion that the principle in question is the worship and cultivation, or, briefly 'the cult' of incompetence or inefficiency...The people favours incompetence, not only because it is no judge of intellectual competence and because it looks on moral competence from a wrong point of view, but because it desires before everything, as indeed is very natural, that its representatives should resemble itself."*

> *~ Emile Faguet*[149]

Elucidation:

One would have to read Faguet's interesting little book, from which the above citation is taken, in order to properly appreciate his thesis; but it is not difficult to understand that an incompetent public chooses the incompetent candidate, not just accidentally, due to the incompetence, but *on purpose*. For if the choice of an incompetent leader were merely the result of incompetence on the part of the chooser, then we would see the accidental choice of a competent leader for the same reason: it would be a coin toss. But the principle of *like unto like* demands that the incompetent voters actively prefer the incompetent candidate, despising a competent one.

In other words, the worst part about the attempt to institute "representative" government is that it often works: the people choose leaders, not because they perceive that they know better or because they have exceptional talents, but because they believe that these men resemble themselves.

If Faguet's reasoning is sound, then we would actually have a better chance of drawing quality statesman if we adopted the Old Testament practice of casting lots, for the system we use presently does not give us the luxury of chance, but ensures that the selection will fail. To lead into our next point, however, we must acknowledge that this is not a

---

[149] Emile Faguet, *The Cult of Incompetence*, pp. 15, 29.

conscious process, but an unconscious one, which is to say it is almost instinctual.

POPULAR INSTINCTS PREFER THE INFERIOR CANDIDATE

Argument:

> *"While the natural instincts of democracy persuade the people to remove distinguished men from power, the latter are guided by no less an instinct to distance themselves from a political career, where it is so difficult for them to retain their complete autonomy or to make any progress without cheapening themselves."*[150]

> ~ *Alexis de Tocqueville*

Elucidation:

Perhaps the most profound thing we can take from this observation is its reference to the operation of instinct in democratic regimes. He does not simply suggest that instincts play a part, but that instinct plays *the decisive* part when it comes to both the selection and the appointment of statesmen. This alone is enough to condemn a regime—that it allows instinct to rule supreme. But what else could have been expected? We knew already that knowledge could not possibly be the determining factor, and so if not knowledge then something else. That something else is instinct, or emotion. Tocqueville follows by citing Chancellor Kent's *Commentaries on American Law*, vol. I, p. 273:

> "It is probable, in fact, that the most appropriate men to fill these places would have too much reserve in the manners and

---

[150] *Democracy in America*, I.2.5.

too much severity in their principles ever to be able to gather the majority of votes at an election that rested on universal suffrage."

The end result is that a candidate must either *actually be* a man formed after the instincts of the mass, or he must be an intelligent and objective man who is willing to degrade himself in such a way that he appears to be so, and in appearing as such is able to win the majority. It is difficult to say which of these two we'd prefer, and it seems to boil down to the situation we find ourselves in at each modern election: a choice between two men of such poor quality that we do not vote *for* the good candidate but rather we inevitably end up voting *against* the one we perceive as more sinister or incompetent. And so, in many ways, we can understand Mencken's frustrations as he prophesied the point of termination for this descending curve: government by morons. As Mencken put it:

"Here is tragedy—and here is America. For the curse of the country, as well of all democracies, is precisely the fact that it treats its best men as enemies. The aim of our society, if it may be said to have an aim, is to iron them out. The ideal American, in the public sense, is a respectable vacuum."[151]

We may also turn here to the always reasonable Aldous Huxley, who reaches similar conclusions:

"In the world of politics, the chances of getting imbecile leaders under an elective system could be considerably reduced by applying to politicians a few of those tests for intellectual, physical and moral fitness which we apply to the candidates for almost every other kind of job. Imagine the outcry if hotelkeepers were to engage servants without demanding a 'character' from their previous employers; or if sea-captains

---

[151] "More Tips for Novelists" in the Chicago Tribune (2 May 1926)

were chosen from homes for inebriates; or if railway companies entrusted their trains to locomotive engineers with arterio-sclerosis and prostrate trouble; or if civil servants were appointed and doctors allowed to practice without passing an examination! And yet, where the destinies of whole nations are at stake, we do not hesitate to entrust the direction affairs to men of notoriously bad character; to men sodden with alcohol; to men so old and infirm that they can't do their work or even understand what it is about; to men without ability or even education."[152]

IN THE ABSENCE OF KNOWLEDGE, EMOTION RULES SUPREME

Argument:

> *"Without a real knowledge of the object we cannot let reason make a judgment. On the other hand, a few external aspects, if perceived, are sufficient to let our emotions react."*

> ~ *Erik von Kuehnelt-Leddihn*[153]

Elucidation:

Kuehnelt-Leddihn's observation is closely related to the problem of propaganda, which is the subject of the next installment in this series. Our comments here, therefore, should be understood as an allusion to arguments that must wait until they can be fully developed in their proper place. Suffice it to say here that a very effective way to get a man to behave irrationally, and to open him in a most degrading way to the power of suggestion, is to pressure him to make a decision that he is not equipped to make. This can be done in various ways—for

---

[152] — Aldous Huxley, *Ends and Means*, Chatto and Windus (London), 1937, p. 174.
[153] *Liberty or Equality*, p. 116.

example either by flattering him into thinking he *is* equipped to make a decision he isn't, or else by instilling him with enough fear that he is driven to express an opinion without respect to its proper formation.

Bertrand de Jouvenel traced the steps leading to this process as well, observing that the Founding Fathers, optimistic humanists that they were, believed that education and rational public discourse could fulfill the requirement of knowledge and thus create a population competent to deal with political questions. While this was perhaps conceivable in the 18th century, it is a far-fetched fantasy in the 21st. If it was possible for the man on the street to grasp the processes—political, economic, or otherwise—that surrounded him in the days of Thomas Jefferson, it is in no way possible for him to understand them anymore. The information age and universal compulsory education has only added to the complexity of things and highlighted the mental deficiency of the public at large. This has resulted in a new attitude being adopted by the Thomas Jefferson's of today:

> "The men of our day, however, being circumspect people, have realized that the cultivation of the electors' intelligence is at least as likely to open a window on the arguments of their opponents as on their own; therefore it is labour lost. The faculty of reason may lie relatively unused in the majority of a people, but there is not a man anywhere who is incapable of emotion. And it is to the emotions, therefore, that appeal must be made."[154]

Thus, we have imposed upon ourselves a regime that enthrones emotion as the driving force of politics by pressing men with questions that they do not have the knowledge to answer. This problem is built into the DNA of democracies in a society so hyper-complex as ours, and this means that propaganda itself is inherent in the democratic regime: it is not an evil inflicted by a group of plotting elites in a dark room, but is a natural product of the system, without which the system

---

[154] Jouvenel, op. cit., p. 273.

could not function, nor could men function within it. Propaganda, then, must be understood if we are to understand ourselves, and our next installment will hopefully form a contribution to that self-understanding.

PART 4: CHURCH AND STATE

"The world has heard enough of the so-called rights of man. Let it hear something of the rights of God."

~ *Pope Leo XIII*[155]

INTRODUCTORY

The relationship between Church and State involves two questions: one of power and one of knowledge. From the point of view of the State, it is a question of power and who is subordinate to whom. From the point of view of the Church it is a question of truth, and whose knowledge is closer to the absolute and which, therefore, must be prior to the other. The failure to understand these differing points of view is the perennial source of conflict between the two spheres. The Church understands itself as the bridge between the absolute and the relative, between Eternity and Present, between Truth itself and temporal confusion. In this role it clearly sees itself as superior from a logical point of view to all other social bodies *in knowledge*, since it is attached to "the source" while others receive the knowledge thus drawn. The State, on the other hand, which tends to conceive of all

---

[155] *De Monarchia*, III, 16.

social institutions in terms of power, cannot help but be jealous of an authority which claims to hold this directing knowledge. It feels this as a threat to the exercise of its power, whether or not the threat is real, and is perpetually seeking to dethrone the spiritual authorities in such a way that it no longer has to reconcile the exercise of its power with the dictates of their knowledge. It loathes being responsible to a body that is, from its unique point of view, so utterly weak. And so the two social groups, which in the end represent two necessary social functions, tend to exist in tension, although at certain periods throughout history they have, by understanding themselves and their respective functions properly, harmonized in their purposes and achieved the unity dreamed of by St. Thomas Aquinas and Dante. The purpose of this installment in our series is to examine the nature of this relationship. We will also seek to understand the problems that arise when the relationship between the two is denied, destroyed, or inverted. This will lead us not only to questions of religion and politics, but to questions regarding the nature of law and justice itself.

KNOWLEDGE AND ACTION

Argument:

> *"All action that does not proceed from knowledge is lacking in principle and thus is nothing but a vain agitation; likewise, all temporal power that fails to recognize its subordination to the spiritual authority is vain and illusory: separated from its principle, it can only exert itself in a disorderly way and move inexorably to its own ruin."*
>
> *~ Rene Guénon[156]*

---

[156] *Spiritual Authority and Temporal Power*, p. 28-29.

To state the question in its simplest form, the Church and the State represent to separate functions, these being *knowledge* and *action*. Understood in this way, it becomes blatantly obvious that there exists between the two a relationship that is not "separate but equal," but rather "hierarchical." This is because human action *must* proceed from knowledge. Knowledge, for rational beings, is the principle of their action in the physical world.

Now clearly one could respond that "action" takes place all the time, through the growth of plant life, for example, that has no origin in thought. This objection can be answered by taking a more comprehensive view of reality.

According to the traditional understanding of the cosmos, all beings are "thoughts" of the Creator, and Creation is the expression through act of the Mind of God. And so, from this point of view, the existence of the world itself has its origin in thought, which is to say in the "knowledge" of God. This is why Christianity says of Christ, the *Logos*, that "through him all things were made." Because Christ is the "Word" of God, he is the mind of God expressed through existence, and hence it can be said that he is "the Lamb of God sacrificed from the beginning of the World." This is the relationship between knowledge and action in terms of the macrocosm.

Man, for his own part, is called a "microcosm," reflecting in himself the structure of the macrocosm. Thus, while brutes (irrational animals) do indeed "act" upon the world in various ways, they do not participate in rationality. The knowledge from which their activity proceeds has its origin in the laws of nature, to which they are passive. Their action has its origin in knowledge, even though it is not their knowledge. That is why plants and animals, although alive and acting, do not reflect the universe in the way that man, who is the "rational animal," contains it within himself.

Human action, if it is properly human, which is to say rational, proceeds from knowledge. Although it is possible for man to act on a brute level, and to go on living on a vegetal level, this is not human action properly speaking. All human action proceeds from knowledge, and this knowledge is found in the human being himself and is not, as was the case with the brute, a passive or "instinctual" participation.

In summary, we can say with Guénon that action without knowledge is not human, but rather an animal type of knowledge. If man does not subordinate his action to knowledge, then his action is disordered. He is acting either irrationally or "non-rationally," and thereby degrades his action to the level of the brute.

THE CASTE SYSTEM

Argument:

> "The principle of the institution of castes, so completely misunderstood by Westerners, is nothing else but the differing natures of human individuals; it establishes among them a hierarchy the incomprehension of which only brings disorder and confusion...In effect, each man, by reason of his proper nature, is suited to carry out certain definite functions to the exclusion of all others...and thus the social order exactly expresses the hierarchical relationships that result from the nature of the beings themselves."
>
> ~ Rene Guénon[157]

Elucidation:

---

[157] *Spiritual Authority and Temporal Power*, pp. 8-9.

The properly ordered social body, because it is a unity of the human order, has a structure that is analogous to that of the human body, composed of differing parts each contributing in a unique way to form a coherent and harmonious whole. This is why throughout traditional societies we find the various members of the social body, along with their corresponding functions, being symbolically represented by the human body.

The traditional world acknowledged the diversity among human beings. No one was born as a blank slate, capable of performing any task with the same aptitude as his neighbor, as if mankind were a homogenous mass of identical "atoms." The egalitarian outlook has no place in the traditional understanding of society. "Caste" is the result of this anti-egalitarian understanding. It is nothing more than the acknowledgement that men differ in aptitude and inclination, and that these differences correspond to the functional needs of society in such a way that, if they are acknowledged and ordered properly, all men in a society can be assigned a "vocation" that fits their nature and allows them to realize their potential to the greatest degree possible.

This system has its equivalents in all traditional societies, from the Christian Middle Ages to Japan. However, the Hindu caste system in India, because it is the only one with which modern men are vaguely familiar, will be used an example here, although its underlying assumptions and its categories must be understood to be universal amongst the other traditional civilizations. The terms for the Hindu castes (*varnas*) are the Brahmins, the Kshatriyas, the Vaishyas, and the Shudras. Returning again to Guénon:

> "...the Brahmins represent essentially the spiritual and intellectual authority; the Kshatriyas, the administrative prerogative comprising both the judicial and the military offices, of which the royal function is simply the highest

degree; to the Vaishyas belongs the whole varied range of economic functions in the widest sense of the word, including the agricultural, industrial, commercial and financial functions; as for the Shudras, they carry out the tasks necessary to assure the purely material subsistence of the community."[158]

If we choose to represent this "social body" symbolically, the Brahmins form the mouth, the Kshatriya the arms, the Vaishya the thighs, the Shudra the feet.[159]

Translating these functional groups into more familiar terms, such as those of the Medieval West, we can speak of the priestly class (Brahmins), the nobility (Kshatriyas), the "third estate" (Vaishyas), and peasantry (Shudras).

While the study of each of these four principal castes would be beneficial for the modern Westerner, our purposes make it necessary to focus on the divergence between the first two only: the priesthood and the nobility, the "Sacerdotum" and "Regnum," or in other words the Spiritual Authority and the Temporal Power. The third and fourth classifications are, after all, subordinate or lesser subdivisions of the nobility.

The Spiritual Authority and the Temporal Power are, as should be clear at this point, the representatives of "knowledge" and "action" respectively, and therefore these are the categories we really ought to have in mind when we are considering problems of "Church and State," even if the latter terms are specific to the modern world.

---

[158] *Introduction to the Study of the Hindu Doctrines*, pp. 154-155.
[159] *Rig-Veda*, x. 90.

SPIRITUAL AUTHORITY AND TEMPORAL POWER

Argument:

"Ineffable providence has thus set before us two goals to aim at: i.e. happiness in this life, which consists in the exercise of our own powers and is figured in the earthly paradise; and happiness in the eternal life, which consists in the enjoyment of the vision of God (to which our own powers cannot raise us except with the help of God's light) and which is signified by the heavenly paradise.

Now these two kinds of happiness must be reached by different means, as representing different ends. For we attain the first through the teachings of philosophy, provided that we follow them putting into practice the moral and intellectual virtues; whereas we attain the second through spiritual teachings which transcend human reason, provided that we follow them putting into practice the theological virtues, i.e. faith, hope and charity.

These ends and the means to attain them have been shown to us on the one hand by human reason, which has been entirely revealed to us by the philosophers, and on the other by the Holy Spirit, who through the prophets and sacred writers, through Jesus Christ the son of God, coeternal with him, and through his disciples, has revealed to us the transcendent truth we cannot do without; yet human greed would cast these ends and means aside if men, like horses, prompted to wander by their animal natures, were not held in check "with bit and bridle" on their journey.

It is for this reason that man had need of two guides corresponding to his twofold goal: that is to say the supreme Pontiff, to lead mankind to eternal life in conformity with revealed truth, and the Emperor, to guide mankind to temporal happiness in conformity with the teachings of philosophy...

But the truth concerning this last question should not be taken so literally as to mean that the Roman Prince is not in some sense subject to the Roman Pontiff, since this earthly happiness is in some sense ordered towards immortal happiness.

Let Caesar therefore show that reverence towards Peter which a firstborn son should show his father, so that, illumined by the light of paternal grace, he may the more effectively light up the world, over which he has been placed by Him alone who is ruler over all things spiritual and temporal."

~ *Dante Alighieri*[160]

Elucidation:

Dante's words speak for themselves here. In the Western world the relationship between the Spiritual Authority and the Temporal Power has been expressed by that between the King and Roman Pontiff at various times in Europe. Indeed, the very title "pontiff," according to St. Bernard, denotes its function:

"The Pontiff, as indicated by the etymology of his name, is a kind of bridge [*pont*] between God and man."[161]

That is to say, the Pope was to represent the tether between the worldly and the eternal. He was a mediator between heaven and earth, and this is why he was able to christen as well as depose noblemen who failed to acknowledge the proper social order.

THE SEPARATION OF CHURCH AND STATE

Argument:

---

[160] *De Monarchia*, III.16.
[161] *Tractatus de Moribus et Officio Episcoporum*, III, 9.

"Men living together in society are under the power of God no less than individuals are, and society, not less than individuals, owes gratitude to God, who gave it being and maintains it, and whose ever-bounteous goodness enriches it with countless blessings. Since, then, no one is allowed to be remiss in the service due to God, and since the chief duty of all men is to cling to religion in both its teaching and practice—not such religion as they may have a preference for, but the religion which God enjoins, and which certain and most clear marks show to be the only one true religion—it is a public crime to act as though there were no God. So, too, is it a sin in the State not to have care for religion, as a something beyond its scope, or as of no practical benefit; or out of many forms of religion to adopt that one which chimes in with the fancy; for States are bound absolutely to worship God in that way which He has shown to be His will. All who rule, therefore, should hold in honour the holy Name of God, and one of their chief duties must be to favour religion, to protect it . . . . "

~ Pope Leo XIII[162]

Elucidation:

The doctrine of the separation of church and state, which is extolled in America by both the religious and non-religious alike, for opposite reasons, is the political result of the victory of the temporal power over the spiritual authority. For there is no such thing as "separate but equal," and once separation by law becomes institutional, then the party responsible for making and maintaining the law immediately rises to supremacy.

---

[162] *Immortale Dei*

In the same Encyclical he cites as reprehensible these views:

> "The State (civitas) does not consider itself bound by any kind of duty towards God. Moreover, it believes that it is not obliged to make public profession of any religion; or to inquire which of the very many religions is the only one true; or to prefer one religion to all the rest; or to show to any form of religion special favour; but, on the contrary, is bound to grant equal rights to every creed, so that public order may not be disturbed by any particular form of religious belief."

Again, in his Encyclical *Libertas*, 20 June 1888, he teaches:

> "This kind of liberty [liberty of cult], if considered in relation to the State, clearly implies that there is no reason why the State should offer any homage to God, or should desire any public recognition of Him; that no one form of worship is to be preferred to another, but that all stand on an equal footing, no account being taken of the religion of the people, even if they profess the Catholic faith.... Civil society [civilis societas, quia societas est] must acknowledge God as its Founder and Parent, and must obey and reverence His power and authority. Justice therefore forbids, and reason itself forbids, the State to be godless; or to adopt a line of action which would end in godlessness—namely, to treat the various religions (as they call them) alike, and to bestow upon them promiscuously equal rights and privileges. Since, then, the profession of one religion is necessary in the State, that religion must be professed which alone is true, and which can be recognized without difficulty, especially in Catholic States, because the marks of truth are, as it were, engraven upon it."

Likewise, Pius X wrote in his Encyclical *Vehementer nos*, 11 February 1906:

> "That the State should be separated from the Church is an absolutely false and most pernicious thesis. For first, since it is based on the principle that religion should be of no concern to the State, it does a grave injury to God, He Who is the founder and conserver of human society no less than He is of individual men, for which reason He should be worshipped not only privately but also publicly."

PROTESTANTISM AND SECULARISM

Argument:

> *If the human race were not condemned to see things reversely, it would select for its counsellors theologians amongst the generality of men, and the mystics among theologians, and amongst the mystics, those who have lived a life most apart from business and the world. Among the persons whom I know, and I know many, the only ones in whom I have recognised an unshaken common sense, and a prodigious sagacity, and an amazing aptitude to give a practical and prudent solution to the most difficult problems, and to discover a means of escape in the most trying circumstances, are those who have lived a contemplative and retired life; and, on the contrary, I have not yet discovered, and I do not expect ever to discover, one of those who are called men of business, despisers of all spiritual, and, above all, divine speculations, who would be capable of understanding any business.*

> *Juan Donoso Cortes*[163]

---

[163] Juan Donoso Cortes, *Essays*, 61.

Daniel Schwindt

Elucidation:

Take the words of Cortes, which represent the old view of knowledge which taught that those men closest to the absolute would obviously be the most discerning in any order, and compare this with Luther's view:

> "...you have people under you and you wish to know what to do. It is not Christ you are to question concerning the matter but the law of your country...Between the Christian and the ruler, a profound separation must be made...Assuredly, a prince can be a Christian, but it is not as a Christian that he ought to govern. As a ruler, he is not called a Christian, but a prince. The man is a Christian, but his function does not concern his religion...Though they are found in the man, the two states or functions are perfectly marked off, one from the other, and really opposed."[164]

And so, in the fashion of Luther, men like Jefferson could learn to see any priest who walked outside the church doors as a trespasser, useless in everything except the administration of the sacraments. And because no right-thinking clergymen would ever accept this absurd limitation, anti-clericalism was the result, and Jefferson, along with his comrades, would have to see priests as enemies of thought and freedom:

> "In every country and in every age the priest has been hostile to liberty; he is always in alliance with the despot, abetting his abuses in return for protection to his own. It is error alone that needs the support of government. Truth can stand by itself."

Thus, the notion of a beneficial "wall of separation between church and state" has its roots in liberal philosophy, and in fact this idea follows very naturally from its basic premises. So inevitable was this conclusion that we find it rearing its head not only in the political

---

[164] *Luther's Works* (Wiemar Edition) XXXII, pp. 391, 439, 440.

philosophies of John Locke and J.S. Mill, but even from religious reformers such as Martin Luther, whose advice we have cited above.

And while the Catholic Church had warned kings that "through this crown, you become a sharer in our ministry,"[165] the secularism of Luther was to become the unconscious *status quo* in all the later liberal-democratic regimes with which Protestantism would form an unhealthy union. In nations built on this philosophy, even those Catholics who wished to participate in public life would have to sacrifice their principles to the liberal altar. Consider the following statements of the Catholic president, John F. Kennedy, which we have mentioned elsewhere but which are worth citing again, and consider how perfectly they mirror the thinking of Luther, while at the same time flatly contradicting the teachings of Kennedy's own Church:

> "I believe in an America where the separation of church and state is absolute... I am not the Catholic candidate for president. I am the Democratic Party's candidate for president, who happens also to be a Catholic. I do not speak for my church on public matters, and the church does not speak for me...Whatever issue may come before me as president—on birth control, divorce, censorship, gambling or any other subject—I will make my decision...in accordance with what my conscience tells me to be the national interest, and without regard to outside religious pressures or dictates."[166]

RELIGION AND ECONOMICS

Argument:

> *"The Catholic Church, that imperishable handiwork of our All-Merciful God, has for her immediate and natural purpose the saving of souls and securing our happiness in heaven. Yet*

---

[165] Jouvenel, op. cit., p. 33.
[166] *Address to the Greater Houston Ministerial Association* delivered Sept. 12, 1960.

in regard to things temporal she is the source of benefits as manifold and great as if the chief end of her existence were to ensure the prospering of our earthly life."

~ Pope Leo XIII[167]

It is common to hear complaints of religious figures such as the Pope making suggestions about economic theory, as today it is assumed that the two spheres have nothing to do with one another. This warrants a comment on the understanding of economic activity and its history, particularly with respect to "origins stories" which go to form modern assumptions about such things. According to the conventional wisdom, money originated in a completely naturalistic fashion—from the ground up, almost like man from ape, based on a purely biological and necessary logic of efficiency. This gives the impression that the transcendent realm of religion is at the opposite end of reality from the science of money. If we ignore Smith's theses, however, which according to contemporary scholars[168] is a reasonable thing to do, we can explore other options that turn this paradigm on its head. For example, we can consider the view that, as readily acknowledged, money was originally in the power of religious authorities. It is well-known that the earliest economic transactions are temple artifacts.

At any rate, even if the economic secularists were correct in their history, the reality is that, as Pope Benedict XVI suggested, *every economic decision has a moral consequence*. Economics is not a science, and while economics are responsible for technical applications, their applications and their approach in general are circumscribed within a moral framework, which is to say they must be circumscribed by the principles of religious truth. Hence, the Catholic Church states with certainty:

---

[167] *Immortale Dei*, 1.
[168] David Graeber refutes the conventional wisdom very well in his *Debt: the first 5000 years*.

"[T]here resides in Us the right and duty to pronounce with supreme authority upon social and economic matters ...Even though economics and moral science employs each its own principles in its own sphere, it is, nevertheless, an error to say that the economic and moral orders are so distinct from and alien to each other that the former depends in no way on the latter."[169]

LIBERALISM AND THE PRIVATIZATION OF TRUTH

Argument:

"For the Liberal the spiritual center of gravity was in the individual, and the realm of private opinion and private interests was the ideal world. Hence, when the Liberal spoke of religion as a purely private matter it was in compliment rather than in derogation. To separate the Church from the State—to keep religion out of politics, was to elevate it to a higher sphere of spiritual values. But today in the democratic world, these values have been reversed. The individual life has lost its spiritual primacy, and it is social life which has now the higher prestige, so that to treat religion as a purely individual and personal matter is to deprive it of actuality and to degrade it to a lower level of value and potency. To keep religion out of public life is to shut it up in a stuffy Victorian back drawing room with the aspidistras and antimacassars, when the streets are full of life and youth. And the result is that the religion of the Church becomes increasingly alienated from real life while democratic society creates a new religion of the street and the forum to take its place."

~ Christopher Dawson[170]

---

[169] *Quadragesimo Anno*, 41-42.
[170] Christopher Dawson, Beyond Politics (New York: Sheed & Ward, 1938).

Daniel Schwindt

Elucidation:

What is observed here by Dawson has also been observed at length by figures such as Alexis de Tocqueville, who said that in liberal democratic regimes religious truth undergoes a transformation in several ways: it becomes a matter of consensus, which is something that happens to all truth in individualistic democracies; it becomes influenced by materialism, since democracy turns men's mind toward the material world overall; and it becomes an oversimplified expression of rationalism and "intuitivism" through which the individual confuses his own prejudices and guesses with "self-evident truths."

THE WEAKNESS OF SECULAR GOVERNMENT

Argument:

> *"Now a government is secure insofar as it has God for its foundation and His Will for its guide; but this, surely, is not a description of Liberal government. It is, in the Liberal view, the people who rule, and not God; God Himself is a 'constitutional monarch' Whose authority has been totally delegated to the people, and Whose function is entirely ceremonial. The Liberal believes in God with the same rhetorical fervor with which he believes in Heaven. The government erected upon such a faith is very little different, in principle, from a government erected upon total disbelief, and whatever its present residue of stability, it is clearly pointed in the direction of Anarchy."*

> *~ Seraphim Rose[171]*

Elucidation:

---

[171] *Nihilism: The Root of the Revolution of the Modern Age*, part II, ch. 1.

What has been said above regarding ambulatory law and divine law is complemented here by the words of Rose. Perhaps the only perspective we need add to the above observation about the self-impoverishment that results from the adoption of liberal principles is that of Donoso Cortes, who added that such societies are not only weakened but plummeted into chaos:

> "Liberalism explains the evil and the good, order and disorder, by the various forms of government, all ephemeral and transitory; when, prescinding, on one side, from all social, and, on the other, from all religious, problems, it brings into discussion its political problems as the only ones worthy by their elevation of occupying the statesman, there are no words in any language capable of describing the profound incapacity and radical impotence of this school, not only to solve, but even to enunciate, these awful questions. The Liberal school, enemy at once of the darkness and of the light, has selected I know not what twilight between the luminous and dark regions, between the eternal shades and the divine aurora. Placed in this nameless region, it has aimed at governing without a people and without a God. Extravagant and impossible enterprise! Its days are numbered; for on one side of the horizon appears God, and on the other, the people. No one will be able to say where it is on the tremendous day of battle, when the plain shall be covered with the Catholic and Socialistic phalanxes."[172]

THE TRUE END OF HUMAN SOCIETY

Argument:

> "It is, however, clear that the end of a multitude gathered together is to live virtuously. For men form a group for the

---

[172] Donoso Cortes, *Essays*, 64.

purpose of living well together, a thing which the individual man living alone could not attain, and good life is virtuous life. Therefore, virtuous life is the end for which men gather together... Yet through virtuous living man is further ordained to a higher end, which consists in the enjoyment of God, as we have said above. Consequently, since society must have the same end as the individual man, it is not the ultimate end of an assembled multitude to live virtuously, but through virtuous living to attain to the possession of God."

~ St. Thomas Aquinas[173]

Elucidation:

The ultimate purpose of social life is not simply the "good life," but lies beyond this life entirely, within the hereafter. This adds to the list yet another reason why the Spiritual Authority must be considered superior to the Temporal Power, since it directs man toward his ultimate end, while the Temporal Power directs him only to a relative end. This is why St. Thomas says that all human functions have contemplation as their superior end, "so that, when considered properly, they all seem to be in the service of those who contemplate truth."

But even while saying this, it is important to remember that this reasoning is only a *secondary* proof as to the superiority of the Nobility over the Priesthood. I stress this because today few in the Western world would agree that the ultimate end of society is the vision of God. I want the reader to understand that, even denying this purpose, the supremacy of knowledge over action still remains a fact, and cannot be refuted even if one adopts a purely atheistic point of view.

---

[173] *De Regno*, Bk. I, Ch. 3.

SYMBOLS OF THE RELATIONSHIP

Argument:

> *"Now it came to pass as they went, that he entered into a certain town: and a certain woman named Martha, received him into her house. And she had a sister called Mary, who sitting also at the Lord's feet, heard his word. But Martha was busy about much serving. Who stood and said: Lord, hast thou no care that my sister hath left me alone to serve? Speak to her therefore, that she help me. And the Lord answering, said to her: Martha, Martha, thou art careful, and art troubled about many things: But one thing is necessary. Mary hath chosen the best part, which shall not be taken away from her."*

> ~ *The Gospel of Luke*

Elucidation:

The account of Mary and Martha from the Gospel is the most well-known illustration of the "two paths," contemplative and active. Jacob's wives, Leah and Rachel, are also symbolic of these two paths. The biblical accounts are instructive in several ways, but the theme is universal in traditional literature.

Merlin, the Druid, and King Arthur represent the same choice between two paths, and identify the hierarchical relationship between the two parties: Merlin has knowledge and acts as Arthur's advisor. Merlin knows all things, even the future, while Arthur has been "chosen" to carry out the plan on the physical plane. St. Thomas himself explicitly refers to the relationship between the Druids and their relationship with their kings when teaching about the proper relationship between royalty and priesthood.[174]

We should also mention the ancient parable of the two men—one blind and one lame. The two form a partnership where the lame man, physically weak but gifted with sight (knowledge), is carried by the blind man who is gifted with physical strength (action). The two are clearly mutually dependent for the exercise of their functions, but it is the lame man who plays the guiding role, and the action of the blind man has its origin in the counsel of the lame man. This is precisely the relationship between the priesthood and the royalty, for while the royalty must depend upon the guidance of the priest, lest he act blindly and in vain, the priest must be protected from disturbance and the vicissitudes of worldly affairs if he is to carry out his function of contemplation and discernment.

REVOLT OF THE ARISTOCRACY

Argument:

> "Just as Martha complained about Mary so in every age active persons have complained about contemplatives...I think that worldly-minded critics who find fault with contemplatives should be excused on account of their ignorance...As certainly as Martha was ignorant of what she was saying when she protested to the Lord, so these people understand little or nothing about the contemplative life."[175]

> ~ *The Cloud of Unknowing*

Elucidation:

---

[174] *De Regno.*
[175] *Cloud of Unknowing*, Ch. 18-19.

In order to understand the historical process that has led to our current situation, we must return again to the story of Martha and Mary. As the account suggests, the contemplative life, being "beyond" the realm of action, is incomprehensible to those whose vocation does not include that sort of knowledge. Thus, while the higher always, at least in potentiality, includes the lower, the lower does not include the higher. This is why men called to action will always display a tendency to usurp, or at least to ignore, the guidance of those responsible for knowledge. The Temporal Power will always attempt to throw off the so-called chains of the Spiritual Authority, so that it can act according to its own desires. This is the revolt of the aristocracy, and it is the first stage in a chain reaction which leads to the ruin of civilization altogether and ends in a return to barbarism. This chain reaction, which begins when the royalty undermines the priesthood and usurps its role, is called the "regression of the castes."

REGRESSION OF THE CASTES

Argument:

> "A progressive shift of power and type of civilization has occurred from one caste to the next since prehistoric times (from sacred leaders, to a warrior aristocracy, to the merchants, and finally, to the serfs)."

> ~Julius Evola[176]

Elucidation:

Although there are examples of this process (the "regression of the castes") everywhere in history (India and Japan present obvious

---

[176] *Revolt Against the Modern World*, p. 327.

examples), let us stick to the phenomenon as it has unfolded in Europe, since that civilization is more familiar to Western audiences.

King Henry VIII provides for us an excellent example of the first stage of regression where a secular power refuses to acknowledge the authority of the sacred, and then claims the role of the spiritual authority for itself. We must remember, King Henry did not simply break from Rome, but also established a new church—the Church of England—of which he himself was the head.

However, as suggested earlier, the process of revolt cannot stop once it has begun. *This the way of all revolutionary movements*: they cannot be stopped, and they sooner or later boomerang and destroy those who initiated them, repaying their hubris with a self-inflicted and violent death. We are reminded here of Phaethon's attempt to take the reins of his father's chariot which led inexorably to his own demise. And so the regression must continue downward until it can go no further, which is to say, until it propagates through all four castes and levels the structure of human society to the ground.

Once Henry VIII's project was complete, it was only a matter of time before the revolutionary spirit took hold of the next caste in the hierarchy, which was the caste responsible for economic activity. In the economic revolution that was to follow, Henry VIII and the rest of the noble class along with him were to be consumed in the very blaze of rebellion which they themselves ignited. This second stage of regression, the revolution of the "third estate," can be seen in the great revolutions of America and France, and in the increasing power of the merchant and financier classes that came during the Industrial Revolution. Their political ideas, it must be remembered, despised the notion aristocracy above all else.

During this period the validity of royal authority was called into question, and rightfully so, for without spiritual authority above it, it had rendered itself completely illegitimate. The third estate, inspired by the successful rebellion they had just witnessed, rebelled in their own turn. Now the roles of priesthood and nobility became dispersed amongst the populace, and the age of democracy began.

Some might protest at this point that the revolutionary period we are describing was a revolution for the "common man," and a victory not for the wealthy, but for all. This thesis is propaganda plain and simple, for any survey of the events reveal that men lost rights and independence both in France and America (by measure of taxes and forced participation in the perpetual wars that would follow). The democratic era benefitted above all the moneyed classes, for democracy has always been a machine fueled by dollars more than by ballots.

This era, because ruled by those whose aptitudes are of the economic order, comes to be dominated by economic ideology, profit, trade, and productivity, because such is the ruling mentality of the merchant caste. All considerations, all political discourse, gravitates toward economic considerations. Government is no longer directed by statesmen but by those with the highest economic aptitudes.

Those who are most economically oriented, which is to say, those who can make the most money for themselves or for society at large, become the new aristocracy and gain for themselves the esteem previously reserved for royalty and priesthood. Society becomes a plutocracy.

Morality itself devolves to promote and esteem the virtues of moneymaking and economic success. Society's highest virtues at this point will be "productivity" and "hard work." Western civilization is currently within this stage of regression, as should be clear enough to the contemporary reader, and is moving slowly but surely to the last and final stage of hierarchical disintegration, which has reared its head intermittently but has thus far been only partially successful. Here we refer to the ideology of socialism.

Socialism, the revolution by which the merchant caste self-destructs and is finally overthrown by the laboring classes, brings the regression to its end. Civilization is then leveled to the ground, both figuratively and literally, for socialism even more than democracy is a leveling obsession.

In short, the Middle Ages marks the last "normal" civilization to exist in the west. It fell at the Reformation when the spiritual authority was displaced and exiled. The royal authority, once rendered illegitimate by its own actions, was eventually dismantled by the rising merchant class, leading to the current age of Capitalism. Next the laboring classes, because they sooner or later perceives the illegitimacy of the authority lorded over them by their moneyed masters, revolt in turn, completing the process and bring civilization to a natural end.

FAITH AND REASON PLACED IN OPPOSITION

Argument:

> *"Reason is directly opposed to faith and one ought to let it be; in believers it should be killed and buried"*

> ~ *Martin Luther*[177]

Elucidation:

Luther's ridiculous statement above can be explained as follows.

---

[177] Erlanger Ausgabe, XLIV, 158.

An interesting consequence of the rise of rationalism is that it renders anything that cannot be strictly "rationalized" irrational, and what is irrational is not true. Thus, any "supra-rational" truths are no long the highest forms of knowledge, but they cannot be considered knowledge at all. And so the work of Aquinas was, it seems, in vain, as Luther teaches us that:

> "You must abandon your reason, know nothing of it, annihilate it completely or you will never enter heaven. You must leave reason to itself, for it is the born enemy of faith. . . . "There is nothing so contrary to faith as law and reason. You must conquer them if you would reach beatitude" (Tischreden. Weimarer Ausgabe, VI, 6718).

KNOWLEDGE VS. BELIEF

Argument:

> *"To him who feels himself preordained to contemplation and not to belief, all believers are too noisy and obtrusive; he guards against them."*
>
> *~ Friedrich Nietzsche[178]*

Elucidation:

Once a proper view of knowledge is destroyed and belief becomes "irrational," it also becomes intolerable. Let us pause to comment again on the traditional view of knowledge.

It has been said that when the gods appear to men they always adopt forms that will be comprehensible to the nature of those to whom they

---

[178] *Beyond Good and Evil*, 112.

appear. This is the differentiation—to adopt Catholic terminology—between the "Church teaching" and the "Church taught." Although the Second Vatican Council modified this teaching, adding that the laity does play a role in the development of doctrine, it is clear that their participation is largely, if not wholly, unconscious. They participate as members of an unerring collectivity:

> "The holy People of God shares also in Christ's prophetic office. It spreads abroad a living witness to Him, especially by means of a life of faith and charity and by offering to God a sacrifice of praise, the tribute of lips which give hour to His name (cf. Heb. 13,5). The body of the faithful as a whole, anointed as they are by the Holy One (cf. Jn 2,20, 27), cannot err in matters of belief. Thanks to a supernatural sense of the faith which characterizes the People as a whole, it manifests this unerring quality when "from the bishops down to the last member of the laity," it shows universal agreement in matters of faith and morals."

When the connection between belief and knowledge is severed and associations, churches, and entire religions are based on nothing but beliefs held in common, which is to say, a religion of consensus rather than of doctrine, then religion becomes what is more properly termed "superstition," which is a "belief" for which there is no longer anyone who understands the reason. When this occurs, the mob of "believers" tends to become assertive and obnoxious, and we can begin to understand Nietzsche's complaint. In fact, we can understand most of Nietzsche's complaints if we allow that he was observing a decadent Christianity—one which had, by rejecting the notion of Spiritual Authority, severed its own spiritual jugular. Nietzsche watched it in disgust as it writhed in its death throws, having become a "faith without knowledge," or as was said earlier, a superstition.

This is the inevitable situation once the caste responsible for knowledge is functional destroyed. Then only ignorance and a sort of "zombie Christianity," dead but still walking, can remain.

WHAT IS BARBARISM?

Argument:

> *"Leveling is the barbarian's substitute for order."*
>
> ~ *Nicolas Gomez-Davila*

> *"Revere the emperor, expel the barbarians."*
>
> ~ *Japanese anti-Western slogan*

Elucidation:

To call a people "barbaric" is to describe the state of its soul, condemning its mentality or philosophy as one of godlessness. The insult may have nothing at all to do with superficial material conditions such as technological development. A rich man can be a barbarian as easily as anyone else.

The Japanese traditionalists expressed just this when they made their anti-western slogan: sonnō jōi or "revere the emperor, expel the barbarians." By barbarians they referred to the Western powers with their extravagant wealth, their vulgar manners, their secular governments, and their materialistic attitudes. In this slogan they not only sought a rejection of these "barbarian" ideals, but also a return to proper spiritual hierarchy, headed by a divine emperor. However, once the flood gates were rammed open by American battleships in 1853 and the forcible modernization of Japan was commenced, a new slogan was created: fukoku kyōhei or "enrich the country, strengthen the military."

The depth of the transformation is evident. Reverence for spiritual authority is dropped in favor of "enrichment," while the growth of a "military"—sheer technological power—is adopted in place of a traditional warrior class. This "barbarian" evolution has also been condemned by another word, "infidel," which means precisely the same thing. Infidel, in Islam, does not refer to Christian or Jew or even to Hindu. Islam considers all these "people of the Book" and calls the revelations they received valid. Infidel is reserved for "unbelievers"—for the godless. Thus, when Islamic extremists call Westerners infidels, the term has nothing to do with religion, but rather the absence of it.

In response, we Americans call our accusers "religious extremists," which is a term the modern world has created for anyone who does anything in the name of God. We use it within our own borders against Christians who reject abortion and homosexuality. Soon, no doubt, the term "religious extremist" will come to mean anyone who expresses any spiritual sentiment at all, which is to say, anyone who is not a barbarian.

RATIONALISM AND THE INVENTION OF RELIGION

Argument:

> *"Embedded in the Enlightenment's (re-)definition and elevation of reason is the creation and subjection of an irrational counterpart: along with the emergence of reason as both the instrument and essence of human achievement, the irrational came to be defined primarily in opposition to what such thinkers saw as the truths of their own distinctive*

historical epoch. If they were the voices of modernity, freedom, liberation, happiness, reason, nobility, and even natural passion, the irrational was all that came before: tyranny, servility to dogma, self-abnegation, superstition, and false religion. Thus the irrational came to mean the domination of religion in the historical period that preceded it."

~Roxanne Euben[179]

Elucidation:

As strange as it sounds, the concept of religion as it has been handed down to us is itself a creation of the modern world. When civilizations were ordered on the basis of action informed by knowledge, which is to say, where the superiority of knowledge to action was acknowledged in the social structure itself, there was no question of "religion" as a separate entity, muscling its way in against other entities vying for power in the social sphere. The traditional world saw reality itself, at all levels, as a sacred experience. There was no level of activity that was not permeated by some higher significance. Everything was connected in a concentric circles, at the center of which sat transcendence, and this is why even crafts such as saddle-making had "theologies" and "initiations" for guild members only. These practices sprung from their perception of reality and not from the dictates of a religious power imposing them where they did not belong. For men of this mentality, there was no such thing as "spiritual life" vs. "ordinary life," with the two cleanly separated into a dichotomy.

With the Enlightenment and the rise of Rationalism, that was all to change. Descartes rationalism is itself based on a mind-body

---

[179] Roxanne L. Euben, *Enemy in the Mirror: Islamic Fundamentalism and the Limits of Modern Rationalism* (Princeton, NJ: Princeton University Press, 1999), 34.

dichotomy, or if not based on it, its practical effects were centered on this either/or. Once this doctrine of division was introduced into philosophy and then to the people, it is easy to understand that any practices, principles, or persons who are concerned with immaterial realities such as the soul would be relegated into the "mind" sphere and away from the realm of the body.

This was in line with the rationalist outlook but it was also very convenient for Enlightenment propaganda. The Enlightenment needed its own "founding mythology" in order to justify itself to itself and to future generations. Because the pride of the Enlightenment was its being "rational," it clearly required an irrational "other" which it could claim to have conquered: this is religion. And so, the rationalists did not conquer religion so much as they re-structured the modern man's view of the world in such a way that religion would be compartmentalized and rendered impotent. In this way, religion, as imagined in the modern world, is a child of rationalist propaganda.

ETERNAL LAW

Argument:

> "Eternal law is the plan of government in the Chief Governor, all the plans of government in the inferior governors must be derived from the eternal law. But these plans of inferior governors are all other laws besides the eternal law. Therefore all laws, in so far as they partake of right reason, are derived from the eternal law. Hence Augustine says (De Lib. Arb. i, 6) that 'in temporal law there is nothing just and lawful, but what man has drawn from the eternal law.'...

174

"Human law has the nature of law in so far as it partakes of right reason; and it is clear that, in this respect, it is derived from the eternal law. But in so far as it deviates from reason, it is called an unjust law, and has the nature, not of law but of violence.

~ *St. Thomas Aquinas*[180]

Elucidation:

When the various humanisms of the Enlightenment era made man the measure of reality, they also reduced law itself to an expression of man's opinion; and where it was not man's opinion that made the law, it was a disfigured form of "natural" law that degraded man by equating his laws with those of biology. Before all these transformations, there was Divine Law.

Divine law was the legal superstructure of all other forms of justice. All other levels of justice, all other types of law, had to make reference to divine law in order to remain legitimate, in order not to deteriorate into nothing more than a "form of violence."

Because in the traditional world it was taken for granted that eternal law was the "given" standard to which human law must conform, any ruler, in order to remain legitimate, had to at least pretend that his law was derived from the divine one. He may have been able to abuse his power, but he could only go so far. He had built-in accountability. This is the primary difference between divine sovereignty and popular sovereignty—that while the former makes absolutism impossible, the latter is by nature absolutist, since it answers to nothing but itself.

---

[180] *ST*, I-II, q. 93, a. 3.

Daniel Schwindt

DIVINE SOVEREIGNTY

Argument:

> *"[P]opular sovereignty may give birth to a more formidable despotism than divine sovereignty. For a tyrant, whether he be one or many, who has, by hypothesis, successfully usurped one or the other sovereignty, cannot avail himself of the Divine Will, which shows itself to men under the forms of a Law Eternal, to command whatever he pleases. Whereas the popular will has no natural stability but is changeable; so far from being tied to a law, its voice may be heard in laws which change and succeed each other. So that a usurping Power has, in such a case, more elbow-room; it enjoys more liberty, and its liberty is the name of arbitrary power."*

> *~ Bertrand de Jouvenel[181]*

Elaboration:

The stock argument has been that divine sovereignty has the effect of fueling the growth of arbitrary power. Yet in its place today's popular governments, if indeed we accept for a moment that they really are popular, make the law follow the "general will," and the general will is the very definition of arbitrariness.

In trying to escape the limited arbitrariness of the king—limited because answerable to a transcendent standard—the modern world has enshrined a sort of collective arbitrariness that is far more powerful since the collective, unlike the king under divine sovereignty, answers to no higher law than the consensus it finds among its members. This,

---

[181] Jouvenel, op. cit., p. 47.

according to Jouvenel, is the weakness of popular sovereignty—that is answers to nothing but itself and is therefore absolute:

> "For a Power which lays down the good and the just is, whatever form it takes, absolute in a quite different way from one which takes the good and the just as it finds them already laid down by a supernatural authority. A Power which regulates human behaviour according to its own notions of social utility is absolute in a quite different way from one whose subjects have had their actions prescribed for them by God. And here we glimpse the fact that the denial of a divine lawgiving and the establishment of a human lawgiving are the most prodigious strides which society can take towards a truly absolute Power. So long as a supernatural origin was ascribed to law, this step remained untaken....All the great civilizations were formed in the framework of a divine law given to society, a law which even the strongest will of all, that of the wielders of Power, was powerless to shatter or replace."[182]

RELIGION AND EGALITARIANISM CANNOT CO-EXIST

Argument:

> "Hierarchies are heavenly. In hell, all are equal."

> ~ Nicolas Gomez-Davila[183]

Elucidation:

---

[182] Jouvenel, op. cit., pp. 220-221.
[183] Davila, 2013 edition, p. 203.

Daniel Schwindt

Hierarchy is the reflection, not only of earthly reality, which is never egalitarian, but also of the celestial order, which is, after all, a *kingdom*.

Many of the prejudices against traditional social structures stem from the modern mania for equality at all costs. Egalitarian systems cannot allow a vertical dimension to exist, and so they are by nature antagonistic to religious principles.

All religion implies transcendence, which implies a vertical dimension, which in turn implies hierarchy. Egalitarian democracy (and socialism, for that matter) denies this dimension, only allowing for differences to exist on a "horizontal" plain. Men can be "different" but they must always be "equal" from a hierarchical perspective. Anything else is repugnant to the egalitarian mind, which abhors vertical diversity, whatever it may preach about diversity in other respects. Religion and egalitarianism are therefore mutually exclusive, although this does not prevent the mass of individuals from attempting to entertain and apply both at the same time. Such is the primary source of what is called "cognitive dissonance" in our contemporaries.

EGALITARIANISM AND CASTE

Argument:

> *"Every non-hierarchical society splits in two."*
>
> ~ *Nicolas Gomez-Davila*[184]

Elucidation:

---

[184] Davila, 2013 edition, p. 169.

We can also point out another major contradiction that should be obvious by now but which, due to the willful blindness of the disciples of modernity, is rarely acknowledged. I am speaking of the fact that the "form" of the caste has not ceased to exist, but has only been reduced in its complexity, and the chasm between its groups widened tenfold. While the castes of India were four, and within those four susceptible to indefinite subdivision, the one that came to replace it and which rules the lives of men today has only two: those who own, and those who do not. This is not a Marxist doctrine, but a commonsense doctrine apparent to anyone who takes an honest look at the present situation. All of the complaints about "inequality" are legitimate, even if those who speak of such things have no idea what the real cause of the inequality might be. They imagine that problem is hierarchy, and that the solution is greater equality. It does not occur to them, because they have been too long imbued with egalitarian propaganda, that it was the desire for equality which brought about this disaster, and that a functionally organized social hierarchy is the only solution for the vast inequality and concomitant injustice that offends them.

ORTHODOXY AND HETERODOXY

Argument:

> "I am becoming orthodox because I have come, rightly or wrongly, after stretching my brain till it bursts, to the old belief that heresy is worse even than sin. An error is more menacing than a crime, for an error begets crimes..."

Daniel Schwindt

~ *G.K. Chesterton*[185]

Elucidation:

Perhaps the reason religion has come to be so despised is because it has been reduced to two things: behavioral standards and emotional comforts. That is to say, it has been reduced to moralism and sentimentality, or at least the sort of religion with which our American churches and religious political activities acquaints us seems to fit this bill. So used to this are we that it is difficult to imagine what else religion could or ought to provide besides judgments about sinful behavior and the comfort that comes from "being saved." But there was once something more, and this missing piece is what is signified by the term "orthodoxy." Orthodoxy is the body of religious truth, be that Scripture or Tradition. It is a supra-moral standard, in the sense that morality can be drawn from it but is not its essence; it is also beyond sentimentality because its purpose has nothing to do with emotional comfort or acceptability.

A civilization loses orthodoxy when it begins to say "I'm spiritual but not religious," or, what's worse, "Christianity is not a religion, it's a relationship!" Neither of these statements is capable of comprehending Chesterton's realization: that there is an evil *worse even than sin*. This evil is embodied in the concept of heresy, which is as foreign to modern society as orthodoxy. This makes perfect sense because the two imply each other and make no sense in isolation. Departure from orthodoxy is heresy, and the absence of heresy is adherence to orthodoxy. Both of these refer to the *truth* of the doctrine held by the believers. It concerns knowledge in its purest form. The loss of orthodoxy and heresy together, therefore, also implies the loss of a

---

[185] G.K. Chesterton, "The Diabolist," *Tremendous Trifles*.

society's concern for knowledge of this order. Such a civilization has descended along the path indicated in the famous Taoist passage:

> "When the Way is lost, there comes goodness, when goodness is lost, there comes morality."[186]

When Protestantism rejected the concept of orthodoxy, which was necessary for its insistence on private interpretation, it predestined itself to descend into the "vague mist of platitudes" that C.S. Lewis warned against. Now it is no wonder the people loathe its presence in their midst. They see it for what it is: a set of shallow conventions adopted to get a set of superficial emotional comforts. In the ages of orthodoxy these had always been secondary products, derivations from the *truth* that was the only truly inviolable thing. Disconnected, they become ends in themselves, pleasant to easily satisfied minds, but slowly losing their appeal to the many.

SLOUCHING TOWARD MEDIOCRITY

Argument:

> *"A decline in courage may be the most striking feature which an outside observer notices in the West in our days. The Western world has lost its civil courage, both as a whole and separately, in each country, each government, each political party and of course in the United Nations. Such a decline in courage is particularly noticeable among the ruling groups and the intellectual elite, causing an impression of loss of courage by the entire society. Of course there are many courageous individuals but they have no determining influence on public*

---

[186] *Tao Te Ching*, ch. 38.

> *life…Should one point out that from ancient times decline in*
> *courage has been considered the beginning of the end?"*
>
> ~*Aleksander Solzhenitsyn* [187]

Elucidation:

St. Thomas characterized democracy as the worst of the good regimes, but the best of the worst. In other words, democracy only has great merit if you place it in the context of tyranny and chaos. If a regime were going to go bad, it would be better if it were a democracy, because democracy, for better or worse, hovers around mediocrity. But for this same reason democracy limits itself, if it is good, to being only slightly good. The floor its nature sets is also a ceiling. This is why St. Thomas ultimately chose monarchy as the best form of government. St. Thomas was not a pessimist. He did not build his philosophy in an effort to escape the possibility of evil, but to offer the possibilities of greatness.

That is the fundamental difference between the democrat and the monarchist: that they both know that the evil monarch poses a greater threat than the evil democrat, but the latter believes that it is worth the risk because of the possibilities for greatness that monarchy opens before society. The horizons for a monarchy are automatically more extended in both directions. When offered the choice between the dual possibility of greatness and evil, on the one hand, and the assurance of a comfortable mediocrity on the other, the man who chooses the first is the monarchist and the man who chooses the security of mediocrity is the democrat.

---

[187]Harvard Commencement Address delivered on June 8, 1978.

When God created the angels he knew that this implied the possibility of devils. He thought it worth the risk. In the act of Creation, God, the cosmic monarch, showed man the path of courage. Modern man chooses instead the path of cowardice. If God had been a democrat, he'd have created very little. He certainly wouldn't have created man. He'd have stopped at the creation of vegetable life, and perhaps a few low animal species: for here he could have been guaranteed a comfortable mediocrity, for animals cannot become devils. But this was not the way of the Creator: he wanted saints, and if he had to suffer death on the cross at the hands of a few devils, he'd suffer it. This was the way of courage—the way of the King. "Power corrupts!" the democrat shouts. "So be it," replies the Creator as He gives him the gift of power. Saints he would have, and devils too, but devils for the sake of the saints. The democrat chooses to have neither (and in fact he has neither heretic nor martyr in his regime), and he pats himself on the back for achieving this comfortable mediocrity where none can rise or fall, and where every horizon is dictated by cowardice.

ORTHODOXY AND HERESY DIE TOGETHER

Argument:

> "Liberalism...transgresses all commandments. To be more precise: in the doctrinal order, Liberalism strikes at the very foundations of faith; it is heresy radical and universal, because within it are comprehended all heresies..."

> ~ Fr. Felix Sarda y Salvany[188]

Elucidation:

---

[188] *Liberalism is a Sin*, ch. 3.

Heresy, from an etymological standpoint, means nothing more than "to choose for oneself." Obviously, then, the word is entirely appropriate for one who departs from orthodoxy to blaze his own trail. Heresy, then, implies the existence of orthodoxy, which is its counterpart. In the past, every heretic believed himself to be orthodox. The two terms are related to one another, in the same way that "to be inside" of something implies the existence of an "outside." But with Liberalism something altogether new was introduced to man. It was a heresy, to be sure, but for the first time it was a heresy that made no pretenses at orthodoxy. It was, in fact, the first heresy to more or less explicitly reject orthodoxy *as a valid conception.* And because orthodoxy signifies *those beliefs which are true*, to render it invalid is to render incomprehensible the traditional notions about truth and error.

To quote again from Fr. Sarda:

> "[Liberalism] repudiates dogma altogether and substitutes opinion, whether that opinion be doctrinal or the negation of doctrine. Consequently, it denies every doctrine in particular. If we were to examine in detail all the doctrines or dogmas which, within the range of Liberalism, have been denied, we would find every Christian dogma in one way or another rejected—from the dogma of the Incarnation to that of Infallibility."[189]

But Fr. Sarda will not leave his analysis incomplete. The explicit denial of the legitimacy of dogma carries with it an implicit affirmation of a "new dogma" which is both universal and negative in its character:

> "Nonetheless Liberalism is in itself dogmatic; and it is in the declaration of its own fundamental dogma, the absolute

---

[189] *Liberalism is a Sin*, ch. 3.

independence of the individual and the social reason, that it denies all Christian dogmas in general. Catholic dogma is the authoritative declaration of revealed truth—or a truth consequent upon Revelation—by its infallibly constituted exponent. This logically implies the obedient acceptance of the dogma on the part of the individual and of society. Liberalism refuses to acknowledge this rational obedience and denies the authority. It asserts the sovereignty of the individual and social reason and enthrones Rationalism in the seat of authority. It knows no dogma except the dogma of self-assertion. Hence it is heresy, fundamental and radical, the rebellion of the human intellect against God."[190]

The victory of liberalism meant the extinction of the concepts of both heresy *and* orthodoxy, which really represented nothing more than the primordial duality of *truth* and *falsity*. The old positive-negative pair was then replaced with a single, universal negative which rendered the previous paradigm illegitimate and, further, assured that anyone indoctrinated into the negative dogma of liberalism would be completely unable to understand the old terms. Man was left to sit alone in the privacy of his home, asking with Pilate "What is truth?"[191]

TOLERANCE AND THE HERETIC

Argument:

> *"Tolerance consists in the firm decision to allow the others to scoff at everything that we pretend to love and respect, provided that they do not threaten our worldly comfort. As*

---

[190] Ibid.
[191] John 18:38.

> *long as others do not tread on his corns, modern man—liberal,*
> *democrat, progressivist—tolerates them to besmirch his soul."*

> ~ *Nicholas Gomez-Davila*[192]

Elucidation:

Religion represents the highest of truths, and so the decision to ignore religion is the decision to subordinate the higher truths to lower ones. One expression of this is an over-zealous belief in the pseudo-principle of *tolerance*, which is passed off as a respect for others, but is really just another kind of materialism.

As Davila suggests, it is a reversal of values and allows disdain to the higher for the sake of peace with respect to the lower orders of life. But there is also a reverse side of this principle of "tolerance" and it is that it cannot be tolerant. Or, to say it another way, tolerance can only tolerate a void. Its only guiding principle is that no one claim to have a principle or at least that no one claim their principle be true.

The result is a censorship of such an extreme degree that anyone who believes in any kind of absolute truth perceives themselves as some sort of persecuted minority. We shall discuss this below.

PERSECUTION MYTH AND PERSECUTION MANIA

Argument:

> *"When opinion is ordained the measure of law in society, then*
> *every individual whose opinion does not align with current*
> *law imagines himself to be (and in fact is) a persecuted*
> *minority."*

---

[192] Davila, 2013 edition, p. 149.

Elucidation:

The notion that the general will, which is to say the general opinion, rules the day and is the engine of law in society, imbues the popular mind with a pronounced sense of inclusion or exclusion depending upon whether or not their opinion falls in-line with that of the majority in the most recent election. Said another way, by defining justice in terms of opinion, it becomes impossible to explain to the individual whose opinion is in the minority that he is justly ruled by the opinions of others. He cannot accept the fact that opinion is the standard of law, but that it happens to be his neighbor's opinion and not his. And so no matter how deeply he believes in democracy, he feels oppressed when it becomes obvious that the general will is not his, and is therefore not as general as it was explained in theory.

The result is that every time the political process does not conform to the will of an individual he feels that injustice has been done. Even if he is only one of six million other voters, he expects to feel at least that the election went $1/6,000,000^{th}$ his way. But it didn't go his way at all. In short: he feels persecuted. He feels what every losing party expresses in every modern election.

When law is tied to an objective standard of justice, then the man who gives his input on the matter knows that, whatever his own opinion, the standard is outside of him and that he cannot change it. If he votes, he attempts to vote in favor of an objective and external truth. It is not his opinion, nor is it the opinion of the majority that determines justice in this case, and even if the man loses he may feel that an offense to justice has been committed, but not that it was offense against him personally. He may condemn the political process, but he will not feel it necessary to play the martyr.

187

Today everyone plays the martyr. Every party, politician, and voter plays the martyr. Even the Christians, who should know a bit about martyrdom, play the martyrs in the petulant game of opinionation. Who can really blame them, though? Once you've adopted the premise of popular sovereignty there is no other possible way that things can end. Anything short of complete consensus creates a persecution mania. That's why gay couples and anti-gay religious groups can carry out demonstrations on the same street at the same time, both crying "persecution!" And they're right.

LAW: SUBJECTIVE AND OBJECTIVE

Argument:

> "The end of political Power is to realize the Law."
>
> ~ Leon Duguit

Elucidation:

Such was the opinion of the political philosophers of old. Today, whatever the rhetoric, there is no such thing as law, in an objective sense. There is only the will of the majority, and the law is a reflection of this will. It is nothing of itself, but changes as the will changes, and there is no political principle to be found which suggests to us that this will adheres to or makes any effort to discover such an objective rule.

AMBULATORY LAW

Argument:

> "The life of democracies has been marked by a growth in the precariousness of laws...anything that might have checked the immediate translation into law of whatever opinion was in

vogue, have everywhere been swept aside or rendered powerless. The law is no longer like some higher necessity presiding over the life of the country: it has become the expression of the passions of the moment."

~ *Bertrand de Jouvenel*[193]

Elucidation:

By attaching the process of legislation to a machinery so fickle as the majority will, democracies develop what can be called "ambulatory law"—a form of law that never stands still, never proceeds along the straight course, but is constantly shifting, reversing, and at war with itself. The Middle Ages knew nothing of this difficulty; for them the law was fixed, the rule a premise. But from the time that the divine law was rejected as superstition, and custom as a mere routine, the law had to be *made*. And so we end where Jouvenel predicted, with a deluge of fictional legislation:

> "Loud and clear we proclaim it— the mounting flood of modern laws does not create law. What do they mirror, these laws, but the pressure of interests, the fancifulness of opinions, the violence of passions? When they are the work of a Power which has become, with its every growth, more enervated by the strife of factions, their confusion makes them ludicrous. When they issue from a Power which is in the grip of one brutal hand, their planned iniquity makes them hateful. The only respect which they either get or deserve is that which force procures them. Being founded on a conception of society which is both false and deadly, they are anti-social."[194]

---

[193] Jouvenel, op. cit., p. 236.
[194] Ibid., 326.

James Madison himself saw this coming, but because the cause lay in his own principles, he could only lament the inevitable effect:

> "The internal effects of a mutable policy are still more calamitous. It poisons the blessing of liberty itself. It will be of little avail to the people, that the laws are made by men of their own choice, if the laws be so voluminous that they cannot be read, or so incoherent that they cannot be understood; if they be repealed or revised before they are promulgated, or undergo such incessant changes that no man, who knows what the law is to-day, can guess what it will be to-morrow. Law is defined to be a rule of action; but how can that be a rule, which is little known, and less fixed?"[195]

LEGALISM AND SOCIAL DECAY

Argument:

> *"Dying societies hoard laws like dying people medicines."*
>
> ~ *Nicolas Gomez-Davila*[196]

> *"Once we suffered from our vices; today we suffer from our laws."*
>
> ~ *Tacitus*[197]

Elucidation:

---

[195] James Madison, *Federalist Papers*, #62.
[196] Davila, 2013 edition, p. 185.
[197] *Annals*, iii. 25.

The great aphorist continues: "There are two symmetrical forms of barbarism: that of the nations who have nothing but customs and that of the nations who respect nothing but laws."[198]

Here Davila argues for a cycle of ascent and descent as civilizations approach justice and then descend away from it. For if we examine the most primitive societies, we find that they are ruled mostly by customs. These customs may be good or bad, and to say that a society is ruled mostly by customs is not necessarily to imply that it is unjust. But the point is that these customs are followed as customs, and that for the most part the communities that live according to their dictates do not have a specific, objective, or transcendent standard of justice by which their lives and institutions are measured. They're system is, in this sense, rigid and relatively mindless. It has no room to change or develop according to the vicissitudes of history.

As a people begin to rise from this arrangement, leaders in both worldly and transcendent affairs begin to raise the standard and begin to form a higher notion of justice than pure custom. Again, the customs may be good, but as the culture develops and the intellectual life flourishes, a philosophy emerges that tells these people *why* the customs are just, and enables them to understand those cases where custom may have become unjust. They have moved "beyond custom" and approached objective law. As an example of a civilization which had reached such an apex, we can look at the Middle Ages, where men of Aquinas' quality were developing the most nuanced understanding of justice the world had yet seen. Again, we stress that this did not replace custom, for custom was in many cases a just and stable reality; but they were able to transfigure custom and place it, when it was good, in an overall and objective system of justice, traceable all the

---

[198] 107

way through nature and to eternal principles. In short, they took what was mindless and connected it to the mind of God himself.

Now let us move forward. Over the next half-century we see a severing of this connection between law and the eternal. We see law, or "sovereignty," divorced from the eternal and connected to the popular—to the general will, without any direct reference to the transcendent. The curve, after reaching its apex and the height of its coherence, begins to descend. Immediately law loses the stabilization that objectivity had provided, and begins to multiply. It rises in complexity and, in addition, becomes the sole standard for life. When law was an aspect of the divine, it was possible for it to be reinforced by the various other forces in man's life, such as his personal conscience and his religious sentiments. However, now that law was answerable only to itself it becomes the sole rule of what a man ought to do. This causes law to be multiplied further because those actions which were once governed by the unwritten laws of religion were nullified and then openly transgressed. Legalism ensues, and whatever moral imperative is left out of the written laws is publicly permissible. And so the society that had once risen to the intellectual heights of Thomism descends into the legalistic superficiality of perpetual lawsuits over spilt coffee and wedding cakes.

Soon the old basis of law is forgotten altogether, and the multitude of laws become once again mindless, and the cycle completes itself—from barbarism to barbarism—entering back into custom. Hence Chesterton's saying that "Over-civilization and barbarism are within an inch of each other."[199] This new custom, however, because it is inorganic, cannot pretend, like the customs of old, to be even a precursor to justice.

---

[199] *Illustrated London News*, Sept. 11, 1909.

MARX'S OPIUM AND AMERICAN CHRISTIANITY

Argument:

> *"Religious suffering is, at one and the same time, the expression of real suffering and a protest against real suffering. Religion is the sigh of the oppressed creature, the heart of a heartless world, and the soul of soulless conditions. It is the opium of the people."*

> *~ Karl Marx*

Karl Marx's immortal jab—that religion is the "opium of the people"—can only be appreciated when placed within a minimum of its original context, which is provided above.

Here Marx was obviously criticizing society more than religion. He did not stand with the New Atheists, who view religion as a disease which, in itself, spawns evil in the world. Instead he suggested that the world has its own evils, and that religion had come to be adopted as a warm blanket in the face of a cold reality. An illusory warmth, to be sure—like a draught of whiskey on a winter night—but the important point is that Marx's condemnation in this instance was not of religion *as such*, but of religion *as an escape from reality.*

For Marx the problem with religion was that it obscured important issues. It held out to the people a false happiness which, if embraced, could obscure the reality of social evils. Such an "illusory happiness" any sane man, atheist or not, would seek to abolish:

> *"The abolition of religion as the illusory happiness of the people is the demand for their real happiness. To call on them to give up their illusions about their condition is to call on them to give up a condition that requires illusions. The*

> *criticism of religion is, therefore, in embryo, the criticism of*
> *that vale of tears of which religion is the halo."*

Taken in this sense, the Marxian diagnosis is pregnant with two implications that are easily overlooked:

First, we are given no reason to believe that the diagnosis applies always and everywhere, but only to a specific case. Religion *may*, under certain conditions, serve the function of an anesthetic; but this is not necessarily the nature of religion itself. In those specific cases, when religion-as-anesthetic becomes the rule, we are to interpret this occurrence as an indication that "soulless conditions" exist in that society. In short, Marx is condemning a diseased society for using religion as a form of escapism.

Second, if we are dealing with a case where a diseased patient is clinging to religion merely in order to delude himself and avoid the reality of his situation, then religion *as it is in that specific case* ought to be abolished, not because it is in itself an evil, but because it is being made use of in a perverse fashion. It is providing a veil behind which an illness is allowed to fester.

It occurs to me that this observation contains a timely insight which, properly applied, would allow us to disentangle the web of chaos, hatred, and confusion that surrounds religion in America. In fact, it allows us to take a somewhat novel position: by adopting the insight of Marx, we can make a case against religion America, while at the same time defending religion in general. The essence of the argument involves making the distinction between diseased and healthy religion, and resembles the surgical necessity of removing diseased flesh so that new, healthy growth can take its place.

To borrow Marx's words, we will argue against "religion as the illusory happiness of the people" in hopes that, in doing so, we can make room for an authentic religious life in a society for which that sort of life is not currently a possibility.

Because the most obvious symbol of religious expression in society is the church building, we might begin with a few comments on the church itself as an independent, dedicated structure.

As members of the "house church" movement are happy to remind us, the early Christians did not worship in churches—buildings constructed for, ornamented toward, and dedicated to, the celebration of a liturgy. They worshiped in homes, we are told. So far, so good.

We do not find actual "churches" until around the time of Constantine and the Edict of Milan (313 AD). Now, regardless of whether or not you accept the authenticity of Constantine's conversion, or how you interpret its cultural significance, it is undeniable based on archeological research that it was during this period that the church-as-dedicated-structure began to appear.

And so, we can say without much room for debate that the church building represents the ornamentation of a society which has become thoroughly infiltrated by the spirit of the faith. It could not have appeared before this point, which is to say that the church is the "fruit-ion" of the long organic process of conversion, and it implies a preceding period of growth and cultural flowering, nourished by real and deep roots.

Such an architectural phenomenon was entirely appropriate to the Roman Empire of Constantine's period, given its stage of cultural development. The construction of these buildings was *proper* to the society where they appeared.

To this period we might also compare the Europe of the Middle Ages, which was even more completely saturated by the Christian religion, so much so that it has been given the name "Christendom." As with the churches which appeared in the Empire of Constantine, the apex of Christendom gave birth to its own structures which were completely appropriate to its personality, and these we call cathedrals.

The point of all this is that the architectural expression of religion springs from the religious life of the civilization as a whole. Churches cannot arise before, or persist after, the religious spirit that gives them birth. Just as every church or temple grows up as the ornamentation of a living organism, so it ought to decay and disappear along with the cultural life that sustained it.

According to this interpretation, it is only natural to expect that with the dissolution of Christendom we should no longer see the construction of cathedrals. In fact, insofar as the cathedral persists in the absence of Christendom, it is an anachronism, of interest only to the antiquarian. Left without roots it can only ossify.

This brings us back to our present situation. No modern nation-state is culturally Christian (and this remains true regardless of what proportion of the citizenry professes the Christian religion). Nonetheless, in countries like the United States, we still see the proliferation of church buildings. In fact, we've even seen the emergence of mega-churches—a phenomenon which flies in the face of everything we've said so far.

If the church building was the final manifestation of a vigorously Christian culture, it ought to have been the first thing to disappear when that culture died out. That it did not do so—that churches and even mega-churches continue to rise on our horizon—demands an explanation. If these structures do not owe their existence of a living, religious culture, then what sustains them?—for by all rights they should be dead and gone.

To answer this question we must keep in mind Marx's lesson: that religion under certain conditions can take on an unnatural form of life which has little or nothing to do with its normal purpose. Even dead religion, corpse that it is, may still be propped up in order to comfort or deceive those who will not accept its death, and who wish not to see the reality of a world where *their* god is dead. In such cases, we find the opiate religion.

UTILITARIAN RELIGION

Argument continued from previous.

In order for religion to be distorted and bent to such a purpose, its original end must be obscured.

In our case, this has been achieved by reducing religion to its *use value*. Once a thing is judged merely by its usefulness, it can be made us of for anything. Tocqueville observed long ago that religion in America almost immediately took on a utilitarian guise. Even among the clergy, he reported, virtue was not taught as something holy or beautiful, but as something *useful to oneself.*

Naturally the utilitarian attitude permeated government institutions as well. The common courtroom practice of "swearing in" the witness before hearing testimony is symbolic of the whole phenomenon: here religion—in the form of an oath on the Bible—is utilized in a way that does not imply any confession whatsoever on the part of the government itself regarding the truth value of the text. The book is used purely as a device to manipulate the conscience of the witness. A more spiritually patronizing situation is difficult to imagine, but it shows us to what degree a secular government can enjoy religion, not as good or true, but as useful. "Useful religion" then leads directly to the situation Marx condemned.

Religion is, etymologically, supposed to be a means of reconnecting with reality (*re-legio*). It is therefore a technique to be condoned or condemned based on whether or not it serves that purpose. But if the value of religion is reduced to its *social use*, both from the point of view of the believer and in the eyes of the government, then it becomes impossible to distinguish between uses that are proper and those that aren't. As Marx perceived, religion can be very useful as an anesthetic, rendering society numb to injustice and compliant in the face of oppression. Such a use is, of course, the opposite of that for which religion is intended, but it is comforting to the believer and helpful to the State, and so both parties drink readily from the Dionysian cup.

Under these conditions, religion has ceased to "re-connect" its followers with reality, and instead it distances them from it. Religion becomes anti-religion; Christianity becomes anti-Christ.

What, then, is to be done? Various movements have appeared which, sensing the artificial nature of Christianity as it is, fight others and each other in favor of a particular form which they believe to be the ideal. On the Protestant side, this movement is represented by the migration toward the "house church." At the opposite end of the spectrum, there are vocal Catholics for whom nothing but the Latin Mass will do.

The mentality that these two very different groups share is their insistence on formalism. They each believe that there is a permanent form of religious expression which is "proper" to Christianity, which has presumably been lost in modern times, and which must be re-instituted in order to return Christianity to health.

Neither of these groups seems willing to take into account the full implications of history as a process—one which contains no two moments that are exactly the same. They each deny the uniqueness, not only of person and place, but also of *time itself.*

The idea that each time and place has its own organic idiosyncrasies, occurring in its period and its period alone, is something that they either cannot or will not take acknowledge when formulating their ideals. The "house church" was *proper* Christianity, and that is all its proponents need to consider. It is seductively simple, but extremely shallow. Again, one may say that the Latin Mass was the ideal form, in which case it becomes irrelevant where we are and who we are and when we are—all that matters is that we ought to conform to that simple norm.

Neither of these will allow for the possibility that what was a completely natural and appropriate religious phenomenon for the first-century or the medieval Church is no longer either ideal or even proper for 20th-century America. And to force such an alien form onto into the present is an act of violence.

Church, as a social phenomenon, if it is to remain valid and healthy, must ultimately take into account to the world-historical conditions of the people whose souls are to participate in it. At one time it would have truly been an offense against the European soul to demolish one of its Cathedrals; in our day it would be an offense to build one.

And yet we are still faced with the reality of the mega-church, and the thousands of other modern churches that continue to rise out of soil which we have declared sterile. On this point, at least, we can agree with both the traditionalist Catholics and the radical Protestants: these churches are unnatural; they should not be here. What are they?

The optimist might claim that the persistence of church buildings in the modern world is a triumph against the times, proof that the Church is immortal and "the gates of Hades shall not prevail against it." That is flattering and noble. But it looks to the keen observer more like playing pretend. More and more isolated from political realities, divorced from the everyday life of the modern world, the church-goer of today tends to leave the sanctuary more naïve than when he entered. If something is happening there, it isn't *re-legio*.

Within the church building itself he engages in strange activities. He volunteers for "ministries"—artificial supplements to the Christian diet, the necessity of which proves how impossible the believer finds it to live a normal Christian life outside the walls of the church. And because these activities are artificial, they tend to be redundant, and because redundant, also tedious. But the supplement must be taken, and new "ministries" must be invented all the time, lest the believer be left with the suspicion that the lifestyle he treasures is not a possibility for him.

This is why, in response to complaint that Christianity is dead in our government, we would be inclined to reply: "Yes, it is, but in the Churches it is *un*-dead." It lives there within those walls, but it is a most unnatural life, hermetically sealed at best.

The post-Christian West has turned out to involve, not a return to pre-Christian barbarism, but instead an advance to a new kind of strangeness. It is the age of what Sam Rocha has dubbed "Zombie Christianity," where Christianity does not go extinct but rather persists as an untimely abomination. It is really no wonder that Christianity is viewed with suspicion by the outside world.

TOWARD AN ORGANIC EXPRESSION OF RELIGIOUS LIFE

Argument continued from previous.

There is no normative form of religious expression, but only that which accords with the doctrine obtained by a civilization and is proper to the men who are participating in it. Any number of arrangements can meet these needs.

The church as a dedicated structure is appropriate only to those civilizations whose spiritual capital is such that it brings these out naturally, of its own accord. In secularized times, church buildings become not only artificial but misleading to both believers and non-believers. It is hard enough to discern the reality of our situation without millions of believers, stumbling-drunk on Marx's opiate-religiosity, arguing to the contrary, congratulating themselves on their "Christian nation," just because it allows them to go about their secular business with a good conscience.

We ought to recoil in disgust from the rising mega-church because, perceiving the absence of sufficient spiritual capital in our cultural substrate, we sense that its growth is unnatural.

Every church building in America is an anachronism. They ought to please only the antiquarian. To everyone else they should appear strange and even repellent. The fact that they are not recognized as such is evidence, not of some remnant of spiritual vigor, but of an unprecedented capacity for self-deception on the part of the American people.

This is why it would perhaps be the healthiest of possible catastrophes if somehow or another all the churches were razed to the ground. The believer would suffer, to be sure, just as the alcoholic suffers when his bottle is taken from him. But perhaps without his church walls to blind him, the believer would finally have to face with courage the cold discomfort of his world as it is.

Then and only then could he hope to conquer the real problems that oppress him; only then could he build something real and proper to himself, because only then will he have truly been "re-connected with reality." He will have escaped the religion of Marx and re-discovered the religion of Christ. Perhaps he will find that a house church is indeed appropriate. So be it. Perhaps someday he will build a cathedral. But the point is that whatever he does will be authentic and natural—and it will be alive with his life.

In summary: Churches only enter the historical scene after Constantine converted. So it is no exaggeration to say that the political presence of Christianity preceded its architectural presence. This order of things, however, is incomprehensible to an era which imagines that Church buildings can and should exist within society but "outside politics," and that the former will somehow influence the latter by some sort of emanation of righteousness. Each new Church built in America is a joke, an example of Christian delusion, an act of imaginary activism and vanity. They serve the same function for society at large that the window garden serves for the average man's home: they give his wife a place to vent her sentiments, while he goes about his business. Churches are the window gardens of a secular civilization. Anachronistic ornaments which look good and make certain individuals feel good, but only imitate the function of the institution they have tried to copy.

SECTION 5: PROPAGANDA

"The majority prefers expressing stupidities to not expressing any opinion: this gives them the feeling of participation. For this they need simple thoughts, elementary explanations, a "key" that will permit them to take a position, and even ready-made opinions. As most people have the desire and at the same time the incapacity to participate, they are ready to accept a propaganda that will permit them to participate, and which hides their incapacity beneath explanations, judgments, and news, enabling them to satisfy their desire without eliminating their incompetence."[200]

~ Jacques Ellul

"I see men assassinated around me every day. I walk through rooms of the dead, streets of the dead, cities of the dead; men without eyes, men without voices; men with manufactured feelings and standard reactions; men with newspaper brains, television souls and high school ideas."

~ Charles Bukowski

INTRODUCTORY

Readers of previous installments in this series will notice that the present work proceeds in a different manner. While earlier portions— Democracy, Liberalism, Knowledge—were structured on the basis of a thesis followed by an elaboration of each thesis, this time the argument

---

[200] Jacques Ellul, *Propaganda*, p. 140.

will proceed aphoristically and will develop in a more logical fashion. This is because, unlike the others, which were merely collections of arguments or theses about a particular subject, our present study requires more explanation. This is due to the alien nature of the subject itself. Rather than challenging preconceptions about something all too familiar to the reader, such as democracy, we are introducing a concept that is assuredly almost entirely new to him. Hence, our argument must take the form of a logical progression if the contemporary reader is to be expected to follow.

Propaganda is one of those caricatured subjects, much like monarchy, that is difficult to talk about today because everyone who hears the term thinks they know what it signifies, while in fact they are acquainted only with a parody of the concept. This confusion is, ironically, often a direct result of propaganda. What I mean is that, while I can't say for sure if the insane know they're insane, I can say that the propagandee does not know he is propagandized.

Again, comparing discussions about propaganda to those about monarchy, it is impossible to speak of these concepts to American audiences because their shallow preconceptions have been so thoroughly reinforced, not by study or by experience, but by the pressure of exaggeration and self-congratulatory myth. At this point, any explanation at variance with their expectations is rejected out of hand as counter to "common sense." Just as all Americans believe that every King is necessarily a tyrant, so also is propaganda a thing of the past, discarded because impotent against an enlightened and informed populace.

This is why the term, if it is used at all, is applied to primitive and obvious attempts to further political positions. When we hear "propaganda," we think of cartoons picturing Uncle Sam spanking Hitler, or something of that sort. We see such devices as so blatant and superficial that to call an effort "propaganda" is to classify it as something so apparent that no reasonable adult would take it seriously.

To make matters worse, the term also brings to mind Hollywood representations of "brain washing" and Manchurian Candidate-style conspiracy plots. All of this mocking confusion undermines a proper discussion of propaganda from the start. Any warnings or claims about the dangers association with it sound to the modern ear like simple-mindedness or paranoia. I hope in what follows to illustrate clearly that the assumption that modern man is exempt from propaganda technique is a very dangerous form of ignorance.

A DANGEROUS SITUATION

Egalitarian society asks much of the men within it; so much in fact that it is difficult to imagine any group of individuals capable of answering the call with success. It is no insult to admit that a single person is not capable of achieving competence on very many matters. This is due to a variety of factors such as time, desire, and aptitude. After all, the names on a ballot really represent a range of very complex questions, and very few men have the time required to understand and answer those questions properly before they enter the voting booth. Of those who do have the time, how many have the desire to carry out their "due diligence?" And of the remaining number who have both the time and the desire, how many of these still lack the proper aptitude for this type of study? Few indeed will be left able to reach the level of knowledge that we could honestly describe as "competent."

This creates a dangerous environment from the outset, because it is everywhere suggested to men that they must express opinions whether or not they are properly equipped to do so, whether or not they even have opinions about a given "issue," and despite the fact that some of them may have never even cared to think about the matter before. (And rightly so!—for a wise men does not attempt to generate opinions on everything under the sun, and particularly on those matters which fall outside of his range of competence and therefore do not concern him).

Democratic civilization goes even to the point of imputing a sort of negligence on to those who, perhaps out of an honest humility, choose not to express their ignorance on the ballot sheet. I ask the reader: can you sense the extreme peril of such a situation? Masses of men are being herded into ballot boxes and pressed to fill out questionnaires about men they do not know and who, ironically, may be as ill-equipped for the task of governance as themselves. Such conditions do not empower the people, but leave them ripe for exploitation.

Deprived of knowledge, pressured into an act of hypocrisy, the voter is often just as likely to answer one way as another. It only takes a nudge to tip the scales and get a vote, and that nudge rarely comes in the form of a rational discourse. The modern election, carried out in this fashion, becomes a large-scale expression of ignorance.

We must proceed, therefore, by asking what, if not knowledge, determines the outcome of the electoral process? Asked another way: what forces influence and direct the mind of the modern democratic man? These are not simple questions, and the subject must be approached from various angles in order to get a sense of the answer.

DEMOCRACY AND THE NEED FOR OPINIONS

Let us take a step back for a moment and look again at the situation where the average American citizen finds himself. Our existences are, for the most part, banal, and so are our social problems. This does not mean they are not important, but it does mean that they are not as obvious as the problem of Huns descending upon our neighbors or the threat of starvation due to draught. Our problems are at the same time much more complex and much more uninteresting.

Were the difficulties of the day to be stated in the chaotic, confused, and ultimately mundane terms where we actually find them, then no one would take an interest in the news, much less in politics. If some did take an interest, they would not feel very compelled to express and opinion on the matter anymore than they feel compelled to philosophize about the process of photosynthesis occurring in the grass on their front lawn.

In order to induce the citizen to *care enough* to go out and vote, he must be convinced that the workings of politics which often seem beyond his comprehension (because they are) and beyond his control (again, because they are) are worth the time he must spend trying to understand them. This is quite a task. In the words of Hans Delbrück:

> *"The experience of thousands of years teaches that the overwhelming majority of peoples does not take sufficient interest in the state to be able to form well-founded opinions concerning either persons or bills to cast its vote accordingly. . . . In most elections, except those of rare popular interests, the party that succeeds through some means or other in hauling a crowd of absolutely indifferent men to the polls is the party that wins. Is it then the people's will that has become manifest through this election? We find ourselves in an evident dilemma. If no parties existed, the vote would be so small that there could be no question of an action of the people. If we have parties, it is true, they drag the people onto the stage, but the verdict is pronounced by the powers, who understand how*

Daniel Schwindt

> *to induce those who have no opinion of their own to vote in the way desired.*[201]

Although this runs counter to the present way of understanding the democratic process, it is an accurate depiction of the truth, and it also explains why every news story is sensationalized as much as possible, and why political issues are framed in terms that inevitably threaten the well-being of the average citizen, otherwise the average citizen would not care. So here we are with a political system organized on the assumption that men want to control their own political processes. When it turns out that really this isn't true of very many people, rather than change the assumption, political parties set about trying to convince the people that they should care, and this always necessitates a distortion of the issues. Nevertheless, and for reasons we will explore below, it always succeeds through propaganda technique in inducing men to become passionate about "the issues."

But there is one serious problem with this success. Having induced the people to care, and care very vehemently, democracy is immediately confronted with the problem of knowledge. Fear and concern has been instilled in the mob, but where shall they find their opinions, which because they never cared they never formed? Clearly these must be manufactured for them, and nothing is more efficient at this process than propaganda. And so we see at this early stage a key feature of propaganda: *it is self-perpetuating.*

---

[201] Hans Delbrück, *Government and Will of the People*, trans, by Roy S. MacElwee (New York: Oxford University Press, 1923), p. 14.

PROPAGANDA IS SELF-INFLICTED BASED ON A NEED

Propaganda, once unleashed, creates in society a need for more propaganda. First the concern of the citizen is inflamed, and when he finds himself in dire need of opinions and "answers" to allow him to express this concern, again propaganda presents itself as the answer. In a way, it is like an addictive drug. This is propaganda in its second stage, and it is this type of "opinion forming" propaganda that we see and experience most in the present context.

What is most important to understand now is that once this point is reached propaganda is catering to a population of consumer who *need it*. They need opinions, for only in opinions can the democratic citizen find any semblance of peace, and the wellspring of opinion in the post-literate age where books no longer matter is the apparatus of propaganda. This is why Jacques Ellul wrote:

> *"[O]ne cannot reach through propaganda to those who do not need what it offers. The propagandee is by no means just an innocent victim... There is not just a wicked propagandist at work who sets up means to ensnare the innocent citizen. Rather, there is a citizen who craves propaganda from the bottom of his being and a propagandist who responds to this craving."[202]*

INDIVIDUAL NEED

We have identified an individual need, but this need can be divided into many aspects, each of which exerts an incessant pressure on the

---

[202] *Propaganda*, p. 121.

persons, a pressure for which propaganda is the most efficient source of relief. The aspects are as follows:

The citizen of today, more than ever before, takes a very serious interest politics. He feels, at the same time, responsible for every event that takes place in the political and helpless to alter these events. By subscribing to the notion that the people rule, and acknowledging that he is one of the people, then he feels the pressure that in previous ages only statesmen and kings knew. This pressure, moreover, is multiplied a hundred times over by the fact that his world is exponentially more complex than what was experienced by the kings of old. He is confronted with unprecedented complexity in his surroundings, combined with unprecedented responsibility for them, and this creates a constant sense of anguish and alienation from the very political system of which he has been assured that he is a part. His mind buys into the notion, but reality is constantly refuting it. He is divided against himself. As a culminating blow, there is no longer a public religious presence to assure him that God is ultimately the one who will control the fate of the nation. On the contrary, God is a thing for the private space, which is a very small thing indeed, while the public space is under the direction of men only. So even religion no longer offers solace when it comes to the problems of daily life. Confused, overwhelmed, frustrated, the man arrives home to hear that an election is approaching and it is up to him to choose wisely, lest the nation be obliterated when the wrong party wins the vote. Where is he to turn? He turns on the television to ease his mind. He watches the news. The circle is complete.

STATE NEED

The individual need is only half the story. The modern state also requires propaganda and is dependent on it, although in a different fashion. It is a problem of responsibility and the assent of the public. Democratic governments depend on the assent of the public in order to govern. Or, in the words of Napoleon: "Power is based on opinion. What is a government not supported by opinion? Nothing." Yet public opinion is irrational, erratic, absent critical faculties, and historically blind. For example, public opinion can in no way formulate long-term foreign policy. The solution, from the position of those who govern, is clear:

> "...a government that is honest, serious, benevolent, and respects the voter cannot follow public opinion. But it cannot escape it either...Only one solution is possible: as the government cannot follow opinion, opinion must follow the government. One must convince this present, ponderous, impassioned mass that the government's decisions are legitimate and good and that its foreign policy is correct."[203]

And so the government must set about manufacturing the consent that it requires in order to do what it must do. In this it has no choice. If any government at any time followed the will of the people for a day, it would be in ruin by nightfall.

CORPORATE NEED

In addition to the individual and the state, which are often mistakenly considered the only two actors in contemporary society, we must

---

[203] Jacques Ellul

211

speak of the role of corporations, or "Big Business" in the phenomenon of propaganda. The so-called Roaring 20's saw a phenomenal degree of prosperity, which brought to light a problem that had not been faced before. In previous periods normal men and women purchased what they needed. Their shopping was, by and large, practical. With the rise of the affluent society producers were faced with the problem of overproduction. They needed to find a way to convince the public to buy things even when they did not necessarily need them, and to replace clothing, cars, and other devices for reasons other than the fact that the old had been worn out. The world of production required the mentality we now call "consumerism" which buys for a range of reasons that have little or nothing to do with practical need. This period also saw the invention of "planned obsolescence." Cars, at the suggestion of the Freudians, could now be purchased as symbols of sexuality and masculine prowess, and when they died early it did not so much matter because the sex appeal needed to be renewed anyhow.

Paul Mazer of the *Lehman Brothers* stated the problem explicitly:

> "We must shift America from a needs to a desires culture. People must be trained to desire, to want new things even before the old had been entirely consumed. We must shape a new mentality in America. Man's desires must overshadow his needs."

And how could this be brought about except by means of propaganda?—or in more familiar terms, by "advertising." We take advertising for granted but it is nothing other than the most common form of propaganda in a commercialist society such as ours. Every commercial is an attempt to propagandize, and considering the known correlation between sales and advertising budgets, this propaganda has become very effective.

PARTIES AS THE COLLUSION BETWEEN STATE AND INDIVIDUAL

The three groups that are today dependent on propaganda for their well-being are therefore the citizen, the state, and the corporation. Before moving on, however, we have to understand that although reflex has taught us that this sets them at odds with one another, in the end we find that they often cooperate in the endeavor. No better example of this collusion for the purposes of "reciprocal propagandizing" can be found than the *political party*.

Thomas Jefferson wrote that political parties were an "addiction." He called them "the last degradation of a free and moral agent," stating further in his letters that, "If I could not go to heaven but with a party, I would not go there at all."

Unfortunately, today we take them as a given, and even as a public good, and party loyalties are so ingrained that a man will often disdain his family or his religion before he will call into question the infallibility of his party. How can we explain this fanaticism for parties which the Founding Fathers despised? The answer lies in propaganda and the thirst for what it provides.

By their fruits you shall know them. What are the fruits of political parties? They provide answers, "platforms," slogans, easily comprehensible and even "common sense" paradigms for the most difficult of social problems. They are educational bodies that condense history, current events, and the loftiest of philosophical problems into clichés. Needless to say, the truth rarely survives the operation, but the individual finds comfort. To return again to Ellul:

"This is the great role propaganda must perform. It must give the people the feeling--which they crave and which satisfies them--'to have wanted what the government is doing, to be responsible for its actions, to be involved in defending them and making them succeed, to be 'with it.' "

If we turn now to the problems faced by the individual as a voter, however, we find that the political party is the answer to his prayers. It soothes his feeling of ignorance by teaching him all the answers to the problems of the day, whether or not he knows anything about them in reality. The party provides him with a leader that he can trust, even though he can never know him personally. The party gives him the sense of belonging, and this satisfies him most of all. It seems to escape his awareness completely that he had absolutely nothing to do with the selection of the leader or the formulation of the platform and cannot understand any of the legislation that will result from his vote.

But all these will be elaborated upon as we proceed. For now we need only acknowledge that party fanaticism is the collaboration between the state, which must have an instrument with which to propagandize, and the individual, which must have an instrument with which to propagandize itself.

Corporations participate also by injecting money, which is the lifeblood of all modern politics. This is the collusion between state and business. President Herbert Hoover can here act as our witness, as we cite the words he spoke to a group of public relations men:

"You have taken over the job of creating desire and have transformed people into constantly moving happiness machines. Machines which have become the key to economic progress."

PROPAGANDA MANUFACTURES PRODUCTS FOR ALL

Clearly propaganda is so accepted, despite the fact that it is degrading to the mind, because it meets the needs of all groups. The individual needs certainty, the state needs consent, and corporations need desire. All these things propaganda provides, and provides very effectively.

THE MYTH OF THE GENERAL WILL

Let us now probe into mind of those who live in democratic ages in order to dispel a certain illusion. If we ask how the democrat thinks, we notice that he has a very particular set of ideas through which he seeks to understand his world. These ideas are always very simplistic because a democracy requires that its precepts be comprehensible to everyone, even those most averse to rational enquiry. Thus, the democrat takes for granted certain concepts that would be alien in any other time or place. For example, the notion of a homogenous and unified "will of the people" or the "general will."

There is no such thing as a "general will" any more than there is such a thing as an "average intelligence." That is to say, if we really did compute the "average intelligence" of an American, this number would probably not correspond to any actual living Americans. Every individual would be either higher or lower than the average. Likewise, when we speak of a "general will," things become even more absurd, and even if we could somehow compute such a thing, this artificial will would be at variance with all the real ones for the same reason just mentioned.

The problem is complicated further by the fact that men work upon each other's minds and so the two minds working together is not the same thing as two isolated minds added together arithmetically. When we transfer this to a larger scale, we arrive at some frightening observations.

When men combine they become, not a collection of individual and insulated selves, but "mass men." When this happens, the mental reactions of the group do not equal a sort of "average intelligence" of all those present, even though this is what one might expect from a purely mathematical standpoint. On the contrary, because masses tend to de-individuate and feed off of one another, and because this de-individuation must proceed toward a level common to everyone present, it cannot move up toward a level present only in the minority, nor can it approach the "average" intelligence. The only way the group can form their aggregate and come to an agreement is by moving downward toward the mental level of the lowest elements present. This phenomenon is the combined result of logical necessity and human psychology. It represents a condition which can be properly termed the "democratic psychosis."

The mingling of minds on a massive scale produces not a unified "mastermind" that contains all answers to all problems, but rather degrades the group to the condition of the herd.

THE AGE OF PROPAGANDA

To say that you live in the "information age" is true but misleading. More precision is needed, because the information where you are immersed is a very specific kind of information which is delivered to you in a very specific way. If you turn on the news you will never see images and hear words at random, but in a planned order and with a purpose; and the purpose is always *persuasive*. There can never be any such thing as an "objective" news broadcast any more than there could ever be an "objective" advertisement. Objectivity in the human order is as impossible as perfection. Even a program properly categorized as "entertainment" carries a persuasive element in it seeking to win the viewers' attention over other programs of a similar type and tenor. It does this by a variety of appeals, either to the emotions or the intellect. Because not every person uses the intellect, while every person alive uses the emotions, emotion appeal quickly becomes the standard technique used to achieve the goal of persuasion. The field known as advertising was the true forerunner of modern political discourse, which is but a perversion of traditional political discourse. When men spoke in person to small crowds of their fellow elites who were as educated as they were, the discourse had no choice but to seek a pure intellectual conviction within the listeners. Clear argumentation was a necessity. If a man was going to be dishonest, he had to trick the mind, but even this required him to appeal to it—he could not bypass it altogether. Advertising, on the other hand, seeks to produce a reflex action which will appeal to the intellect only secondarily, if at all. Needless to say, for the reasons already mentioned, the techniques of advertising eventually proved themselves far more efficient in regard to "persuasion" than those of traditional political discourse. Appeals to the intellect require not only certain levels of education within the person, but also a certain degree of truth must be contained within the "argument" itself. Advertising requires none of this; it only asks that the subject be alive and equipped with certain standard human reactions. Its successes or failures can teach anyone what sort of responses can be expected from various words, colors, situations, images, etc. Thus, while traditional political discourse favored rhetoric and reason, the modern form of discourse, modeled on advertising, favors a purely pragmatic method which, while based in psychology, does not achieve its goals by working on the critical faculty. Advances in psychological understanding have also given immense powers to the media planners, as there are stimuli the response to which can now be predicted with a very high degree of certainty. This knowledge about the mind, combined with the machine of dissemination which we call "the media" forms a very finely tuned apparatus which directs itself toward the persuasion of the viewer's mind—and the apparatus never sleeps. It runs at every hour and through the entire year.

ANONYMITY

Here I should clarify that I am not suggesting that a certain man, or even a panel of men, sit behind a curtain turning the gears of the great apparatus, engineering responses to certain predefined goals in a humanly calculated program of exploitation and mind control. That is far too simple-minded, although it makes for exciting conspiracy tales. No, this apparatus moves of its own accord, having divorced itself from conscious guidance long ago. If anything it might be described as something guided by man's collective and unconscious will-to-death, and we could even go further and say that it is a result of modern man's "collective possession," but we are getting ahead of ourselves. For now, to return to our point, we should say that man does not simply live in the "age of information," but rather than he lives in the "age of propaganda." And let it not be said that propaganda ceases to be propaganda just because the individuals utilizing it are not fully aware of what they are doing. Guénon said truly that "it is not easy to judge the degree of sincerity of those who become the propagators of such ideas, or to know to what extent they fall prey to their own lies and deceive themselves as they deceive others; in fact, in propaganda of this sort, those who play the part of the dupes are often the best instruments, as they bring to the work a conviction that others would have difficulty in simulating, and which is readily contagious."[204]

---

[204] Guénon, Crisis, 71

PROPAGANDA AS TECHNIQUE

Propaganda is nothing more than a term used to describe specific techniques of persuasion which seeks to gain the assent of the human subject while bypassing or overriding his or her rational faculties. There is nothing in this definition which requires the techniques be wielded by any particular person, or with explicit knowledge of the nature of the manipulations. Propaganda is in many respects an "impersonal" phenomenon, even if its action always begins with persons. Like an avalanche, or the age-old concept of the *egregore*, propaganda technique can be initiated and nurtured by individuals who are more or less conscious of what they are doing, but at a certain point is become disconnected from their conscious direction and takes on a life of its own as a sort of artificial demonic entity, loosed to wreak havoc on its creators just as much as anyone else.

MAN AS A MEANS

Even when kept under conscious control, it is important to acknowledge that the kind of mental manipulation that propaganda involves is inherently subhuman. It is therefore to be rejected on every level as a means of achieving one's goals. It does not matter whom the technique of propaganda is applied to, it is unacceptable because it seeks to coerce the will not through the mind but by short-circuiting the mind. It achieves its end by bypassing the consciousness of the person and directing them toward an end of which they are unaware, incapable of understanding, or cannot reasonably resist.

The result is that the human subject is turned into an object, which is to say, into a mere means to an end. According to any morality which acknowledges the freedom of the will and the dignity of the person, this sort of degradation is a crime even to one's enemies. And yet we open ourselves to this daily from many directions.

Make no mistake, every time you turn on the television, every time you watch or hear "the news," know that you are unleashing this technique upon yourself, and be on your guard.

EFFICIENCY

Propaganda exists due, among other things, to the tendency of modern man to always follow the most efficient means for any goal he sets for himself. This is a reflection of the industrial mentality, of which our industrialized society is but a reflection. I will not say whether or not the industrialization of civilization is a result of this mental transformation, or if the mental transformation is a result of economic industrialization. It is enough to simply say that the two have grown together, and to conclude that the industrial focus on efficiency without regard to any subtle human factors characterizes modern politics just as much as the production line. The most efficient means will be adopted in an enterprise unless some obstacle is erected to prevent its path, thus effectively rendering it inefficient.

REDUCTION TO SIMPLICITY

One consequence of the "efficient mentality," when applied to communication, is a preference for the reduction of concepts to their most simplistic form. An idea that is difficult, subtle, or multifaceted cannot be easily transmitted to masses of varying dispositions, nor can it be communicated in the almost instantaneous fashion required by the modern lifestyle. Some concept which presupposes familiarity with distant historical factors, for example, is impossible to present to a democratic population. The mass of men may not have the time, and perhaps not even the aptitude, for the required comprehension, and so this renders the effort inefficient in the utmost. How then to proceed? Associations here are central for the propagandist, and so he must appeal to pre-existing mental constructs, as well as universal reflex actions, within his audience. What this means, in short, is that entire subjects must be reduced to agendas, agendas reduced to "platforms," and platforms reduced to mere slogans and catchphrases. Any experience with contemporary politics is enough to see that slogans are a favorite of modern mass man. Consider President Obama's 2008 slogan, "Change we can believe in," which is in every way meaningless if analyzed from a rational point of view, but becomes very powerful if analyzed from a purely emotional standpoint devoid of intellectual meaning. The vague notion of "change" has universal appeal to a nation that is almost always dissatisfied with present circumstance, and the notion of something which we can "believe in" creates in those already predisposed a response akin to "faith," or at least signals to them that this slogan represents not a particular truth, but "truth" in the abstract, which obviously deserves unquestionable loyalty of all. In 2012, Obama's slogan changed simply to "Forward," which, again, is not only meaningless from a rational standpoint, but is actually in direct contradiction to the 2008 slogan. Nonetheless, it prevails on an emotional level regardless of any contradictions it might entail.

KEYWORDS

Beyond slogans, there has also been developed an array of specific keywords which merely by being invoked can create a desired response. These are such words as *democracy, freedom, equality.* These are terms which, elevated to the status of "values" in and of themselves, give impression of thought and argument each time they are invoked, yet are completely devoid of meaning if left without qualification and further explanation. For example, one might consider the oft-repeated statement that America's enemies "hate our freedoms." This statement, empty of meaning in itself, has nonetheless proven sufficient to explain to the American people every hostile action by a foreign nation in the last 50 years, perhaps more. Never mind that the statement is really so fluid that it could be applied to any situation and any military action, including those of the United States. For example, the Allies in WWII hated Hitler's freedom to exterminate Jews. Therefore, such statements as "they hate our freedoms," while giving the impression of thought, end up ensuring that there is no thinking involved in the matter. "Freedom," as a haloed concept in the modern civil religion, is to be revered. Any hatred toward freedom is received as if it were hatred toward God. Thus, we see that such slogans really only serve to bypass the mind and create a reflex action of anger and fear, which are very persuasive factors, especially in the absence of reason.

SEMANTIC BREAKDOWN

A variety of observers have noted with frustration the natural outcome of these trends, which is a sort of prevailing "semantic breakdown." What this means is that language is decaying and proper definitions are systematically replaced with sentimental responses. Another way of saying this is that everything becomes slang and slur: certain words which have a valid meaning become impossible to use in their proper sense because they have been "hijacked" by abuse with sufficient frequency as to render the original meaning obsolete. The term "liberal" is an excellent example of this. Having originally been used to signify a specific philosophical bent, emphasizing the freedom of individuals, closely linked to humanism and the Enlightenment, the term "liberal" now means nothing more than one of the two American political parties fighting perpetually for control. It may or may not signify any of the actual doctrines of "liberalism" in the historical and philosophical sense. In fact, it cannot be used in this way because it would then apply to conservatives as well, because the two opponents are in fact two modern branches of the liberal tree, each adhering to the philosophy in a different manner and degree. This means, of course, that conservative also has no objective meaning. Conservative and liberal are not simply relative terms which can only be said to describe two enemy parties whose actual philosophical positions may be here, or there, or nowhere, depending on the year. Thus you will see that you can use such terms if you dare, but you will never be able to use them in their proper sense. The climate of propaganda where you are saturated forbids it, and any attempt to communicate using the intellectual meanings of words will only lead you into frustration and confusion.

STATISTICS: FACT OR TRUTH?

Davila said that "statistics is the tool of those who give up understanding in order to manipulate."[205] When he said this, Davila had recognized that statistics, as form of propaganda, have come to wield too much power in public discourse.

Statistics, in a way, lead inevitably to fallacious thinking. This is because no single statistic carries any truth value in itself: it must be

---

[205] 115

interpreted; and in order to properly interpret any statistic, we usually need a great many more statistics, as well as experience, reasoning skills, and objectivity.

The problem is that because all of those "interpretive" requirements happen in the background, usually without our even thinking about it, we forget that it is even occurring. Because the only part of the process we notice is the "fact," we operate on the assumption that the fact "interprets itself." We forget that a naked fact carries no truth with the interpretation, and multiple interpretations are always possible. And so we encounter two problems with statistics—two forms of deception: first, we forget that they always require interpretation; and second, we forget that in order to arrive at a valid interpretation, we usually need more data.

The following two case examples are drawn from modern political conversation, and they illustrate that this deception is used by both sides of the political war.

Example 1: Planned Parenthood's Budget

The scenario:

Planned Parenthood is accused by political opponents of being a significant provider of abortion services. Planned Parenthood responds by claiming that, of all the services they provide, only 3% are abortions.

The deception:

The statistic itself is true, but only when the calculations are performed in a certain way. Consider this: Planned Parenthood also administers pregnancy tests. A pregnancy test, as most people know, requires almost no time, no money, does not require a physician, and is minimally invasive. An abortion is a different matter entirely.

However, if we so desire, we can consider a pregnancy test as "1 service" and an abortion as "1 service." This treats them as mathematically equal, even though no honest person would say they are equal in reality. If we do the math in this manner, Planned Parenthood can administer 97 pregnancy tests and 3 abortions in one hour, and then claim that only 3% of their services are abortions. This is true, mathematically. But realistically?—it is so misleading as to be an outright lie. It is a fact, but it hides the truth.

Example 2: The Tax Burden of the Rich

The scenario:

Politician X claims the wealthy pay a disproportionate and unjust amount of taxes to the government. In support of this claim, he explains that the wealthiest 1% of Americans pay a whopping 36% of the taxes. If we expand this to the top 10%, the group pays almost 70% of the taxes. These figures, it is implied, suggest massively unjust demands being made on rich. We are then told that the lower classes (the bottom 50%) are getting off easy, paying a scant 3.3%.

The deception:

Planned Parenthood was guilty of interpreting data in a misleading way. The politician above, on the other hand, is guilty of a partial presentation of data which, in the end, is equally dishonest. To see why, we need to incorporate some supplementary data in order to achieve a necessary point of reference. So, in addition to the distribution of taxes, let's include also the distribution of wealth. We then see that the top 1% holds 35% of the wealth, and the top 10% holds about 70%. So if by "just taxation" we mean that each person should pay an equal share of his income, then it only makes sense that he who has much will pay much, and he who has almost nothing will pay almost nothing.

But these partisan debates do not really concern us here. The point is simply that statistics are by and large, as we encounter them today, an expression of propaganda. Like any other piece of information, they are only useful insofar as we truly understand their depth, history and context. For most of us, this means that statistically are mostly useless.

Unconsciousness of Propaganda

Always keep in mind that the propagandistic climate is so familiar to your contemporaries, so all-pervasive, that it has ceased to be consciously felt for what it is, and is now as natural as breath. The air indeed would smell stale to them if it were cleared of the propagandistic technique and delivered via pure intellectual appeal. They would find it alien and appalling. See, for example, how many men you can persuade to read Aristotle's *Politics*, and you will quickly understand. Intellectual foundations for arguments cease to be necessary when arguments cease to be intellectual. Emotions do not require a foundation; they only ask to be felt. Again, this all proceeds on a level outside of conscious acknowledgement and your neighbor will all the while deny the existence of the drum even as he dances to its beat.

No More Demagogues

Frequently today we hear so-and-so accused of being a demagogue. This is an important error for us to correct, which we will now do. In the words of Theodor Geiger:

> "The typical leader by no means influences the masses in one direction, he finds the undercurrent and is himself a possessed among the possessed. The typical mass-leader is not a 'demagogue,' he does not consciously and with a cool brain direct the masses in one way, he most of all is gripped by the ecstasy of mass-experience, he is himself among the most unconscious of all." [206]

The modern political leader is really only the first dupe. He is truly the first among equals amidst a mass of equally ignorant and deluded individuals, whether we are speaking here of a president or a *Fuhrer*. Remember that we are speaking here not of theory or any articulated law as to the "powers" invested here or there, but rather of the actual effective role of such leaders in the flow of political events. Here, with few exceptions, the individual melts into passivity.

The Verbal Universe

Quoting Davila again, we can agree with him that: "Daily news is the modern surrogate of experience." [207]

To illustrate this point, I am reminded of an anecdote from Milan Kundera:

---

[206] *Die Masse und Ihre Action.*
[207] 203

"My grandmother, who lived in a Moravian village, still knew everything through her own experience: how bread is baked, how a house is built, how a pig is slaughtered and the meat smoked, what quilts are made of, what the priest and the schoolteacher think about the world; she met the whole village every day and knew how many murders were committed in the country over the last ten years; she had, so to speak, personal control over reality, and nobody could fool her by maintaining that Moravian agriculture was thriving when people at home had nothing to eat. My Paris neighbor spends his time at an office, where he sits for eight hours facing an office colleague, then he sits in his car and drives home, turns on the TV, and when the announcer informs him that in the latest public opinion poll the majority of Frenchmen voted their country the safest in Europe (I recently read such a report), he is overjoyed and opens a bottle of champagne without ever learning that three thefts and two murders were committed on his street that very day."

This is the result of propaganda, that it plummets men into a purely verbal universe that is completely disconnected from reality. What is constructed within this abstract world begins to guide political development and cultural ethos in such a way that the nation no longer makes decisions based on what they see but on what they imagine.

PROPAGANDA DOES NOT REQUIRE UNITY

Because propaganda thrives on disorder and confusion within the mob, it does not, as one would assume from watching movies about brainwashing and manipulation, have to be carried out with precise planning and through flawless execution. Remember, propaganda operates through confusion, and through relentless conditioning achieves its ends. It does not need a "plan," because it does not need a planner. There may be a multiplicity of parties and organizations each employing the same means to batter the subject population with conflicting ideas, undermining each other's particular agenda at every turn. No matter. This does not change the nature of the propagandistic climate, for it is not characterized by calculated ends, but by a conflagration of nervous agitation and mental bewilderment, suppressing man's higher faculties in favor of irrational impulse and, more specifically, conditioned reflex.

EXPLOITATION OF HATE

Everyone feels hatred, resentment, and anger. This means that there is also in each person a need for an outlet or a means of expressing these emotions that will not result in guilt or negative social consequences. Normally a man has to find a way, usually by religious practice and self-discipline, to restrain and diffuse this hatred, or else he will suffer consequences. Not so in the age of propaganda. Propaganda excels in providing men with official enemies, at the same time ensuring that even the most puerile and shameful resentments against "the opposition" are socially sanctioned. Anyone familiar with party systems has seen the disgust one party member is apt to show toward another whom he may really know nothing about other than that he is one of "the enemies." He cannot afford to know much about the person, for then he risks finding some redeeming feature in his enemy, and this is unacceptable. Any redemption for the enemy is a failure for propaganda which seeks separation between individuals; communion is defeat. For such reasons, it matters little what scapegoat is chosen. They need not be powerful or of a different color. The Jews were made easily to serve this purpose by Hitler, so badly does man need someone whom he can hate with impunity.

DEPENDENCE

It has been suggested that the adherents of one party are commanded not to read the literature of other parties because they might find something agreeable in their reading and might therefore change allegiance; but I have found this to be untrue. In the end, the propagandized man becomes dependent on the propaganda, needing it and feeling something akin to fear in its absence. He abstains from all literature not sanctioned by the party authority, not because the authority forbids it, but because he himself fears it. He begins to return daily to the altar of propaganda because he has come to require it as sustenance. In the beginning propaganda may have had to assail him so thoroughly that it became as natural to him as air, but once this acclimation was complete it had to assail him no longer. Having identified it with air, he has come to need it like air, and he feels suffocated in its absence. The human person thus becomes assimilated with propaganda—there may be no turning back.

THE MORAL PAINTBRUSH

Closely linked to the desire to hate is the desire to feel justified in one's own opinions and behavior. Each man wants to be affirmed, wants to be "right," and wants to claim for himself the banner of truth. And this is not a matter of simple theoretical truth, but ultimate truth, which is to say, moral truth. He does not want to be "right" as one is right about a math problem; he wants to be "justified" not only in regard to rational error, but also in regard to sin itself. He wants to be righteous!

Here again propaganda is more than happy to accommodate him. As it provides him with an enemy toward which he may express his hatred, so also he is encouraged to impute to this enemy all evils in the world. Every social problem, every human suffering, will be traced in some way to "the enemy," so that nothing remains a simple difference of opinion. Party allegiance becomes an ultimate question—a spiritual question. Philosophical differences become religious differences. It becomes impossible to conceive of two men who seek truth but come to different conclusions. There is only good and evil, and the line is clearly drawn. This process is an immense simplification of the kind carried out by Hitler against the Jews. Great masses of individuals who may themselves vary greatly in character and opinion are group indiscriminately into one entity as "the enemy," and all must be despised together as if they were so many limbs of the devil himself. Again, although this does rely on the exploitation of hate, we have no gone further and are seeing the exploitation of pride. This is not simply a sanctioned resentment of one's neighbor; it is a sanctioned claim to self-righteousness. Who can resist such an offer?

COLLECTIVE TRANSFERENCE

Another way to look at the previous point is this: there is technique in psychoanalysis called "transference," whereby the physician seeks to redirect feelings of guilt and self-loathing, which the patient originally aims at himself, in such a way that the patient begins to attribute those feelings to the physicians. By this method the physician "frees" the patient from guilt. The idea is that, while initially this results in the patient loathing the physician, it completes a first necessary step of allowing the patient to love himself, and the physician then seeks to train the patient to properly direct the negative feelings consciously, so that they are neither aimed at neither himself nor the physician.

Propaganda exploits this technique, albeit on a collective scale and without the goal of mental health. Propaganda, by its relentless pulverizations and suggestions, allows the collective to "transfer" its guilt feelings onto a designated enemy, who then carries not only his own sins, but also the sins of the entire society.

ABSOLUTISM

Only in under these sorts of pressures could situations arise where the enemy is always "absolutely evil" and is a creature in whom no redeeming qualities exist; opposed to the enemy is the body of the "affirmed" who are "absolutely good" and who embody all that is good and virtuous in civilization.

CAUSES AND CONDITIONS

Remember we had said that the propagandistic climate resulted from certain ambient conditions without which it could not exist. Here we may briefly enumerate some of those conditions which combine to reinforce or exacerbate the propagandistic climate.

INDIVIDUALISM

The dispersion of tightly-knit social groups into that of isolated "individuals" allows the mechanisms of propaganda to then regroup them as potent and organic associations, but rather as abstract "teams," thus offering the feeling of camaraderie without the power or relationship implied in such solidarity. The family must decay so that the company can prosper; the clan must die so that the party can achieve its ends. In truth, propaganda could not operate in societies where the traditional forms of solidarity were central. Peasant and village peoples are impervious to propaganda methods. We can conclude then that widespread individualism and atomization is on pre-condition of propaganda.

TECHNOLOGICAL DEPERSONALIZATION

Propaganda presupposes not only the separation of individualism, but also the depersonalization of those around us once we conceive of them as separate and unrelated to ourselves. As technological means become the medium for all communication, discourse itself becomes less human and therefore serves this end with great efficiency. There is no possible way propaganda could exert its force in an organic setting of interpersonal dialogue. Natural face-to-face conversation has both advantages and limitations, but in almost every way it is hostile to propaganda. It implies an inescapable personal contact which excludes the possibility of seeing your "opponent" in the abstract as the devil himself. In such scenarios we cannot help but see the man across from us as a limited human being as susceptible to error and ignorance as anyone else. We find then that he could not possible be the evil mastermind that we had pictured in our abstract generalizations, and against which we had directed so much disdain. It is even likely, although not guaranteed, that we may sense some likeable quality in the man. Indeed, we may realize, with abject horror, that the man actually harbors a good will! We may be forced to explain his opinions as a matter of ignorance pure and simple, which renders our hatred somewhat impotent, because who can really hate someone seen as good-willed but wrong-headed? At worst we are left with a frustration at our inability to meet intellectually, but, having met personally, much of our insanity has been expelled.

EXISTENTIAL INSECURITY

As suggested already, the modern man has unprecedented expectations laid at his feet in regard both to discernment and behavior. Never before has the common man been so "free" from guidance from the wisdom of tradition or religion. Never before has he been so privileged as to have a say in all of the most complex of political, economic, social, and scientific matters. Having been liberated from all the traditional limitations, he suffers under the weight of his the plethora of new responsibilities which threaten to overwhelm him. Divorced not only from traditional supports, but also even from his neighbor, he must discern for himself in every matter. When the perennial problems of existence assail him, he must formulate his own explanations. He knows he is a sinner and he feels his own weakness, both physically and mentally, and yet he is deprived of any recourse. He is ripe for propaganda. Propaganda is more than happy to offer him simplistic explanations for the most complex social phenomena. These he must accept because the real explanations are impossibly far removed from his competence, and he must have an explanation!—so he takes the only one that is within his reach, however absurd. It is more honorable in this age to be arrogantly ill-informed than to be honestly about one's ignorance. So much for the struggle with his ignorance. And the struggle with his sinfulness?—with the knowledge that he is weak and that there are ever-present evils in the world with which he must struggle? The wings of the church can no longer shelter him. Again, he must find his own solutions. Propaganda is here again, teaching man how to project his own evils onto an abstract opponent, focusing all of his spite on the enemy. He is taught to separate himself from sin, freeing him of his guilt and his need for repentance, which simultaneously frees him from any obligation to deal charitably with his enemies. Propaganda offers him truth and salvation in a terrifying world that denies the existence of both.

FEAR AND ANGST

As Mencken wrote, this creates a vicious circle:

> "Civilization, in fact, grows more maudlin and hysterical; especially under democracy it tends to degenerate into a mere combat of crazes; the whole aim of practical politics is to keep the populace alarmed (and hence clamorous to be led to safety) by an endless series of hobgoblins, most of them imaginary. Wars are no longer waged by the will of superior men, capable of judging dispassionately and intelligently the causes behind them and the effects flowing out of them. They are now begun by first throwing a mob into a panic; they are ended only when it has spent its ferine fury."[208]

MATERIALISM

As suggested above, propaganda tends to create a new order of sacred objects. More accurately, for those civilizations where materialism has created a spiritual void, propaganda seeks to populate that void with new concepts, persons, and pseudo-doctrines. This elevation of inferior objects to the status of sacred could obviously never be achieved in the presence of a valid spiritual authority. Thus, propaganda presupposes a practical materialism. Even if the society where it works continues to remain nominally religious, the forces of propaganda will still succeed if the spiritual authority is excluded from the social order. Again, even

---

[208] *In Defense of Women*, p. 53.

if the society claims and even theoretically desires religion to remain supreme, if it is excluded from all socio-political matters it becomes, in a practical sense, subordinate. This creates the aforementioned spiritual vacuum which is then easily populated as described. It is a strange irony then that materialism does not eliminate the sacred sphere, but merely displaces it and sweeps it clean before populating it with something else, namely, civil religion. This new faith is just as dogmatic and twice overbearing as any church state, because its members are not tied to any rationally enunciated set of principles. The new order of the sacred is an order of irrationality and tribalism.

ATROPHY OF THE CRITICAL FACULTY

It has been observed that "there is no such thing as a collective critical faculty." As "man as individual" slowly disintegrates, losing himself to "man as teeming throng," the less the critical faculty will be able to operate in any way. This is precisely the reason that men lose themselves during riots. Since the critical faculty can only operate on an individual level, and because the passions once inflamed can only be checked by that very faculty, when men de-individuate within the herd and the reason is suppressed, there is nothing left to check the passions. Thus, the same passion, which might have inflicted minimal damage through a man in isolation, becomes violent and catastrophic when that same individual is immersed within the collective. It is not so much that he takes on the passions of others, as you might expect, but that his aptitude for moderation becomes paralyzed, and so he becomes helpless before his very own passions—and that is more than enough.

RESULTANT PREDISPOSITION

When propaganda succeeds, which it always will within mass civilization, it creates in the people certain predispositions. It agitates and ensures that a certain level of tension, short of riot but only just, will remain constant. Man must never feel at ease, and whether it be awareness of death, injustice, war, natural disaster, political strife, or economic downturn, he must always exist in a state of anxiety. In this way he will maintain the necessary openness to suggestion. When the suggestion comes, it sends him down a path which is wholly predictable and is really now only a matter of reflex. When the signal comes, he knows exactly where to go, what to say, and, most importantly, who the enemy is. Ironically, however, what this usually means is not war or some dramatic act of revolt. It usually means simply that he accepts this candidate or piece of legislation while rejecting the other; that he hates this nation and loves another; that he believes this doctrine while accepting another; all without the exercise of his own reason. He will start no wars. He will not become a radical. He will probably do nothing shocking, nothing that a fully aware and un-propagandized man wouldn't do.

THE FINAL PRODUCT

Perhaps the only real difference between the man of propaganda and the conscious man is that the former will not do anything in his daily life simply because he has considered the action in its essence—questioned and examined it—and decided that it was best. He will simply do it, and that is all, whether that involves spending his money, voting, shooting a gun, or flaying the flesh off his neighbors back. And to the degree that he just does these things, any of them, to that same degree does he cease to be human. Propaganda is, at its essence, the animalization of man. It manufactures men who are, as the scientists say, without wills. As a differentiated man, propaganda will perhaps cause you more pain than any other single modern phenomenon. This is not because it will touch you, for you have a natural immunity or else you would not be reading this book. No, it will agonize you because it will touch everyone around you, and there will be nothing you can do to overpower it. Set before it the greatest work of philosophy and wisdom—it will be trampled into the dust by a thousand feet marching, chanting meaningless slogans. Produce the most eloquent of speeches!—it will be drowned out by an idiot talking nonsense on the television. Then you will realize one day that communication has become impossible. This will perhaps be the loneliest day of your life. But you must learn to accept it, to transcend it, and to accept the challenge, which is that you must speak in the small places, the secret places, the places where few will hear and none will remember your name. The age of famous philosophers is gone— the philosopher is as dead now as God. But that does not mean you cannot find, here and there, a lover of philosophy. It does not mean that you cannot find, even in the silence that is chaos, communion with God.

MASS MEDIA: APPARATUS FOR PROPAGANDA

We can conclude with a note on the press.

There is no press for you; there is only propaganda. Here as everywhere the laws of subversion have transformed a mechanism designed for truth into one which perpetuates deceit. Here again you must maintain the proper perspective: the information given you by the media will always be useless, even malicious, in the raw form in which it will come to you. Until you work upon it, disseminating its half-truth, its misinterpretation, and its grossly misplaced emphasis, which will inevitably tinge everything which passes through its machinery, it can offer you no sustenance. In fact, the degradation of the press has gone so far that you will have to think long and hard about whether it is even worth the effort to make of it something useful, asking yourself if it is not wiser to discard it completely, as Spengler suggested, writing that:

> "To-day we live so cowed under the bombardment of this intellectual artillery (the media) that hardly anyone can attain to the inward detachment that is required for a clear view of the monstrous drama. The will-to-power operating under a pure democratic disguise has finished off its masterpiece so well that the object's sense of freedom is actually flattered by the most thorough-going enslavement that has ever existed"[209]

The media today exists for no other social function that to allow the audience to be informed about everything without understanding anything.

TOOLS OF THE TRADE

I feel compelled, before closing this installment, to provide at least a brief enumeration of the methods of propaganda. The list is obviously not complete, nor could it be, but at least in the few sections that follow the reader might learn to recognize some of the most common ploys used to undermine his reason.

---

[209] Oswald Spengler, *Decline of the West: Perspectives of World History* (New York: Knopf, 1928), p. 455.

AD HOMINEM

I will mention the ad hominem fallacy first because it is one of the simplest and most popular. We're all familiar with it, if not in theory then at least in practice. It means to argue against the person or "to the man," and it involves trying to refute an argument by attacking the person who makes it rather than the argument itself.

For example, if you were to go before the public and attempt to disprove one of the statements made in this pamphlet, I might respond by going before the public and explaining to them that you are a brain-dead hell-spawn; I might tell them that you have dozens of unpaid parking tickets, and that these are not just any parking tickets, but that you are a habitual violator of handicapped spaces. I may then conclude that I have personally witnessed your crime forcing wounded veterans to traverse vast stretches of parking lot in order to get groceries.

Well that all may be true, and more. But it has nothing to do with your argument or mine. It has to do with you, yours actions, or your character. My response commits the ad hominem fallacy in spades.

AD NAUSEAM

There is a common saying, that "you can repeat something as many times as you like, but that won't make it true." The saying is, strictly speaking, accurate. Unfortunately, in practice we find that ceaseless repetition, while it does not actually make a statement true, can give it the appearance of truth.

The problem is largely psychological: we tend to take familiar things for granted as normal. And so a questionable statement, repeated to the point of numb familiarity, ceases to seem questionable.

One significant example of this process took place during the Middle Ages. At that point in history, taxes were largely unknown. If the king wanted to wage war, dower a daughter, or buy a new set of armor, he had to go on a "begging campaign" to raise money for his project. This process was normal—but it was normal as an exception.

Then the Hundred Years War occurred. This "war" was actually a series of many short forays, each of which required a separate "begging campaign." The handouts became so frequent that by the end of the Hundred Years War, the king had achieved a first: the poll-tax. How did he achieve this? By arguing for financial gifts ad nauseam.

APPEAL TO FEAR

In the novel Dune, author Frank Herbert has his characters repeat a mantra that has stuck with me through the years. It is called the "Litany Against Fear" and its first lines are: "I must not fear. Fear is the mind-killer." A truer word was never spoken. Fear is an extremely powerful emotion, and while not necessarily a negative one, it almost always causes critical thought to suffer. This is why the "appeal to fear" is another popular fallacy.

Appeal to fear is used especially during war, usually in connection with threat of death, extermination or loss: Either "the Germans want to destroy us all," or "President Obama wants to take your guns and enslave your family," or some other such thing.

Yet this technique is much more commonplace than that. Anyone who has been through Driver's Ed has been exposed to it in the form of bloody videos of auto collisions caused by driver negligence. It's even present in advertising. I once saw a pharmaceutical commercial warning viewers to "ask your doctor" about drug X, because disease Y might be upon you this very minute and you'd have no idea until it was too late. These tactics may sound a bit silly, but we may assume that they wouldn't be used if they did not get results.

REDUCTIO AD HITLERUM

This fallacy was named by conservative thinker Leo Strauss and is one of my favorites, simply because it is so common and, once you become aware of it, it seems so wickedly silly when used.

It involves "playing the Hitler card," and claiming that this or that policy is similar to, the same as, or would lead to, a policy supported by Hitler and the Nazis. It tries to trick us into the following fallacious thought process:

Hitler was evil. Hitler supported policy X. Candidate A also supports policy X. Therefore: Candidate A is evil like Hitler.

The error is obvious. Similarity in one respect does not imply similarity in all respects. Furthermore, just because Hitler held a certain opinion does not mean that the opinion is wrong or evil. Maybe he liked cats. Does this mean that those who share his feline affinity share also his anti-Semitism? Of course not—and yet we could assemble hours of television footage showing how willingly people will compare the opponents with Hitler. The Right says Obamacare, abortion, etc., are "things Hitler would have done." The Left says the same about those who oppose same-sex marriage. And it goes on and on, until everyone, it seems, is Hitler.

RENAMING VICES

Words change with time. This is natural and inevitable. But it is also convenient, especially if you can guide and even engineer the change to your advantage. This has been the case with several words, particularly those which happen to be morally loaded. For example, the term "individualism" has come to signify a positive, almost virtuous attitude in our culture; yet there was a time when it did not exist. It did not need to exist because there was already a word for that attitude: it was called egoism. Yet egoism is laden with negative connotation because it describes the vice of self-centeredness. "Individualism" became popular when society began looking upon egoism as a good, in which case the negative connotations had to be discarded. Because this is usually not possible, the word is discarded and replaced with something new—"individualism"—which is then colored with positive moral undertones.

This also happened in the area of political corruption in America. We took the practice of "bribery," obviously despicable within a democracy, and began calling it "lobbying." Precisely the same practice, and yet now it is seen as normal and accepted without a thought.

Words will always be changing, but it is a process we ought to watch closely.

FALSE DICHOTOMY

"Dichotomizing means pathologizing; and pathologizing means dichotomizing" said Abraham Maslow.

In certain instances, it is true to say that there are two options and no more—that the answer is either black or white. Yet those instances are

243

rare, and most of the time reality provides a colorful bouquet of possibilities, some very good, some very bad, and most a mix of both. You should be automatically suspicious, then, when someone demands that you limit yourself to either left or right, for even at a fork in the road you have more than just two option: it is often possible, and sometimes wise, to turn around and go back.

The purpose of the "false dichotomy" fallacy is to hide all other alternatives beyond the two currently placed directly before you. It is a fallacy of oversimplification.

This one is most prevalently exercised by the party system in America. As we've all been assured, you may choose either the Right or the Left, but if you choose anything else you are wasting your time. History itself refutes this bad logic, but it has proven extremely effective for our two parties, both of which benefit from this sort of thinking.

THE "LESSER OF TWO EVILS"

A counterpart to the false dichotomy, the "lesser of two evils" usually follows directly in its trail, reinforcing and solidifying its work. Using the contemporary political situation again as our example, the false dichotomy presents the public with only two options, and then the "lesser of two evils" argument tells voters that, rather than voting for the candidate or party they actually like, they must settle for the one they dislike the least. This tells the electorate that they must not hold out for an acceptable option, but that they must choose the option that is least unacceptable.

The success of this argument comes to the forefront during every election, when our friends tell us (and perhaps we tell ourselves): "I don't really care for Joe Goober or Bill Smiley, but I've got to pick the lesser of two evils. Ideally I'd choose someone else entirely, but I've got to be realistic: this country is in trouble and I've got to make the best of it."

And so it happens that the quality of our candidates slowly deteriorate because they no longer have to offer something desirable; they simply have to show that their man is "less evil" than the other. The words of St. Paul, that we must never "do evil that good may come of it," is to us naïve and unworkable. And we reap the fruit of our compromise.

COMMON SENSE

We quoted Mencken above, saying that: "For every complex problem there is an answer that is clear, simple, and wrong."

In case you hadn't noticed, many of fallacies we've mentioned so far involve the oversimplification of reality. Reality is rarely obvious and never simple, especially in our technological, globalized, age where everything is intermingled and travelling at supersonic speed. If there was ever a time when the most complex aspects of human life were easily discernable at first glance (I doubt there ever was such a time), that age is far behind us.

Yet we still wish that our mysterious, often contradictory reality was this straightforward and accessible; and this desire, so strong within us, makes us extremely susceptible to the "common sense" fallacy. This fallacy suggests to us that the answer to a complex problem, because it is simple, easy, obvious, and seemingly intuitive, must be correct. It also teaches us to look with suspicion on any solution that intimidates us or exceeds our comprehension. The result is that, because many issues are complex to the point of inaccessibility, anyone who wishes to defend their case must employ oversimplifications, or else have their idea rejected, not because it is wrong, but because it is difficult.

CULT OF PERSONALITY

If you turned ad hominem upside-down and inside-out, you'd get the Cult of Personality. Instead of refuting an argument by assaulting a person's character, this fallacy goes the opposite direction by building some person into an idealized, celebrity-hero whom the people can embrace as savior. This person, who may even have a special title— "Führer" or "Ill Duce" for example—is then used to garner support for a particular position.

For example, when John Wayne spoke on some political topic, his words carried great weight because of the heroic ideal which he symbolized in his person and character. Now, while I, personally, love John Wayne movies, it is nonetheless fallacious to accept a proposition simply because John Wayne accepted it.

The mass media is often a significant component in the cult of personality, because it allows the entire population to be incessantly bombarded with portraits, videos, and slogans relating to the hero. For this reason, although present in every age, we can say that this trick is chiefly a modern technique. Using the mass media as a vehicle, various regimes have exploited this procedure, from Adolf Hitler to Benito Mussolini to Saddam Hussein.

DEMONIZING THE ENEMY

Hitler could not have become who he was without the Jews. As strange as it might sound, they were his greatest asset, and the reason why is psychological.

It is not possible to build up such extreme levels of irrational enthusiasm in the people without also, at the same time, fueling an equally powerful force of aggression. Think of small children who are prone to become "over-excited": it always begins with enthusiasm and laughter, but if allowed to go too far it turns into hysteria, tears, and tantrums. Because masses, in many ways, operate like psychological children, a government which fuels irrational enthusiasm runs this very same risk. Hence, if you are going to build a hero you must also have an enemy, and the greater the worship your hero claim, the greater must be the demonization of the enemy. If your hero is a god-king, the enemy must be represented as the embodiment of evil itself. This is the only way to exploit the enthusiasm while avoiding the aggressions that come with it.

The Jews were Hitler's "enemy." This explains much in regard to how seemingly "normal" people could commit such atrocities against a group. They did not begin that way—but they ended that way through the process of demonization.

THE SCAPEGOAT

Think of "The Scapegoat" as the everyday, milder version of the previous fallacy. It exploits the same human weaknesses, but on a less extreme level. We may not all reach violent levels of enthusiasm and hysteria, but we all desire self-justification—we all desire a personal entity on which to place blame for our troubles, frustrations, and failures. This desire, subtle as it may be, is what makes us susceptible to the Scapegoat.

For example, if I am struggling to find employment, I might blame immigrants. Now, immigrants may indeed be the reason I am unemployed; but it may also be that I've made some bad decisions, or that I have an unpleasant personality, or maybe the economy is just lagging. On a psychological level, however, only one of the former options will satisfy my deep need to personalize evil and project it on some person or group outside of myself (because, God knows, I can't blame myself).

This is perhaps one of the main reasons our two-party system survives: They provide one another with a perfect scapegoat. They need each other. The Right could not do without the Left, because then they would have no one to hate.

DIVIDE AND CONQUER

Just the other day I saw a political poster on the Internet depicting an American soldier in Iraq, with a caption saying something along the lines of: "I make less than minimum wage, and a guy who flips burgers thinks he should be paid $12 an hour?" The obvious intent is, of course, to induce disgust toward anyone who might suggest that minimum wage workers deserve higher pay. The implication is that fry cooks have no business asking for more, because then they'd be making more than soldiers.

Now here's the problem: What if the soldier in the photo is drastically underpaid as well (and it is fairly obvious to most people that he probably is)? If this is the case, then the fry cooks are the natural allies of the soldiers. They have common ground, which is the desire for just pay for their labor. They would gain much by uniting, but they are weak when divided. Neither can hope to benefit by hating one another.

So we might do well to ask: Who does benefit from this scenario?—a scenario where two large segments of the lower working class are taught to see each other as enemies? Obviously this works to the great advantage of those who write the checks, who should be at the center of the conflict, but who can now stand comfortably aloof.

FLAG-WAVING

We could also call this the "Appeal to Patriotism." Whether or not a person is sufficiently "patriotic" can be a life or death point in political matters, particularly in nations like the United States where national self-awareness has reached in incredible degree.

Flag-waving is an attempt to win support for one's position by showing either that a particular person or action is patriotic or that supporting a policy will benefit the nation. It also works in the opposite direction: If you can prove to Americans that an action is unpatriotic, then you've all but handed it a death sentence. How often do we hear the accusation that such-and-such a person "hates America," in attempts to attach negative associations to that person.

As the name "flag-waving" implies, this technique is usually attached to symbols, such as the American flag or the Statue of Liberty or some other universally recognized image. A politician who appears in a photo with a flag wrapped around his shoulders, or with a flag blowing in the background, this is an attempt to cause the viewer to take all the positive feeling associated with the flag and then, consciously or

Daniel Schwindt

unconsciously, apply them to the person, even if they may have no rational cause for making such an association.

MANAGING THE NEWS

This involves orchestrating a coordinated effort to present the same few, simple points to a population, ceaselessly and from all directions. It involves incorporating all media formats including newspaper, television and radio. Jacques Ellul called this process "encirclement"; I call it "pulverization by the media." It is similar to what is called "classical conditioning" in psychology, because it plants and reinforces associations by sheer repetition.

Adolf Hitler said: "The most brilliant propagandist technique will yield no success unless one fundamental principle is borne in mind constantly—it must confine itself to a few points and repeat them over and over."

The media machines of today have taken Hitler's advice to heart. The key to this technique is relentlessness: No one must have a moment's peace in order to find himself in the din.

SLOGANS, CATCHPHRASES, CLICHéS

Although we've already mentioned this above, it warrants mention again. Bertrand de Jouvenel said that, instead of rational discourse, modern audiences were best reached through,

> "Stupid slogans, which come trippingly to the tongue and are a pleasure to repeat, songs which exalt the 'comrades' and ridicule the 'enemy,' these are the stuff of politics. Mix with it

a little doctrine, but only a very little, and reduce it to the simplest propositions."

The reason people might lean this way is not hard to discern. In a democracy everyone cares about politics, and everyone wants to engage in intelligent political discourse. Yet not everyone can understand and absorb the many complex arguments necessary to refute the hypotheses of their opponents. After all, most of us can barely defend our own opinions.

The answer to this problem occurs almost naturally through a process of reduction: philosophies become "programs," programs become platforms, platforms become slogans, slogans become catchphrases, and catchphrases become clichés. The story ends with an environment where men talk at one another without speaking, and hear without listening. And both participants get to walk away under the impression that they engaged in meaningful conversion.

VIRTUE WORDS

Certain words, depending on time, place, and culture, wield an unbelievable amount of power over the minds and emotions of a people. These are usually the words which represent the supreme values of the society. In American society, examples might be words like: "liberty," "freedom," or "equality." There are also vice words which correspond to these: "tyranny," "slavery," or "hate."

The problem is that these words, while surrounded with an almost holy aura, are at the same time extremely vague. If someone says that "freedom is under attack," everyone recoils in disgust, and yet we do not really know what this means—it could mean almost anything depending on the speaker. What if the speaker is referring to the "freedom to have an abortion"? What then?

But that is the beauty of virtue words: it draws the audience, almost irresistibly over to your side even before they know what exactly you are arguing for, because the response has become a reflex. The words "freedom" and "equality" act as invocations to the modern mind, producing an almost guaranteed effect. After reflection, of course, we may realize that we don't agree with the speaker after all, but how many of us remember to pause and reflect?

IDEOLOGY

Ideologies are what we get when we try to explain reality—which is vast, complex, and mysterious—with a few simple formulas. It is another fallacy of oversimplification, although this one is particular to democracies. Alexis de Tocqueville observed that in such societies "the craving to discover general laws in everything, to include a great number of objects under the same formula, and to explain a mass of facts by a single cause, becomes an ardent, and sometimes an undiscerning, passion in the human mind."

He said that, because we see everyone as equal politically, we also treat everyone as equal mentally. Thus, we act as if we should need no recourse to outside sources in order to understand life's problems. He says we "would fain succeed brilliantly and at once, but they would be dispensed from great efforts to obtain success. These conflicting tendencies lead straight to the research of general ideas, by aid of which they flatter themselves that they can figure very importantly at a small expense."

The popular ideologies in America are: capitalism, liberalism, and democracy. Each of these pretends to provide intuitive, simple explanations to overwhelmingly complex problems. But they are rigid and always incomplete. Thus, they create minds equally rigid and incomplete.

SECTION 6: ODDS AND ENDS

ABOUT THIS SECTION

This section serves as a catch-all for remaining subject and ideas which did not easily fit into other categories and did not take up enough space to warrant a category of their own. Items presented here will generally stand on their own feet, grouped together by topic, and are presented without commentary.

EQUALITY

"Equality as it is currently pursued is incompatible with true liberty; for liberty involves an inner working with reference to standards, the right subordination, in other words, of man's ordinary will to a higher will. There is an inevitable clash, in short, between equality and humility."[210]

"… it suffices to say that the artificial establishment of equality is as little compatible with liberty as the enforcement of unjust laws of discrimination…"Nature" (i.e., the absence of human intervention) is anything but egalitarian; if we want to establish a complete plain we have to blast the mountains away and fill the valleys; equality thus presupposes the continuous intervention of force which, as a principle, is opposed to freedom. Liberty and equality are in essence contradictory."[211]

---

[210] Irving Babbitt, *Democracy and Leadership*.
[211] *Liberty or Equality*, 3.

I think that democratic communities have a natural taste for freedom; left to themselves, they will seek it, cherish it, and view any privation of it with regret. But for equality their passion is ardent, insatiable, incessant, invincible; they call for equality in freedom; and if they cannot obtain that, they still call for equality in slavery. They will endure poverty, servitude, barbarism, but they will not endure aristocracy.[212]

"Egalitarianism is only the counterfeit of justice; it can be the exact opposite, we have seen that. Neither are all inequalities unjust. Which means that equality or inequality is one thing and justice is another. Justice consists in giving everybody his due."[213]

"This certainly does not apply to Christian equality, the proper name for which is equity, but to that democratic and social equality which is only the exaltation of envy, the mirage of jealous incapacity, which was never anything but a mask and which could become a reality only after the destruction of all merit, of all virtue."[214]

"Only by setting hierarchies shall we be able to restrict the imperialism of ideas and the absolutism of power."[215]

Blake: "one law for the lion and the ox is oppressive."

"In a classless society, unanimity does not result from the absence of classes but from the presence of the police."[216]

---

[212] DiA, bk. 2, ch. 1.

[213] Agenor de Gasparin, *L'Egalite*, Paris.

[214] Comte de Monalembert, Speech at a public meeting of the French Academy, Feb. 5, 1852.

[215] Dávila, 2013 edition, p. 207.

[216] Dávila, 2013 edition, p. 185.

"Shigalyov is a man of genius. He invented equality. In his copybook it is well described. He provides for a mutual espionage. Each member of the society has to supervise the others and to denounce them. Everybody belongs to all and all belong to each individually. All are slaves and are equal in their serfdom. In the extreme case there is calumny and murder, but the most important thing is equality."[217]

"Another error, due to the confusion of the concepts of human being and individual, is democratic equality. This dogma is now breaking down under the blows of the experience of the nations. It is, therefore, unnecessary to insist upon its falseness. But its success has been astonishingly long. How could humanity accept such faith for so many years? The democratic creed does not take account of the constitution of our body and of our consciousness. It does not apply to the concrete fact which the individual is. Indeed, human beings are equal. But individuals are not. The equality of their rights is an illusion. The feeble-minded and the man of genius should not be equal before the law. The stupid, the unintelligent, those who are dispersed, incapable of attention, of effort, have no right to a higher education. It is absurd to give them the same electoral power as the fully developed individuals. Sexes are not equal. To disregard all these inequalities is very dangerous. The democratic principle has contributed to the collapse of civilization in opposing the development of an elite. It is obvious that, on the contrary, individual inequalities must be respected. In modem society the great, the small, the average, and the mediocre are needed. But we should not attempt to develop the higher types by the same procedures as the lower. The standardization of men by the democratic ideal has already determined the predominance of the weak. Everywhere, the weak are preferred to the strong. They are aided and protected, often admired. Like the invalid, the criminal, and

---

[217] Fyodor Dostoyevski, *The Possessed.*

the insane, they attract the sympathy of the public. The myth of equality, the love of the symbol, the contempt for the concrete fact, are, in a large measure, guilty of the collapse of individuality. As it was impossible to raise the inferior types, the only means of producing democratic equality among men was to bring all to the lowest level. Thus vanished personality."[218]

"All government, in its essence, is a conspiracy against the superior man: its one permanent object is to oppress him and cripple him. If it be aristocratic in organization, then it seeks to protect the man who is superior only in law against the man who is superior in fact; if it be democratic, then it seeks to protect the man who is inferior in every way against both. One of its primary functions is to regiment men by force, to make them as much alike as possible and as dependent upon one another as possible, to search out and combat originality among them. All it can see in an original idea is potential change, and hence an invasion of its prerogatives. The most dangerous man to any government is the man who is able to think things out for himself, without regard to the prevailing superstitions and taboos. Almost inevitably he comes to the conclusion that the government he lives under is dishonest, insane and intolerable, and so, if he is romantic, he tries to change it. And even if he is not romantic personally he is very apt to spread discontent among those who are."
The Smart Set (December 1919)

Aristotle, Politics, bk. 5, pt. 1: Democracy, for example, arises out of the notion that those who are equal in any respect are equal in all respects.

"Satan was the first Whig." – Samuel Johnson

"That no love of equality, at least since Adam's fall, ever existed in human nature, any otherwise than as a desire of bringing others down

---

[218] Alexis Carrel, *Man the Unknown*, ch. 7.

to our own level, which implies a desire of raising ourselves above them, or depressing them below us."[219]

THE BOURGEOIS

"Inside the feudal frame, the bourgeoisie is localized at small urban centres, where it structures and civilizes itself. Once the frame is broken, the bourgeoisie expands over the entire society and invents the national State, the rationalistic technique, the multitudinous and anonymous metropolises, the industrial society, the mass production of man, and finally the oscillation between the despotism of the populace and the despotism of experts."[220]

ARISTOCRACY

"Among superior societies let us limit ourselves to the consideration of a single one, that of old France; here the hierarchy of birth was considered but one notion among many others; besides imposing duties on those favored by it, it was balanced everywhere by the hierarchy of merits and that of virtues; and in the foundations of a constitutional society religion annulled the inequality which it respected on the surface. In an organization whose most precious quality consisted precisely in the fact that it is not built up systematically but results from an established compromise throughout the centuries between

[219] John Adams, *The Works of John Adams, Second President of the United States: with a Life of the Author, Notes and Illustrations, by his Grandson Charles Francis Adams* (Boston: Little, Brown and Co., 1856). 10 volumes. Vol. 6. Retrieved 1/21/2015. http://oll.libertyfund.org/titles/2104.
[220] Dávila, 2013 edition, p. 295.

forces of different order, power is much more apparent in its majesty than in its exigence, in this authority rather than in its domination, and august as this organization may seem it deserves to be called benign, discrete and even modest considering the liberty which it gives to man to know and fulfill himself outside of its bounds. Everybody developed his personality without leaving behind his life. The artisan in employing the tools for his work was seizing the instruments for his own perfection. Whoever did his duty was working at the perfection of his soul. To every lord in society there was a master craftsman in a workshop, on a farm. The king was the father of his people only because every father was king in his family."

~ Abel Bonnard[221]

"The leaders must stand for life, and they must not ask the simple followers to point out the direction. When the leaders assume responsibility they relieve the followers forever of the burden of finding a way. Relieved of this hateful incubus of responsibility for general affairs, the populace can again become free and happy and spontaneous, leaving matters to their superiors. No newspapers—the mass of the people never learning to read. The evolving once more of the great spontaneous gestures of life.

"We can't go on as we are. Poor, nerve-worn creatures, fretting our lives away and hating to die because we have never lived. The secret is, to commit into the hands of the sacred few the responsibility which now lies like torture on the mass. Let the few, the leaders, be increasingly responsible for the whole. And let the mass be free: free, save for the choice of leaders.

"Leaders—this is what mankind is craving for.

---

[221] Les Modérés.

"But men must be prepared to obey, body and soul, once they have chosen the leader. And let them choose the leader for life's sake only.

"Begin then—there is a beginning.[222]

"Our leaders have not loved men: they have loved ideas, and have been willing to sacrifice passionate men on the altars of the blood-drinking, ever-ash-thirsty ideal. Has President Wilson, or Karl Marx, or Bernard Shaw ever felt one hot blood-pulse of love for the working man, the half-conscious, deluded working man? Never. Each of these leaders has wanted to abstract him away from his own blood and being, into some foul Methuselah or abstraction of a man.

"And me? There is no danger of the working man ever reading my books, so I shan't hurt him that way. But oh, I would like to save him alive, in his living, spontaneous, original being. I can't help it. It is my passionate instinct.

"I would like him to give me back the responsibility for general affairs, a responsibility which he can't acquit, and which saps his life. I would like him to give me back the responsibility for the future. I would like him to give me back the responsibility for thought, for direction. I wish we could take hope and belief together. I would undertake my share of the responsibility, if he gave me his belief.

"I would like him to give me back books and newspapers and theories. And I would like to give him back, in return, his old insouciance, and rich, original spontaneity and fullness of life."

~ D. H. Lawrence[223]

---

[222] D.H.Lawrence, *Fantasia of the Unconscious*, ch. 7.
[223] D.H. Lawrence, *Fantasia of the Unconscious*, ch. 9.

"...they have a sense of equality among themselves, and of constituting in themselves what is greatest and most dignified in the realm, which makes their pride revolt against the overshadowing greatness and dignity of commanding executive. They have a temper of independence, and a habit of uncontrolled action, which makes them impatient of encountering in the management of the interior concerns of the country, the machinery and regulations of a superior and peremptory power."

~ Matthew Arnold[224]

"And that race which has once lost the seed of aristocracy can never again recover it. For that seed is produced only in the garden of God, and when God purposes the destruction of a nation He destroys its Lords, and does not renew the sacred stock. Thus the nation deprived of leaders may not progress. It cannot even stay where it is, but must sink back to the marsh and the forest whence it has painfully and under guidance emerged."

~ A. Carthill

"Nobility preserves subjects from oppression merely by its existence. A despotic Power is one which can change, destroy and overthrow as it pleases; a Power which can overthrow as it pleases is an unlimited Power. Nobility sets a limit to Power, for the monarchy cannot obliterate a nobility which lives beside it, is the child, like itself, of the constitution and is, again like itself, linked to society by indissoluble ties..."

~ Vicomte de Bonald

---

[224] Matthew Arnold, "Democracy," *Mixed Essays* (New York: Macmillan, 1880), p. 4.

"Such a regime wears, it is true, an essentially militarist air because the business of the ruling class is war. But then, war is the business of no other class."

~ Bertrand de Jouvenel[225]

"Nothing was more alien than this [conscription] to the genius of aristocratic societies; it is natural to them to be defended only by the aristocrats. That is the interest, the office, and the privilege of aristocracy. It is as warriors that they make themselves, taken as a whole, indispensable to the monarch who is their chief and to the common people who depend on them. As champions of the one and protectors of the other, they gain both the good opinion of the nation and the respect due to their position, and they are no less able to defend national interests against the foreigner than their own interest against encroachment from above and agitation from below."

~ Bertrand de Jouvenel [226]

INDIVIDUALISM

"Individualism is a recently coined expression prompted by a new idea, for our forefathers knew only of egoism.

"Egoism is an ardent and excessive love of oneself which leads man to relate everything back to himself and to prefer himself above everything.

"Individualism is a calm and considered feeling which persuades each citizen to cut himself off from his fellows and to withdraw into the circle of his family and friends in such a way that he thus creates a

---

[225] Jouvenel, op. cit., p. 127.
[226] Ibid., p. 161-162.

small group of his own and willingly abandons society at large to its own devices. Egoism springs from a blind instinct; individualism from wrong-headed thinking rather than from depraved feelings. It originates as much from defects of intelligence as from the mistakes of the heart.

"Egoism blights the seeds of every virtue; individualism at first dries up only the source of public virtue. In the longer term it attacks and destroys all the others and will finally merge with egoism."

Alexis de Tocqueville[227]

"Despotism, suspicious by its very nature, views the separation of men as the best guarantee of its own permanence and usually does all it can to keep them in isolation. No defect of the human heart suits it better than egoism; a tyrant is relaxed enough to forgive his subjects for failing to love him, provided that they do not love one another...he gives the name of 'good citizens' to those who retreat into themselves."

~ Alexis de Tocqueville[228]

"Individualism and personality are not the same: the one belongs to the formless world of quantity, the other to the world of quality and hierarchy. The Americans are the living refutation of the Cartesian axiom, "I think, therefore I am": Americans do not think, yet they are. The American 'mind', puerile and primitive, lacks characteristic form and is therefore open to every kind of standardisation."

~ Julius Evola[229]

---

[227] Tocqueville, op. cit., p. 587-588 [emphasis mine].
[228] Ibid., 591.

"In the beginning the legislator did not have to concern himself at all with the son, the daughter, and the salve, for these fell within the exclusive jurisdiction of the father. Step by step they all became subject to the law: the state had broken through into a world from which it was at first excluded, and had claimed as subject to its own jurisdiction those who had in former days been subjects of the father alone."

~ Bertrand de Jouvenel[230]

"Doctrinaire individualism is not dangerous because it produces individuals but because it suppresses them. The product of the doctrinaire individualism of the 19th century is the mass-man of the 20th."

~ Nicolas Gomez-Davila[231]

The following lengthy selection is taken from Jacques Pirenne's great work on Egypt, and pertains directly to our subject here:

> "In an individualist society in which no family or social group exists, every public duty is performed exclusively by the State. First among them is that of assuring external security. To guarantee it the State disposes of an up-to-date military organization, which is distinct from the civil authorities and of which the king is the supreme head. The army is divided into tactical units which are placed under the command of regular officers; it is equipped, victualled and supplied by a commissariat service; the fleet, composed of large ships, is built

---

[229] Julius Evola's article *"Civilta" Americana* (American "Civilization") was first published in 1945, and reprinted in 1983 by the Julius Evola Foundation in Rome.
[230] Jouvenel, op. cit., p. 180.
[231] Davila, 2013 edition, p. 111.

in the shipyards of the State; the frontier forts are built by the military labour corps. In addition, the army is formed out of recruits; and the only security the Nation knows is that which it gets itself by supporting the burden of military service imposed on it by the State.

"Internal peace is assured by the judicial body, which holds pride of place among all the administrative bodies. All justice emanates from the king, in whose name the various courts of first instance and appeal pronounce their judgments. The litigants may, it is true, resort to arbitration, which, however, derives all validity and authority from the assurance that the State will execute its awards.

"The social life, whose external and internal security is assured by the army and the judicial body respectively, rests on the service of the civil departments, which give to each and preserve for each his place in Society, of the land-survey, which is the foundation of all property rights, and of the registry of documents, which, by transcribing all conveyances and contracts, can assure at need respect for the pledged word and guarantee to each the free disposal of his own goods and rights.

"The economic life largely depends on the service of the inland waterways. The ever more powerful State is ever more lavishly housed by the public works administration. The coordination of the various departments is the work of the chancery.

"The offices of all these various services are spread over the country; in all parts of it officials of all grades write minutes on papyrus rolls, which are then collected and filed in the State archives.

"In this way the administration makes itself not only the foundation but the very condition of existence in this individualist society; that society owes life itself to the supremacy of a State which guards, but, for that very reason, encroaches further and further.

"And so, in the act of developing, the administration fastens closer and closer the grip of the State and multiplies incessantly the number and importance of its services and officials.

"All these functions must be paid for. The State, it is true, possesses vast estates with enormous revenues. But the charges which it has to meet grow unceasingly. Not only does the administration itself cost more and more, but the growing authority of the State increases continually the prestige of the king, who, now canonized not only into a god but into the god of gods, surrounds himself with a Court the measure of whose luxury calls for an ever more numerous retinue of priests, courtiers, employees and servants. Thus the requirements of the State come to exceed by far the revenues of its estates. Recourse is then had to taxation.

"The civil departments, the land-survey, the registry of documents, thanks to which each single Egyptian is secured in his property and in his rights, have the further effect of giving the State a very good idea of what each possesses and of levying taxation on it accordingly. The administration of the finances and the taxation service then assumes an importance second to none, for, if Egyptian Society, from the third to the fifth dynasty, is viable only by reason of its competent and complicated administrative machine, that machine itself lives only on the strength of the taxation yield. So that the fiscal weapon is seen as an essential feature of the Egyptian Empire under the fourth dynasty.

"All Egyptians are equal before the Law, but this equality of theirs levels them all into an equal subservience to a more and more omnipotent State as represented in the king."

~ Jacques Pirenne[232]

WAR

"In time of actual war, great discretionary powers are constantly given to the Executive Magistrate. Constant apprehension of War, has the same tendency to render the head too large for the body."

~ James Madison

"War is a monster whom there is a conspiracy not to throttle, so that it may continue always as the opportunity of those who abuse the royal authority."

~ Omer Talon

"A new disease has broken out in Europe: it has infected our rulers and caused them to maintain armies which are out of all proportion. It has its recurrences and soon becomes contagious; inevitably, because as soon as one State increases the number of its troops, as they are called, the others at once increase theirs, so that the general ruin is all that comes out of it. Every monarch keeps permanently on foot armies which are as large as would be needed if his people were in imminent

---

[232] History of Ancient Egypt.

danger of extermination; and this struggle of all against all is called peace..."

~ Montesquieu

"There are instruments so dangerous to the rights of the nation and which place them so totally at the mercy of their governors that those governors, whether legislative or executive, should be restrained from keeping such instruments on foot but in well-defined cases. Such an instrument is a standing army."

~ Thomas Jefferson

"The spirit of this country is totally adverse to a large military force."

~ Thomas Jefferson

"Standing armies [are] inconsistent with [a people's] freedom and subversive of their quiet."

~ Thomas Jefferson

"In this country, [conscription] ever was the most unpopular and impracticable thing that could be attempted. Our people, even under the monarchical government, had learnt to consider it as the last of all oppressions."

~ Thomas Jefferson

"The State is all in all. Everything is referred to the production of force. It is military in its principle, in its maxims, in its spirit and in all its movements... Were France but half of what it is in population, in compactness, in applicability of its force, it would be too strong for most of the States of Europe."

~ Edmond Burke[233]

"During the past century and a half civilization has re-created the armed horde. Previously a rarity, it has become the accepted instrument of any great military effort. It has not however come alone. Exactly a hundred and fifty years ago, in 1789 — shortly after the United States had sought to protect themselves against democracy by their federal constitution — the French Revolution began. From that time to our own day democratic ideas have come to dominate politics just as the mass army has dominated war. It is the thesis of this book that the two are inseparably connected with each other and with a third thing, barbarism."

~ Hoffman Nickerson[234]

"At the end of the Napoleonic Wars there were 3,000,000 men in Europe under arms. The 1914-1918 war killed or mutilated five times as many. And in the 1939-1945 war there is no counting the men, and the women and children, engaged in the struggle— as long ago those on Ariovistus's chariots were counted…

"We are ending where the savages began. We have found again the lost arts of starving non-combatants, burning hovels, and leading away the vanquished into slavery. Barbarian invasions would be superfluous: we are our own Huns."

~ Bertrand de Jouvenel[235]

---

[233] *Letters on a Regicide Peace.*
[234] *The Armed Horde*, New York, 1940.
[235] *On Power.*

"The Revolution has deployed in its entirety the national strength of the French people... The other European States must draw on the same reserves with a view to restoring the ancient balance of Europe."

~ Gneisenau, Prussian General in the War of Liberation

"Whereas the Capetian kings made war with a few seignorial contingents whose service was for no more than forty days, the popular states of today have power to call to the colours, and keep there indefinitely, the entire male population. Whereas the feudal monarchs could nourish hostilities only with the resources of their own domains, their successors have at their disposal the entire national income. The citizens of medieval cities at war could, if they were not too near to the actual theatre of operations, take no notice of it...How is it possible not to see in this stupendous degradation of our civilization the fruits of state absolutism? Everything is thrown into war because Power disposes of everything."

~ Bertrand de Jouvenel

"But it must be emphasized that the warrior spirit is one thing and the military spirit quite another. Militarism was unknown in the Middle Ages. The soldier signifies the degeneration of the warrior, corrupted by the industrialist. The soldier is an armed industrialist, a bourgeois who has invented gunpowder. He was organized by the state to make war on the castles. With his coming, long-distance warfare appeared, the abstract war waged by cannon and machine gun."

~ José Ortega y Gasset[236]

---

[236] Esþaña Invertebrada, trans, by Mildred Adams (American Edition), New York, 1937.

"Before the French Revolution, wars scarcely affected the masses. They were fought out between sovereigns — the emperor, the kings, or the aristocratic republics which were still numerous in the eighteenth century — between ruling classes few in numbers, homogeneous, cultured, and refined. These classes could fight each other without excessive animosity; they could recognize that the enemy's cause was as righteous as their own; they could wage war as a game, respecting its rules even when it would be more advantageous to break them; and admit defeat as soon as it became too dangerous to keep on. Today it is the people who fight. . . . This mass cannot keep up the efforts of a war unless it is fired by some passion common to it all. A nation at war must therefore hate the enemy, which means that it must be convinced that it is defending the most righteous of causes against the most infamous aggression; that it represents innocent Right fighting against Evil armed with the most diabolical of long-premeditated designs."

~ Guglielmo Ferrero[237]

"Nevertheless there is a real distinction between professional and temporary fighting men. The professional form a guild or corporation of their own, distinct from other citizens. They fight from disciplined habit. Their esprit de corps is not unlike a strongly developed school or college spirit. Their sense of honour of arms has much in common with that of a clergyman who will not disgrace his cloth or a good workman who would be ashamed to do a bad job. Thus they are ordinarily obedient instruments of the governments which pay them. The French Foreign Legion or the United States Marines have fought in many quarrels about the merits of which their individual members cared little. They need no violent emotions to make them fight. It has

---

[237] *Peace and War* (London: Macmillan, 1933), pp. 57-58, trans, by Bertha Pritchard.

been well said that the grenadiers of Maria Theresa did not have to be told that Frederick the Great was a Sodomite, or those of Frederick that Maria Theresa, ate babies."

~ Hoffman Nickerson[238]

"To the enemies of America, the US military has long been a metaphorical woman hiding behind its air power and technology while bewailing any tiny losses with a whole culture of soul-searching and tear-wringing. To actually bring women into the so-called "front line" units of this organization is nothing more than realizing the inner logic of this unmilitary military and non-imperial empire."

~ Collin Liddell[239]

POLITICAL PARTIES

"Your party man, however excellent his intentions may be, is always opposed to any limitation of sovereignty. He regards himself as the next in succession, and handles gently the property that is to come to him, even while his opponents are its tenants."

~ Benjamin Constant[240]

---

[238] Op. cit.
[239] Colin Liddell, "Not The Spartans," http://alternative-right.blogspot.com/p/not-spartans.html.
[240] *Cours de politique constitutionelle*, ed. Laboulaye (Paris: 1872) Vol. I, p. 10.

"Monarchy is *by its nature* dissociated from party rule...Democracy is *by nature* party rule. The President (or Prime Minister) is a 'party man.' He lacks originally—and often permanently—*general* backing."

~ Erik von Kuehnelt-Leddihn[241]

"Under democracy one party always devotes its chief energies to trying to prove that the other party is unfit to rule — and both commonly succeed, and are right...The United States has never developed an aristocracy really disinterested or an intelligentsia really intelligent. Its history is simply a record of vacillations between two gangs of frauds."

~ H.L. Mencken

"What is any political campaign save a concerted effort to turn out a set of politicians who are admittedly bad and put in a set who are thought to be better. The former assumption, I believe is always sound; the latter is just as certainly false. For if experience teaches us anything at all it teaches us this: that a good politician, under democracy, is quite as unthinkable as an honest burglar."

~ H.L. Mencken

"The fathers of democracy held the view that an election campaign was a season of popular education by means of the full exposition of contrary policies; they attached special importance to the publication of parliamentary debates which would, by being reported, enable the citizen to follow the activities of government and so fit him more and more to pass judgment. If the participation in sovereignty of an ill-informed man was not without its drawbacks, these would in large measure be compensated for by the gradual mitigation of the prevailing ignorance through the medium of discussion, to which even

---

[241] *Liberty or Equality,* p. 150.

the meanest intelligences could not help paying heed. The fact that the larger spirits would have to solicit the votes of the smaller would mean that the latter, their intelligences once formed in such a school, would at long last be fitted for the leading part which had been assigned to them without exception. Of all the arguments in favour of democracy this was the noblest.

"The men of our day, however, being circumspect people, have realized that the cultivation of the electors' intelligence is at least as likely to open a window on the arguments of their opponents as on their own; therefore it is labour lost.

"The faculty of reason may lie relatively unused in the majority of a people, but there is not a man anywhere who is incapable of emotion. And it is to the emotions, therefore, that appeal must be made. Rouse in your behalf trust, hope, and affection; rouse against your rival indignation, anger, and hatred— and success is yours. It is truly complete when a public meeting can be induced to cheer a speech which it cannot understand, and to greet the other side's reply with stampings of the feet. Its path of duty is marked out for it by the proceedings of the national assembly itself. The result is that good citizenship, so far from being awakened among those who are as yet without it, gets extinguished in those who already have it.

"To stifle the curiosity which may be aroused by an outstanding orator on the other side, to kill the desire for the knowledge which comes from an understanding of the arguments on both sides, to destroy the natural amiability which predisposes a man favourably to his neighbour, the chord of party loyalty is struck. To read the enemy's newspaper becomes a treason, no less than to attend his meetings except for the purpose of drowning his voice and afterwards confuting him with the help of a manual for hecklers. For the political battle is a war in the true sense. Baudelaire, even in his day, marvelled at the military jargon employed in it: "The advance guard of democracy, in the forefront of the battle for the republic, and others." The poet was right. The electors had been transformed into soldiers engaged in a campaign, the reason being that their leaders were out to take possession of Power.[...]The more powerful the machine becomes and the tighter the bonds of party discipline are drawn, the less does debate matter: it no longer changes votes. The hangings of desks take the place of arguments. Parliamentary debates are no longer a school for citizens but a circus for boobies.

~ Bertrand de Jouvenel[242]

"[Political parties] are organizations composed of blocs of major investors who come together to advance favored candidates in order to control the state. They do this through direct cash contributions and by providing organizational support through the making available of sources of contacts, fundraisers and institutional legitimization. Candidates are invested in like stocks. For them electoral success is dependent on establishing the broadest base of elite support. Candidates whom have best internalized investor values see their 'portfolios' grow exponentially at the expense of candidates who have not internalized these values. So what you have is a filtering system in which only the most indoctrinated and business friendly of the intellectual class advance to state power. The higher you go up the ladder the more you've appealed to elite interests. Representatives of the major investors are also often chosen to fill political appointments after a favored candidate has achieved office. This political-economic model helps explain why the state largely functions to serve elite business interests on the domestic and international stages.

---

[242] *On Power,* p. 303-304.

Daniel Schwindt

" ... So what would we expect from a system like this? One thing we would expect is that on issues which the public cares about but on which there is cross-party investor agreement no party competition will take place. That means that the issues the public is most interested in will not appear on the agenda."

~ Thomas Ferguson[243]

LIBERTY

"Liberty and democracy are eternal enemies, and every one knows it who has ever given any sober reflection to the matter. A democratic state may profess to venerate the name, and even pass laws making it officially sacred, but it simply cannot tolerate the thing. In order to keep any coherence in the governmental process, to prevent the wildest anarchy in thought and act, the government must put limits upon the free play of opinion. In part, it can reach that end by mere propaganda, by the bald force of its authority — that is, by making certain doctrines officially infamous. But in part it must resort to force, i.e., to law. One of the main purposes of laws in a democratic society is to put burdens upon intelligence and reduce it to impotence. Ostensibly, their aim is to penalize anti-social acts; actually their aim is to penalize heretical opinions. At least ninety-five Americans out of every 100 believe that this process is honest and even laudable; it is practically impossible to convince them that there is anything evil in it. In other words, they cannot grasp the concept of liberty. Always they condition it with the doctrine that the state, i.e., the majority, has a sort of right of eminent domain in acts, and even in ideas — that it is perfectly free, whenever it is so disposed, to forbid a man to say what

---

[243] *The Golden Rule: The Investment Theory of Party Competition and the Logic of Money-Driven Political Systems.*

he honestly believes. Whenever his notions show signs of becoming "dangerous," ie, of being heard and attended to, it exercises that prerogative. And the overwhelming majority of citizens believe in supporting it in the outrage. Including especially the Liberals, who pretend — and often quite honestly believe — that they are hot for liberty. They never really are. Deep down in their hearts they know, as good democrats, that liberty would be fatal to democracy — that a government based upon shifting and irrational opinion must keep it within bounds or run a constant risk of disaster. They themselves, as a practical matter, advocate only certain narrow kinds of liberty — liberty, that is, for the persons they happen to favor. The rights of other persons do not seem to interest them. If a law were passed tomorrow taking away the property of a large group of presumably well-to-do persons — say, bondholders of the railroads — without compensation and without even colorable reason, they would not oppose it; they would be in favor of it. The liberty to have and hold property is not one they recognize. They believe only in the liberty to envy, hate and loot the man who has it."

~ H.L. Mencken[244]

"The democratic idea proceeds toward the fabrication of a human type fit for slavery in the most delicate sense of the word. Every democracy is simultaneously an involuntary institution for the breeding of tyrants in every sense of the word, even in the spiritual sense."

~ Friedrich Nietzsche[245]

"Without any censorship, in the West fashionable trends of thought and ideas are carefully separated from those which are not fashionable;

---

[244] "Liberty and Democracy" in the Baltimore Evening Sun (13 April 1925).
[245] *Beyond Good and Evil.*

nothing is forbidden, but what is not fashionable will hardly ever find its way into periodicals or books or be heard in colleges. Legally your researchers are free, but they are conditioned by the fashion of the day. There is no open violence such as in the East; however, a selection dictated by fashion and the need to match mass standards frequently prevent independent-minded people from giving their contribution to public life. There is a dangerous tendency to form a herd, shutting off successful development. I have received letters in America from highly intelligent persons, maybe a teacher in a faraway small college who could do much for the renewal and salvation of his country, but his country cannot hear him because the media are not interested in him. This gives birth to strong mass prejudices, blindness, which is most dangerous in our dynamic era. There is, for instance, a self-deluding interpretation of the contemporary world situation. It works as a sort of petrified armor around people's minds. Human voices from 17 countries of Eastern Europe and Eastern Asia cannot pierce it. It will only be broken by the pitiless crowbar of events."

~ Aleksandr Solzhenitsyn[246]

"To believe that one should be happy just to be alive, despite leading a hideous existence, is to think like a slave; to think that it is pleasant to have an ordinary and comfortable life, is to have the emotions of an animal; men, however, become so blind that they cannot even see that they do not live or think like human beings. People squirm in agitation before a dark wall and dream about buying washing machines and television sets; they anxiously look to tomorrow, even though it will bring nothing."

~ Yukio Mishima

---

[246] *Harvard Commencement Address.*

"To the strong there is no such thing as free will; for free will implies an alternative, and the strong man has no alternative. His ruling instinct leaves him no alternative, allows him no hesitation or vacillation. Strength of will is the absence of free will. If to the weak man strong will appears to have an alternative, it is a total misapprehension on his part.

"To the strong there is also no such thing as determinism as the determinists understand it. Environment and circumambient conditions determine nothing in the man of strong will. To him the only thing that counts, the only thing he hears is his inner voice, the voice of his ruling instinct. The most environment can do is to provide this ruling instinct with an anvil on which to beat out its owner's destiny, and beneath the racket and din of its titanic action all the voices of stimuli from outside, all the determining suggestions and hints from environment, sink into an insignificant and inaudible whisper, not even heard, much less heeded, therefore, by the strong man. That is why the passion of a strong man may be permanent, that is why the actions of a strong man may be consistent; because they depend upon an inner constitution of things which cannot change, and not upon environment which can and does change. If the strong man is acquainted with determinism at all, it is a determinism from within, a voice from his own breast; but this is not the determinism of the determinists."

~ Anthony Ludovici

"The meanest of the multitude magnify liberty as if the height of human felicity were only to be found in it--never remembering that the desire of liberty was the cause of the fall of Adam."

~ Sir Robert Filmer

"Liberty has always been an aristocratic ideal."

279

Daniel Schwindt

~ Christopher Dawson[247]

ECONOMY

"To be always seeking after the useful does not become free and exalted souls."

~ Aristotle[248]

"Money, money, always money — that is the essence of democracy. Democracy is more expensive than monarchy; it is incompatible with liberty."

~ P. J. Proudhon[249]

"So we can understand how Calvinism helped to create that curious product, the modern business man, who works like a slave, and sometimes rules like a slave driver, in accumulating money, which his tastes and principles forbid him to enjoy, and about the value of which to himself or to others he asks no questions. It has been said that the successful money-maker of today is either a child of the Ghetto or a grandchild of John Calvin. No system was ever so effectual in promoting that kind of progress which is measured by statistics. If you can convince a nation that steady industry in profitable enterprise is eminently pleasing to God, but that almost all ways of spending money unproductively are wrong, that nation is likely to become very rich. We can study the working of this system best in America and Scotland."

---

[247] *Beyond Politics.*
[248] Aristotle, *Politics*, 1338b.
[249] *Solution Du Problême Social.*

~ Dean Inge[250]

"It may be plausibly argued that the faults of the bourgeois are no greater than those of the leading classes in other ages, while his virtues are all his own. But the fact remains that the typical leaders of bourgeois society do not arouse the same respect as that which is felt for the corresponding figures in the old regime. We instinctively feel that there is something honourable about a king, a noble, or a knight which the banker, the stockbroker or the democratic politician does not possess. A king may be a bad king, but our very condemnation of him is a tribute to the prestige of his office. Nobody speaks of a bad bourgeois; the Socialist may indeed call him a 'bloody bourgeois,' but that is a set formula that has nothing to do with his personal vices or virtues.

"This distrust of the bourgeois is no modern phenomenon. It has its roots in a much older tradition than that of socialism. It is equally typical of the mediaeval noble and peasant, the romantic Bohemian and the modern Proletarian. The fact is that the bourgeoisie has always stood somewhat apart from the main structure of European society, save in Italy and in the Low Countries. While the temporal power was in the hands of the kings and the nobles and the spiritual power was in the hands of the Church, the bourgeois, the Third Estate, occupied a position of privileged inferiority which allowed them to amass wealth and to develop considerable intellectual culture and freedom of thought without acquiring direct responsibility or power. Consequently, when the French Revolution and the fall of the old regime made the bourgeoisie the ruling class in the West, it retained its inherited characteristics, its attitude of hostile criticism towards the traditional order and its enlightened selfishness in the pursuit of its

---

[250] Dean Inge, *Protestantism.*

interest. But although the bourgeois now possessed the substance of power he never really accepted social responsibility as the old rulers had done. He remained a private individual — an idiot in the Greek sense — with a strong sense of social conventions and personal rights, but with little sense of social solidarity and no recognition of his responsibility as the servant and representative of a super-personal order. In fact, he did not realize the necessity of such an order, since it had always been provided for him by others, and he had taken it for granted.

"This, I think, is the fundamental reason for the unpopularity and lack of prestige of the bourgeois civilization. It lacks the vital human relationship which the older order with all its faults never denied. To the bourgeois politician the electorate is an accidental collection of voters; to the bourgeois industrialist his employees are an accidental collection of wage earners. The king and the priest, on the other hand, were united to their people by a bond of organic solidarity. They were not individuals standing against other individuals but parts of a common social organism and representatives of a common spiritual order. "The bourgeois upset the throne and the altar, but they put in their place nothing but themselves. Hence their regime cannot appeal to any higher sanction than that of self-interest. It is continually in a state of disintegration and flux. It is not a permanent form of social organism, but a transitional phase between two orders."

~ Christopher Dawson[251]

"Democracy is only a continually shifting aristocracy of money, impudence, animal energy and cunning, in which the best grub gets the best of the carrion; and the level to which it tends to bring all things is not a mountain tableland, as its promoters would have their

---

[251] *Enquiries Into Religion and Culture.*

282

victims think, but the unwholesome platitude of the fen and the morass, of which black envy would enjoy the malaria as long as all others share it."

~ Coventry Patmore

MISCELLANEA

"I have formed a very clear conception of patriotism. I have generally found it thrust into the foreground by some fellow who has something to hide in the background. I have seen a great deal of patriotism; and I have generally found it the last refuge of the scoundrel."

~ G.K. Chesterton[252]

"How could a blind multitude which often does not know what it wants because it seldom knows what is good for it, carry out unaided an undertaking as large and as difficult as is a scheme of legislation? Left to itself the people always wills what is good, but left to itself it does not always perceive it. The general will is always righteous, but the judgment guiding it is not always clear-sighted. It needs to be made to see things as they are, sometimes as they ought to seem to it; it needs to be shown the good road which it seeks, to be safeguarded from the seductions of private wills, to be made aware of places and times, to be taught to weigh the attraction of the immediate, concrete advantage against the danger of the latent and distant evil."

~ Rousseau[253]

---

[252] G.K. Chesterton, *The Judgement of Dr. Johnson*, Act III.
[253] *The Social Contract*, Book XI, chap. vi.

"Woe to the thinker who is not the gardener but only the soil of the plants that grow in him!"

~ Friedrich Nietzsche[254]

"The taste of the populace is not characterized by their dislike of excellence but by the passivism with which they delight equally in the good, the mediocre, and the inadequate. The populace does not have bad taste—it is, simply, tasteless."

~ Nicolas Gomez-Davila[255]

"Through money, democracy becomes its own destroyer, after money has destroyed intellect."

~ Oswald Spengler[256]

"I do not look upon equal voting as among the things which are good in themselves, provided they can be guarded against inconveniences. I look upon it as only relatively good; less objectionable than inequality of privileges grounded on irrelevant or adventitious circumstances, but in principle wrong, because recognizing a wrong standard, and exercising a bad influence on the voter's mind. It is not useful, but hurtful, that the constitution of a country should declare ignorance to be entitled to as much political power as knowledge."

~ John Stuart Mill[257]

---

[254] *Daybreak*, s. 382, R.J. Hollingdale transl.
[255] Davila, 2013 edition, p. 109.
[256] Oswald Spengler, *Decline of the West: Perspectives of World History* (New York: Knopf, 1928), p. 464.
[257] Considerations on Representative Government, New York, 1882, p. 188.

"What is really necessary for a reform of the reform? For my generation to die. The ideals my cohort held are not the kind that sustain themselves and will likely be forgotten. *Apres moi, le printemps.*"

~ John Medaille, Distributist

"Liberalism is essentially the belief that there can be a reconciliation of all difficulties and differences, and since there can't, it is a misleading way to approach politics."

~ Maurice John Cowling[258]

"Bourgeois are by nature people who hate and destroy heavens. When they see a beautiful site, they have no more pressing dream than to cut the trees, dry up the springs, build streets, shops and urinals. They call this ceasing a business opportunity."

~ Léon Bloy

"The true gravitation-hold of liberalism in the United States will be a more universal ownership of property, general homesteads, general comfort -- a vast, intertwining reticulation of wealth. As the human frame, or, indeed, any object in this manifold universe, is best kept together by the simple miracle of its own cohesion, and the necessity, exercise and profit thereof, so a great and varied nationality, occupying millions of square miles, were firmest held and knit by the principle of the safety and endurance of the aggregate of its middling property owners. So that, from another point of view, ungracious as it may sound, and a paradox after what we have been saying, democracy looks

---

[258] Interviewed in Naim Attallah, Singular Encounters (Quartet Books, 1990), p. 136.

with suspicious, ill-satisfied eye upon the very poor, the ignorant, and on those out of business. "

~ Walt Whitman[259]

"The world is weary of statesmen whom democracy has degraded into politicians."

~ Benjamin Disraeli[260]

"Real kingship — hard as it may be to get this idea into the heads of our narrowminded democrats — seems to be created by God for the special purpose of protecting the vast masses of a people against the possibility of violation by a popular elite. " . . . The popular elite, be it a cultural, a social or an economic one does not want, under ordinary, normal circumstances to recognize a master or at least only the semblance of one, a fact which is forgotten again and again or which is purposely kept quiet. Only in extreme danger and distress this elite suffers a master and king, should one be at hand. But for the masses a king standing above all classes and parties is under all circumstances necessary and desirable."

~ Dr. Schmidt-Gibichenfels[261]

"Civilization is by its nature bourgeois in the deepest spiritual sense of the word. 'Bourgeois' is synonymous precisely with the civilized kingdom of this world and the civilized will to organized power and enjoyment of life. The spirit of civilization is that of the middle classes; it is attached and clings to corrupt and transitory things; and it fears eternity. To be a bourgeois is therefore to be a slave of matter and an

---

[259] Walt Whitman, *Democratic Vistas*.
[260] *Lothair*, Chapter XVII.
[261] Die demokratische Luge und der Krieg. Berlin, 1915.

enemy of eternity. The perfected European and American civilizations gave rise to the industrial capitalist system, which represents not only a mighty economic development but the spiritual phenomenon of the annihilation of spirituality."

~ Nicolas Berdyaev[262]

"If only one country adopts conscription it automatically forces the rest of the world to imitate its practice. The "abyss calls to the abyss." The United States has been so forced, against her best tradition, to adopt conscription and so becomes a victim of circumstances. Yet, though the majority dislike conscription, still the majority recognize it as a grim necessity of these times."

~ Erik von Kuehnelt-Leddihn[263]

"The very support which republican doctrine finds in "democracy" has been handed down directly from the royal tradition: the king, ever since the early Middle Ages has ruled against the privileged classes, allying himself with the common people, later on with the third estate. And it is precisely the rupture of this alliance which brought about the fall of the monarchy."

~ Lucien Romier[264]

"Democracy obviously has need of politicians, has need of nothing else but politicians, and has need indeed that there shall be in politics nothing else but politicians."

~ Emile Faguet[265]

---

[262] *The Meaning of History*, trans. George Reavey, New York, 1936.
[263] *Menace of the Herd*, note 106.
[264] *Explication De Notre Temps*, Paris, 1925, p. 195.
[265] Emile Faguet, *Cult of Incompetence*

Daniel Schwindt

"It is a pleasant form of government *in which equality reigns among unequal as well as among equal things*. Moreover, when a democratic State, athirst for liberty, is controlled by unprincipled cupbearers, who give it to drink of the pure wine of liberty and allow it to drink till it is drunken, then if its rulers do not show themselves complaisant and allow it to drink its fill, they are accused and overthrown under the pretext that they are traitors aspiring to an oligarchy; for the people prides itself on and loves the equality that confuses and will not distinguish between those who should rule and those who should obey. Is it any wonder that the spirit of licence, insubordination, and anarchy should invade everything, even the institution of the family? Fathers learn to treat their children as equals and are half afraid of them, while children neither fear nor respect their parents. All the citizens and residents and even strangers aspire to equal rights of citizenship.

"Masters stand in awe of their disciples and treat them with the greatest consideration and are jeered at for their pains. Young men want to be on the same terms as their elders and betters, and old men ape the manners of the young, for fear of being thought morose and dictatorial. Observe too to what lengths of liberty and equality the relations between the sexes are carried. You would hardly believe how much freer domestic animals are there than elsewhere. It is proverbial that little lap-dogs are on the same footing as their mistresses, or as horses and asses; they walk about with their noses in the air and get out of nobody's way."[266]

"The physical change in the thickness of walls since the Middle Ages could be shown in a diagram. In the fourteenth century each house was a fortress. [Today each many storied house is a beehive. It is a city in itself, and its walls are thin partitions which barely shut us off from the street.] Man spent the major portion of his day in them, in secret and well-defended solitude. That solitude, working on the soul hour after hour, forged it, like a transcendent blacksmith, into a compact

---

[266] Quoted in Emile Faguet, *Cult of Incompetence*, 128-129.

288

and forceful character. Under its treatment, man consolidated his individual destiny and sallied forth with impunity, never yielding to the contamination from the public. It is only in isolation that we gain, almost automatically, a certain discrimination in ideas, desires, longings, that we learn which are ours, and which are anonymous, floating in the air, falling on us like dust in the street."

~ José Ortega y Gasset[267]

"He has studied the form and spirit of republics — but the result in his mind from that investigation has been and is, that neither England nor France, without infinite detriment to them, as well in the event as in the experiment, could be brought into a republican form; but that everything republican which can be introduced with safety, into either of them, must be built upon a monarchy — built upon a real, not a nominal monarchy, as its essential basis."

~ Edmond Burke (about himself)

"To be ruled by a superior is not contrary however to human liberty, dignity and equality. Only the despot offends thus . . . even in the state of innocence there would have been political subjection, there would have been a difference of sexes, faculties and power; therefore an order of precedence and subjection. Among the angels there is a hierarchy of order with precedence and succession; why not among men? Therefore it is not contrary to liberty, nor humiliating to the dignity of man to be ruled by his legitimate superiors...There is a difference between political subjection and servile subjection."

~ St. Robert Bellarmine[268]

---

[267] *España Invertebrada*, American Edition, trans, by Mildred Adams, New York, 1937, p. 168.
[268] De Laicis VII:

"If by 'democracy' we mean the form which the Third Estate as such wishes to impart to public life as a whole, it must be concluded that democracy and plutocracy are the same thing under the two aspects of wish and actuality, theory and practice, knowing and doing. It is the tragic comedy of the world improvers' and freedom-teachers' desperate fight against money that they are ipso facto assisting money to be effective. Respect for the big number - expressed in the principles of equality for all, natural rights, and universal suffrage - is just as much a class-ideal of the unclassed as freedom of public opinion (and 'more particularly freedom of the press) is so. These are ideals, but in actuality the freedom of public opinion involves the preparation of public opinion, which costs money; and the freedom of the press brings with it the question of possession of the press, which again is a matter of money; and with the franchise comes electioneering, in which he who pays the piper calls the tune. The representatives of the ideas look at one side only, while the representatives of money operate with the other. The concepts of Liberalism and Socialism are set in effective motion only by money. It was the Equites, the big-money party, which made Tiberius Gracchus's popular movement possible at all; and as soon as that part of the reforms that was advantageous to themselves had been successfully legalized, they withdrew and the movement collapsed."

~ Oswald Spengler[269]

"The liberal bourgeois mind is proud of the abolition of censorship, the last restraint, while the dictator of the press - Northcliffe 1- keeps the slave-gang of his readers under the whip of his leading articles, telegrams, and pictures. Democracy with its newspaper has completely

---

[269] Oswald Spengler, *Decline of the West: Perspectives of World History* (New York: Knopf, 1928), pp. 401-402.

expelled the book from the mental life of the people. The book-world, with its profusion of standpoints that compelled thought to select and criticize, is now a real possession only for a few. The people reads the one paper, "its" paper, which forces itself through the front doors by millions daily, spellbinds the intellect from morning to night, drives the book into oblivion by its more engaging layout, and if one or another specimen of a book does emerge into visibility, forestalls and eliminates its possible effects by "reviewing" it…What is truth? For the multitude, that which it continually reads and hears."[270]

"There can be no true peace except where the appetite is directed to what is truly good, since every evil, though it may appear good in a way, so as to calm the appetite in some respect, has, nevertheless many defects, which cause the appetite to remain restless and disturbed. Hence true peace is only in good men and about good things. The peace of the wicked is not a true peace but a semblance thereof, wherefore it is written (Wisdom 14:22): 'Whereas they lived in a great war of ignorance, they call so many and so great evils peace.' "

~ St. Thomas Aquinas[271]

"Democrats are always happy. Democracy is a sort of laughing gas. It will not cure anything, perhaps, but it unquestionably stops the pain."

~ H.L. Mencken[272]

---

[270] Oswald Spengler, *Decline of the West: Perspectives of World History* (New York: Knopf, 1928), p. 461.

[271] Thomas Aquinas, *Summa Theologica*, II-II, q. 29, a. 2.

[272] "The Master Illusion" in the The American Mercury (March 1925), p. 319

Daniel Schwindt

OTHER WORKS BY THE AUTHOR

Nothing To Vote For: The Futility of the American Electoral Process

The Papist's Guide to America

Catholic Social Teaching: A New Synthesis

There Must Be More Than This: Identity and Spiritual Renewal in the Kingdom of 'Whatever'

Holocaust of the Childlike

The O'Reilly Function: A Short Study on Propaganda and Talking Heads

Made in the USA
Middletown, DE
11 January 2018